Trade Unions in Renewal

Employment and Work Relations in Context Series

Series Editors

Tony Elger
Centre for Comparative Labour Studies
Department of Sociology
University of Warwick

Peter Fairbrother
Centre for Critical Research on
Economic and Social Transformation
Cardiff School of Social Sciences
Cardiff University

The aim of the *Employment and Work Relations in Context Series* is to address questions relating to the evolving patterns and politics of work, employment, management and industrial relations. There is a concern to trace out the ways in which wider policy-making, especially by national governments and transnational corporations, impinges upon specific workplaces, occupations, labour markets, localities and regions. This invites attention to developments at an international level, marking out patterns of globalization, state policy and practice in the context of globalization and the impact of these processes on labour. A particular feature of the series is the consideration of forms of worker and citizen organization and mobilization. The studies address major analytical and policy issues through case study and comparative research.

Other titles published in the series include:

Changing Prospects for Trade Unions: Comparisons Between Six Countries
Peter Fairbrother and Gerard Griffin

Work and Employment Relations in The High Performance Workplace
Gregor Murray, Jacques Bélanger, Anthony Giles and Paul-André Lapointe

Unionization and Union Leadership: The Road Haulage Industry
Paul Smith

Reshaping the North American Automobile Industry: Restructuring, Corporatism, and Union Democracy
John P. Tuman

Trade Unions and Global Governance: The Quest of Trade Unions for a Social Clause
Gerda van Roozendaal

Globalization, Social Movements and the New Internationalisms
Peter Waterman

TRADE UNIONS IN RENEWAL

A Comparative Study

**Edited by
Peter Fairbrother and Charlotte A. B. Yates**

LONDON • NEW YORK

Continuum
The Tower Building, 11 York Road, London, SE1 7NX
370 Lexington Avenue, New York, NY 10017–6503

First published 2003

British Library Cataloguing-in-Publication Data
A catalogue record for this book is available from the British Library.

ISBN 0–8264–5436–4 (hardback)
    0–8264–5437–2 (paperback)

Typeset by YHT Ltd, London
Printed and bound in Great Britain by MPG Books Ltd, Bodmin, Cornwall

CONTENTS

TABLES

Contributors

Huw Beynon. Professor and Director, Cardiff School of Social Sciences, Cardiff University, Wales, UK.

Kate Bronfenbrenner. Director of Labour Education Research, School of Industrial and Labour Relations, Cornell University, New York State, USA.

Bob Carter. Senior Lecturer, Department of Sociology, University of Leicester, England, UK.

Aaron Crawford. Former Senior Research Fellow, Industrial Relations Centre, School of Business and Public Management, Victoria University of Wellington, New Zealand; currently adviser, Industrial Relations Unit, Ministry of Education, Wellington, New Zealand.

Peter Ewer. Research Fellow, Union Research Centre on Organisation and Technology, Royal Melbourne Institute of Technology University, Victoria, Australia.

Peter Fairbrother. Professor, Cardiff School of Social Sciences, Cardiff University, Wales, UK.

Gerard Griffin. Professor, Faculty of Business and Economics, and Director of National Key Centre of Industrial Relations, Monash University, Victoria, Australia.

Pradeep Kumar. Professor, School of Industrial Relations, Queen's University, Ontario, Canada.

Gregor Murray. Professor, Department of Industrial Relations, Université de Laval, Quebec, Canada.

Sarah Oxenbridge. Senior Research Associate, Department of Applied Economics, University of Cambridge, England, UK.

Belinda Probert. Professor and Director, Centre for Applied Social Research, Royal Melbourne Institute of Technology University, Victoria, Australia.

Christopher Schenk. Research Director, Ontario Federation of Labour, Ontario, Canada.

Rachel Sherman. PhD student, Department of Sociology, University of California, Berkeley, California, USA.

Rai Small. Former Research Fellow, National Key Centre in Industrial Relations, Monash University, Victoria, Australia; currently lawyer with Gill, Kane & Brophy Solicitors, Melbourne, Australia.

Paul Stewart. Professor, Employment Studies Research Unit, Bristol Business School, University of West of England, England, UK.

Stuart Svensen. Former Research Fellow, National Key Centre in Industrial Relations, Monash University, Victoria, Australia.

Kim Voss. Associate Professor, Department of Sociology, and Associate Director of Institute of Industrial Relations, University of California, California, USA.

Pat Walsh. Professor, Industrial Relations Centre, School of Business and Public Management, Victoria University of Wellington, New Zealand.

Charlotte A. B. Yates. Professor, Labour Studies Programme and Department of Political Science, McMaster University, Ontario, Canada.

ACKNOWLEDGEMENTS

The contributors would like to thank all the trade unionists who have helped and assisted in their work over the years, and for whom this book is a tribute and hope for the future.

The research for this book has been undertaken by members of the Future of Unions Research Network (FUN) and their colleagues. The network was established in 1999 to encourage systematic, comparative research on union organizing and renewal. It aims to foster collaboration between academic researchers and trade union activists across several countries, including the UK, Australia, New Zealand, Canada and the USA. The network is dedicated to widespread dissemination of its research findings and an ongoing dialogue on questions of union organizing and renewal between workers, unions and researchers. This publication is the first collaborative output of the network. For further details see http://www.socserv.socsci.mcmaster.ca/fun

The authors thank the Social Science and Humanities Research Council in Canada for financial support in the start-up of FUN.

ABBREVIATIONS

ABS	Australian Bureau of Statistics
ACTU	Australian Council of Trade Unions
ACTWU	Amalgamated Clothing and Textile Workers Union
AEEU	Amalgamated Engineering and Electrical Union
AEU	Amalgamated Engineering Union
AFL-CIO	American Federation of Labor–Congress of Industrial Organizations
AIRC	Australian Industrial Relations Commission
ALP	Australian Labor Party
ASTMS	Association of Scientific, Technical and Manufacturing Staffs
ATEA	Australian Telecommunications Employees Association
ATL	Association of Teachers and Lecturers
ATPOA	Australian Telephone and Phonogram Officers' Association
AWIRS	Australian Workplace Industrial Relations Survey
AWU	Australian Workers Union
BCFL	British Columbia Federation of Labour
CALURA	Corporations and Labour Unions Return Act
CAW	Canadian Autoworkers Union
CEP	Communications, Energy and Paperworkers Union of Canada
CEPU	Communications, Electrical and Plumbing Union
CEWU	Communication and Energy Workers Union
CLBC	Canadian Labour and Business Centre
CLC	Canadian Labour Congress
CPSU	Community and Public Sector Union
CCSU	Council of Civil Service Unions
CSN	Confederation des syndicats nationaux
CTU	(New Zealand) Council of Trade Unions
CUT	Central Unica dos Trabalhores
CWA	Communications Workers of America
CWU	Communication Workers Union
ECA	Employment Contracts Act
EETPU	Electrical, Electronic and Engineering Unions
FAT	Frente Autentico del Trabajo

FCA	Fonds pour la formations de chercheurs et d'aide à la recherche
FDA	Association of First Division Civil Servants
FIMEE	Federation of Industrial Manufacturing and Engineering Employees
FinSec	Financial Sector Union
FTE	full-time equivalent
GMB	General, Municipal and Boilermakers Union
H&HU	Hotel and Hospital Unions
HERE	Hotel and Restaurant Employees Union
HRDC	Human Resources Development Canada
ICFTU	International Confederation of Free Trade Unions
ILO	International Labour Organization
IMF	International Monetary Fund
IPMS	Institution of Professional Managers and Specialists
ISTC	Iron and Steel Trades Confederation
ITF	International Transport Federation
IU	International Union
KFAT	National Union of Knitwear, Footwear and Apparel Trades
LHMWU	Liquor, Hospitality and Miscellaneous Workers Union
MPO	Management and Professional Officers Union
MSF	Manufacturing Science and Finance
NAFTA	North American Free Trade Area
NATFHE	National Association of Teachers in Further and Higher Education
NDC	Network Design and Construction
NLRA	National Labour Relations Act
NLRB	National Labour Relations Board
NSW	New South Wales
NUM	National Union of Mineworkers
NZ	New Zealand
OECD	Organization for Economic Co-operation and Development
PCS	Public and Commercial Services Union
PFI	Private Finance Initiative
PMG	Post Master Generals Department
PSA	Public Service Association
SFWU	Service and Food Workers Union
SHOT	Shareholders of Telstra
SIEU	Service Employees International Union
SLA	service level agreement

SPA	scheduled paid absence
SPUR	Special Projects Union Representative
SSHRC	Social Sciences and Humanities Research Council
STE	Society of Telecom Executives
SWU	Service Workers Union
T&S Group	Technical and Services Group, Communications Division, Communications, Electrical and Plumbing Union
TASS	Technical and Supervisory Staffs
TGWU	Transport and General Workers Union
TINA	there is no alternative
TUC	Trades Union Congress
TUTA	Trade Union Training Australia Inc.
UAW	United Auto Workers
UE	United Electrical Workers
UFBWU	United Food and Beverage Workers Union
UFCW	United Food and Commercial Workers
UFW	United Farm Workers
UK	United Kingdom
UNISON	British public service union
UNITE	Union of Needletrades, Industrial and Textile Employees
USA	United States of America
USDAW	Union of Shop, Distributive and Allied Workers
USWA	United Steelworkers of America
STE	Society of Telecom Executives (Connect – The Union for Professional Communications)
WOC	workplace organizing committee
WTO	World Trade Organization

1 Unions in Crisis, Unions in Renewal?[1]

Peter Fairbrother and Charlotte A. B. Yates

In many of the advanced economies, unions are in a situation of uncertainty and some disarray. This is particularly evident in the Anglo-American countries, namely the United States (USA), Australia, New Zealand (NZ), United Kingdom (UK) and, to a lesser extent, Canada. Union memberships are stagnant or declining and new workers are slow to join unions. These trends are in part a consequence of structural factors, in particular major changes in the labour market, involving the increased flexibility of labour, deregulation and a shift from manufacturing to services. In some countries they are also the result of broad political and cultural changes associated with growing ethnic, racial and cultural diversity of working populations and the failure of unions to adapt to these developments. Declining union memberships are also a consequence of the strategic responses of employers, governments and unions themselves to new competitive pressures and the declining legitimacy of social democratic ideas and strategic interventions. Employers in all five countries, albeit to varying degrees, have responded to the economic instability beginning in the early 1970s and continuing into the 1980s by shifting the balance of power in their favour, thus taking the opportunity either to rid their workplaces of unions or undermine union influence. Employers have been helped in these endeavours by governments choosing to restore economic competitiveness through the advancement of neo-liberal policies, in part aimed at restricting union political and economic influence. Further, many governments have abandoned Keynesian full-employment policies in favour of reducing inflation, deregulating labour markets, restricting union growth through changes to industrial relations institutions and eroding the welfare state.

For their part, unions have been caught unprepared by these political and economic shifts. Partially arising from their understanding of these changes as temporary setbacks to the post-World War II order, unions initially clung

1

onto existing institutions and practices in the expectation that better days lay ahead. Faced with declining memberships and accelerated employer and government assaults on unions, articulated by some as a crisis of union representation (for example on Britain and the USA see Towers, 1997), many unions and national labour movements have recently undertaken a reassessment of their strategic responses to the current crisis. This reassessment has ushered in a period of rapid change for many unions, which are now experimenting with a host of new ideas and practices designed to rebuild their memberships and restore unions to a position of strength *vis-à-vis* employers and governments. In the five Anglo-American countries this strategic realignment by unions has in various measures included rationalization through mergers between unions, renewed emphasis on organizing the unorganized and in some cases experimentation with new forms of partnership between unions and employers.

This book examines the issue of union renewal in the five Anglo-American countries by focusing on national federations and individual union's responses to organizing strategies, aimed both at increasing union memberships through organizing the unorganized and restoring union influence through internal reorganization and in some cases remobilization (activating existing members, facilitating member representation, promoting membership education and raising union consciousness). The book's chapters are presented by country, but this introductory chapter aims to provide a comparative examination of some of the challenges, issues and debates about union renewal in these five countries.

Legacies of the past

The trade unions of each country are located in different industrial relations systems, which provide the context for the routinized relationships between trade unions, employers and the state. Over the past 100 years the union movements in each of these countries have struggled to establish themselves, often in the face of marked employer hostility, supported and at times encouraged by the state. By the mid-twentieth century the trade unions in each country were part of the political firmament, either as partners of labo(u)r parties (Australia, New Zealand and the UK) or working in alliance with progressive parties (Canada and to a more limited extent, the USA). The result was the emergence of institutionalized sets of relations between unions, employers and governments, premised on notions of responsible unionism but articulated in different forms depending largely upon the political and economic strength of organized labour in each country. These relations were often contentious, but it was not until the 1980s that these relationships were questioned and eventually challenged. So as to explore these relationships and provide an understanding for the contemporary moment, we look first at the past in each country, drawing out the inter-relationships and parallels between them.

Australia, Canada, New Zealand, UK and the USA constitute a social, political and economic cluster that remains distinct from other advanced liberal and social democratic economies, such as mainland Europe. These states comprise economies linked together as part of the same broad trading group with a common language and predominance of liberal ideas. Perhaps not surprisingly, models of trade unionism and ties between labour movements also flourished at different points in their histories across these countries. Trade unions in Australia and New Zealand were modelled on British unions, with relatively close and ongoing informal links. Deepening economic ties between the USA and Canada led in the nineteenth century to the emergence of international unions representing workers in both the USA and Canada, which persist in influencing current trade union developments. Welfare state development in the post-World War II period also exhibited strong similarities across these five countries. All emerged as liberal welfare states with weak to moderate commitments to universalism, which informed the setting of benefits at low enough levels to enforce attachment to the paid labour market (Esping-Andersen, 1990). This tendency towards liberal welfare state development was at least in part a consequence of the limits to working-class organization and mobilization in these countries, which prevented the emergence of a more universalistic and transformative welfare state.

Despite the broad similarities in macro-economic and welfare policies, the legal regulation and juridical arrangements governing industrial relations differs between these five countries, with Canada and the USA following one model, Australia and New Zealand another, and the UK offering its own system. Both Canada and the USA developed a model of industrial relations in the 1930s and 1940s defined by a set of regulations, applied and adjudicated by government-appointed tribunals known as labour relations boards. Bona fide unions, defined as those that had collective bargaining as their primary focus, had to prove to their respective labour boards that the majority of workers in some portion of an enterprise, legally defined as a bargaining unit, supported representation by a particular union. Closed-shop provisions were rarely allowed outside the building trades, and in many US states were expressly prohibited. Thus union membership had to be built workplace by workplace. Once a union proved its majority status in a work-place, a process often fraught with conflict as a result of legal rights of employers to contest union recognition, the union was granted a certificate by the labour board. This certificate legally recognized the union as the exclusive bargaining agent for all workers in the bargaining unit, whether union members or not. Negotiations for a collective agreement were con-ducted between the employer and the certified union, most often at the enterprise level although some powerful unions forced more centralized company or sector-wide negotiations of a collective agreement. Strikes by unions and/or lock-outs by the employer became a primary means for increasing pressure on the opposing industrial party to negotiate an agree-ment, the result of which was often lengthy strikes/lock-outs, not uncom-monly upwards of several weeks. Once a collective agreement was reached between the union and employer, this became a contract to which both parties were legally bound. Interim disputes over the application and inter-pretation of the contract were most often resolved through a grievance procedure. This workplace-based certification procedure encouraged the emergence of hundreds of unions and a decentralized bargaining system. (On the USA, see Tomlins, 1985; Goldfield, 1987; on Canada, see Jamieson, 1973; Cornish and Spink, 1994.) Yet, these complex legal-juridical proce-dures, combined with particular labour board practices, also encouraged the growth of large, industrial and public service unions.

Although the Canadian legislative framework was initially modelled directly on the US experience, the conclusion of World War II saw the ascendancy of right-wing political forces in the USA and their revision of industrial relations legislation, which curbed the rights of unions and enhanced those of employers (Tomlins, 1985). Thus, although similar, the two legislative systems were seen to have differential effects on the growth of the labour movement, with the US system restricting union growth and the Canadian system offering greater opportunity for expanded union mem-bership (Card and Freeman, 1993). Only in the last ten years, have several Canadian provincial governments initiated changes to the industrial relations regime based on the US model.

Unions in the UK were similarly decentralized and focused on direct bargaining with employers, although the industrial relations system was quite distinct from that in the USA and Canada. What emerged in the UK, and was repeatedly defended by unions, was a voluntarist industrial relations system, which relied not on state regulation, but on the relative strength of unions and managers in the workplace for union recognition and bargaining out-comes. The consequence of this system was a highly decentralized union movement in which shop stewards and local union branches exercised considerable power, often with weak ties to the regional and particularly the national union. A further feature of this system was that multiple unions existed in workplaces, and workers in the same area often belonged to different unions. Agreements between the two parties were not legally binding, leading to both a more fluid process of collective bargaining and the greater likelihood of strikes or lock-outs by unions and employers in a bid to bolster their bargaining positions. The one exception to this pattern was in the highly unionized public sector, where a tradition of centralized unionism, reliant on state boards and cooperative employers, developed. Many of these unions were founded in the early twentieth century, but established themselves in the late 1940s and 1950s, with minimal forms of local representation, unlike their private sector counterparts (Carter and Fairbrother, 1999). From the 1970s onwards, as repeated Labour and Conservative governments targeted unions in both private and public sectors as a key factor in Britain's economic woes, restrictions were placed on strikes, although broader institutional changes were limited (Bornstein and Gourevitch, 1984).

The Australian and New Zealand system of industrial relations developed around the turn of the twentieth century. In both of these countries, there developed an awards-based system of setting wages and working conditions through conciliation and arbitration. Governments, whether national as in the case of New Zealand, or at both the national and state (provincial or regional) level as in Australia, established state agencies whose task it was to regulate unions. Here unions applied for recognition through one of these state agencies and upon receiving this had exclusive jurisdiction over an entire segment of the workforce, whether they were union members or not. Unions served claims on employers, and, after negotiation with employers (successful or otherwise), the unions and employers registered these claims with arbitral bodies whose job it was either to impose an agreement or to recognize an agreement acceptable to both parties. The resulting award specified wage rates and various employment conditions (such as hours of work, or provisions for leave and vacation), which would cover an entire occupational grouping, industry or specified group of workers. Given the potential free-rider problem associated with this model of industrial relations, unions in both Australia and New Zealand relied upon *de facto* (Australia) and *de jure* (New Zealand) compulsory membership provisions within significant and leading awards for securing their memberships. For more powerful unions, awards acted as minimum standards, which were then supplemented with sectoral and/or local agreements. To reduce competition over wages and terms of employment, arbitral bodies used provisions in one award as the basis for inclusion of similar provisions in awards in other occupations or industries. As arbitral bodies both awarded and enforced awards, disputes between industrial parties tended to be resolved by these bodies. When unions did resort to strike action these were usually outbursts of short duration (a matter of days) and were designed to demonstrate the support of union memberships for their union's bargaining position. Occupational unions became dominant and multi-unionism in one workplace was the norm. Under this system, hundreds of small unions developed with weak financial bases and memberships dependent upon arbitral award provisions. A number of analysts of unions in Australia and New Zealand have argued that unions grew as wards of the state rather than independent working-class organizations, dependent upon award provisions for membership and, in the case of New Zealand, direct state sponsorship for resources. (On Australia, see Howard, 1977; Wooden, 2000; on New Zealand, see Hince, 1993; Walsh, 1997.)

With the exception of the USA, all these countries have experienced significant changes to the legal and juridical framework governing their industrial relations systems in the last ten to fifteen years. In the case of the USA, labour law revisions restricting unions began as early as the late 1940s. Yet, what is important is the decisive and enduring influence that post-World War II industrial relations frameworks had on the development of union memberships, the relationship and strategic focus of leadership and members, and on union organization and activity. By examining the effects of national industrial relations frameworks on the growth and development of unions, we can begin to appreciate the different ways in which unions and labour federations in the five countries have approached strategic responses to a membership crisis that was evolving, particularly from the 1970s onwards.

The legislative frameworks under which unions grew in all these countries had long-term structural effects on the relationship between union leaders and members as well as unions and the state. The conciliation and arbitration systems of industrial relations in Australia and New Zealand delivered high union densities. The corollary was that union memberships in significant industries were not expanded through activist union strategies. Under these conditions, union leaders gained little experience with mobilizing activities centred on memberships and instead developed specialized arbitral skills and became preoccupied with procedural issues. Hince and Harbridge describe New Zealand union leadership as 'in the hands of officials who were solid and accountable administrators, well versed in industrial law and the practices of conciliation and arbitration' (as quoted in Harbridge and Honeybone, 1995: 3). Except for unions with more ardently left-wing leaderships committed to union democracy, unions typically developed with relatively passive and weak membership bases. Unions became characterized by a service relationship between leaders and members, whereby members looked to their unions for job protection, wage increases and regulations governing employment conditions. In both Australia and New Zealand, the relative brevity of strike duration in most industries, associated with and in part an objective of the conciliation and arbitration system (Hill *et al.*, 1984, Chapter 10), reinforced this passivity, rarely requiring the mobilization of members for sustained periods of time. Unions looked to the state for membership protection and fair settlements with employers. This dependence on the state was even more acute in New Zealand where many unions were so small as to make their existence impossible outside the conciliation and arbitration system.

Once governments in Australia and New Zealand began stripping away their institutional and legislative support for unions, these organizations were ill-prepared to respond to declines in union membership. Weak membership attachments to unions, combined in New Zealand with the loss of compulsory membership provisions in 1991, contributed significantly to precipitous declines in union memberships. Unions had few existing structures and little or no recent historical experience to call on for rebuilding their membership base. Finally, unions had so long been 'captured' by their institutionalized relations with the state and employers, it took them some time to articulate strategies that lay outside dependence on a regime of state support.

Despite the differences between the voluntarist British system and the more state-regulated system of industrial relations in the USA and Canada, both systems encouraged a more organic connection between union leaders and their members. In the UK, this was most highly developed as union capacity to bargain, particularly outside the public sector, relied exclusively upon the strength and power of the union in the workplace. Extensive shop steward networks and powerful workplace organization, with the capacity to attract and mobilize members behind strike action, were the defining characteristic of UK unions; they were essential in sustaining power in a voluntarist system. This structure reinforced close ties between union activists, local branches and workers, ties that were not, however, always translated to national union structures or leaders.

Legal regulations in Canada and the USA, which required that unions sign up the majority of workers in each workplace to gain recognition, initially encouraged a strong connection between unions and members. Further, workers had to approve collective agreements through majority votes, something that needed ever-greater attention to membership mobilization once economic conditions deteriorated after 1980. When strikes became the only way for unions to secure a collective agreement, whether in the UK, USA or Canada, the need for active membership support for the union became even more acute. These conditions required leaders to pay attention to membership involvement and concerns and encouraged internal union structures to facilitate communication, if not mobilization. Yet, unlike the UK where unions had to maintain this organic connection to exercise their power, once certified, unions in Canada and the USA could and did rely upon stabilized collective bargaining relationships with employers to maintain their presence – a situation that, except during periods of strike activity, encouraged a more passive relationship between unions and their members.

Yet, these greater organic connections between unions and leaders did not immediately lay the conditions for a remobilization of unions once they came under attack. The centrality of collective bargaining in post-World War II industrial relations in Canada, the UK and the USA directed unions' energies to economic issues and 'responsible' unionism in an effort to lay the conditions for union success at the bargaining table. These developments encouraged unions to distrust membership mobilization and encourage a more passive servicing relationship between union officials and members.

In the UK, where unions faced a prolonged period of sustained political and economic attack, partly as a result of relatively poor national economic performance, the workplace-based power base of unions combined with weaker national union bodies meant that local union branches were often isolated and vulnerable to employer pressures and concessions. Even if they had the organic membership connection to mobilize opposition to attacks, UK unions lacked the resources and concerted institutional structures needed to rebuild memberships and their organization. In Canada and the USA, the problems were somewhat reversed. The organic connection to members had been muted by the growth of institutionalized collective bargaining relationships, which in turn had led to the growth of several powerful, national or international unions with considerable resources. Thus, although these unions had the means to mount a sustained comeback, these resources needed to be channelled into rekindling the organic connection between leaders and members. The greatest blockages to this change lay in union leaders dominated by a business unionism perspective that relied upon professionalized and bureaucratic union processes, a passive hierarchical relationship with members and 'friendly' relations with management and capital more generally. The extent to which union leaders abandoned this view of their role in the economy tempers their application and interpretation of alternative strategies. Radical union leaderships were more likely to break with the past to remobilize their memberships, thus undoing the constraints of existing institutions and practices.

The demobilization of unions in the USA and the UK was never complete and it was even less so in Canada. The decentralization of labour movements in these three countries, in part a consequence of the enterprise-based industrial relations system, left open more political space for local divisions of unions and clusters of activists to initiate change in unions. For this reason it is often at the local or branch levels that new organizing initiatives are spearheaded and most successful. In Canada, the revival in the late 1980s of militant, nationalist politics in unions further tempered demobilization. Competition and ideological debate within some unions encouraged membership mobilization, thus positioning these unions to abandon entrenched institutions and practices in favour of strategies that would rebuild memberships.

While unions in Canada and the USA may have had some structural preparedness for engaging in a strategy of renewal through organizing workers, their decision to embrace such strategies was in large part a consequence of the fact that no other strategic option existed for them to rebuild union membership (on these strategies, see Bronfenbrenner *et al.*, 1998). The state had never proven a steadfast ally, in large part due to the absence of labour or social democratic alternatives. Unions in Canada and the USA had nothing to lose in rebuilding memberships through mobilizing and confrontation with employers and governments. This contrasts with the situation in Australia, New Zealand and the UK where the elections of more sympathetic Labour governments still hold out some hope for state support in rebuilding unions. Thus unions in these countries perceive that they have more to lose in mounting all-out opposition to employers and governments, a situation which likely tempers the adoption of more radical organizing initiatives. This applies in the UK and in some states in Australia where Labor governments have been in power since the mid-1990s. The recent election of a Labour government in New Zealand (1999) may have similar consequences for union strategy. Certainly, the character of the industrial relations legislation enacted by the most recent New Zealand Labour government during its first year in office showed unions the value of state support in creating an environment which is potentially conducive to union renewal (on the UK, see Fairbrother, 2000a; 2000b; McIlroy, 1997; 2000; on Australia, Pocock, 1998; Peetz, 1998; and for New Zealand, Oxenbridge, 1997).

PETER FAIRBROTHER AND CHARLOTTE A. B. YATES

Converging political-economic conditions across the Anglo-American countries

One must be cautious not to highlight too strongly either the similarities or differences in working-class and union developments in these countries in the period after 1945. Unions in the UK, Australia and New Zealand all secured much higher levels of union membership in the post-World War II period than did unions in the USA or Canada, as indicated in Table 1.1.

Further, unions in these three countries mobilized fairly successfully behind their respective labour parties, securing them a position of influence and periodic power in government in the post-World War II period. Opposing conditions held in the USA where union membership never reached above 35 per cent and went into relative decline from 1946 onwards. Any kind of labour party was noticeably absent from the US political scene. As in the USA, Canada's unionization rates only briefly exceeded 35 per cent but have remained steady for much of this period up to the present. Although a social democratic party with ties to unions did emerge in Canada in the 1930s, it failed to secure a position of political influence at the national level, tending to achieve power only in select provincial jurisdictions.

Despite these political and membership differences, none of the labour movements in these five countries was able to secure the same institutionally privileged position of political and economic influence achieved by labour movements in many European countries. Unions in the Anglo-American countries negotiated pay and working conditions with employers and played a role in regulating labour markets, but left political management of the economy to labour parties, where they existed, over which they exerted influence but rarely control. The lack of concerted political and economic influence by unions in Canada, the USA and more recently New Zealand was quite simply a consequence of their relative weakness in their respective economies. Unions in the UK were much more ambivalent about the state, with the Trades Union Congress (TUC) and national union leaderships supporting corporatist-type economic management, but unable to deliver restrictions and secure sacrifices from members when faced with tight labour markets and confident pockets of trade union organization in key sectors of the economy (Royal Commission on Trade Unions and Employers' Associations, 1965–68, 1968). Australia in the 1980s came closest to establishing an institutionalized role for labour in managing the economy. Under a Labor government, Australian unions engaged in 'Accord' politics wherein the central labour body, the Australian Council of Trade Unions (ACTU), negotiated national wage settlement schemes and played a role in 'managing' the economy. However, the timing of this experiment under-mined the labour movement's capacity for securing a long-term place for unions in influencing the discourse and practice of economic management. Low-paid, less strategically located workers did reasonably well out of the Accord, but the effects of the Accord were uneven and many unions grew increasingly sceptical of Accord-style politics (Peetz, 1998; Ewer *et al.*, 1991). Coming at the time when international competitive pressures were mounting on the Australian economy and Keynesian management strategies had lost their legitimacy, unions operating in the Accord environment found them-selves partners in a neo-liberal agenda of restructuring the Australian econ-omy. Rather than securing a position of influence through which to counter anti-union neo-liberal policies, the ACTU was compromised by the erosion of the welfare state, deregulation of the labour market and the decline of union memberships.

The inability of labour movements in the Anglo-American countries to secure an institutionalized and privileged role in policy-making and the increasing emphasis on a neo-liberal agenda of labour market reform in the late 1970s and early 1980s set the stage for unions to become prime targets of restructuring by employers and governments. In the neo-liberal lexicon, impediments to the free market in all spheres were to be eliminated. Given the private market-based power of unions in the Anglo-American countries, it became 'logical' to argue that unions were institutions that impeded the operation of market forces. In Australia this process unfolded in a different manner, although the outcome was not dissimilar. Here the federal Labor government elected in 1983 reintroduced a centralized wage-fixing system and attempted to reform rather than deregulate labour markets. However, during the 1980s there was a slow and cumulative shift in government policy that eventually resulted in a union movement that was circumscribed and constrained in its strategic capacity. Significantly, via the Accord the union movement became a partner in this shift, albeit reluctantly on the part of a number of leading trade unionists and their unions (Ewer *et al.*, 1991). The outcome was that unions and existing industrial relations systems were eventually identified as barriers to international competitiveness and in need of reform.

With the exception of Australia, governments in these countries tended to combine coercive strategies with ideological assaults on unions to deregulate labour markets and restructure industrial relations institutions with the goal of containing or eliminating union influence. Governments were aided in these efforts by sustained high levels of unemployment, often itself a political choice of governments, which had a disciplinary effect on labour. The most

Table 1.1 *Union membership density by country, 1960–99*

Year	USA[1]		Great Britain[2]		Canada[3]		Australia[4]		New Zealand[5]	
	Members ('000s)	Density (%)[a]	Members ('000s)	Density (%)[b]	Members ('000s)	Density (%)[c]	Members ('000s)	Density (%)[d]	Members ('000s)	Density (%)[e]
1960	18117.0	31.4	9437	44.0	1459	32.3	1912.4	58.0	332.4	38.0
1970	20751.0	27.2	10672	48.5	2173	33.6	2314.6	50.0	378.5	34.7
1980	20095.3	23.0	12239	54.5	3397	37.6	2952.1	55.0	516.3	39.4
1990	16739.8	16.1	8835	38.1	4031	34.5	2660.0	40.5	611.3	41.5
1998	16211.4	13.9	7152	29.6	3938	32.5	2037.5	28.1	306.7	17.7
1999	16477.0	13.9	7257	29.5	3600	30.0	1878.2	25.7	302.4	17.0

Notes:

[a] US union density data refers to all full- and part-time workers who are members of a labour union or an employee association as a percentage of all full- and part-time workers, excluding self-employed workers.

[b] British union membership density is calculated on the basis of all employees in Great Britain. Similar data for the UK are not available.

[c] Canadian membership measured as number of paid employees in the workforce who are members of a union and density calculated as union membership as the percentage of non-agricultural workforce.

[d] Australian union density is measured using the size of the employed labour workforce, including agriculture, forestry and fishing, as the denominator.

[e] New Zealand union density is measured using the size of the employed labour force as the denominator.

Sources:

[1] U.S. Department of Labor (1960–99) *Bureau of Labor Statistics, Employment and Earnings*, Washington D.C.: Government Printing Office.

[2] J. Waddington (2000) 'United Kingdom: Recovering from the Neo-Liberal Assault', in J. Waddington and R. Hoffmann (eds) *Trade Unions in Europe: Facing Challenges and Searching for Solutions*. Brussels: European Trade Union Institute, p. 585.

[3] Statistics Canada, *Labour Force Survey*, Catalogue No. 75-001, selected years.

[4] Australian Bureau of Statistics, *Trade Union Statistics Australia*, Catalogue No. 6323.0 (1960–80). Catalogue subsequently discontinued. Australian Bureau of Statistics, *Trade Union Members Australia*, Catalogue No. 6325.0 (1990). Catalogue subsequently discontinued. Australian Bureau of Statistics, *Employee Earnings, Benefits and Trade Union Membership Australia*, Catalogue No. 6310.0 (1998–9). The pre-1990 data is not directly comparable with the 1990 and post-1990 data because of different collection methods.

[5] New Zealand Department of Labour (1991) *Annual Reports*. Wellington, Government Printer and Crawford A., Harbridge R., and Walsh P. (1999) 'Unions and Union Membership in New Zealand: Annual Review for 1998', *New Zealand Journal of Industrial Relations*, 24 (3): 383–96.

dramatic example of restructuring of labour market and industrial relations systems occurred in New Zealand in 1990. There, the National government, elected in 1990, introduced legislation that eliminated centralized bargaining, tilted the balance towards individual employment contracts and ended the legal protections upon which unions had always depended. The result, as can be seen in Table 1.1, was a collapse of union membership. In the USA, the legislative environment in which unions have operated has, since 1947, been inimical to union interests. The election of Ronald Reagan as US President in 1980, his changes to the National Labor Relations Board and the firing of striking air controllers, chilled the environment further, contributing to continued steady decline in union membership. In the UK, the mobilization of state power to defeat the 1984/5 miners' strike played a similar but even more significant role. Governments under Margaret Thatcher, first elected in 1979, radically restructured the labour market, instituted restrictions on trade unions through new employment legislation and did the greatest damage by waging an ideological war against unions. Thatcher successfully mobilized popular opinion against unions, which she blamed for Britain's economic ills and, in the aftermath of the miners' strike, vilified union leaders as undemocratic and authoritarian. As in the USA, this led to gradual erosion of union membership rather than a free fall like that exhibited in New Zealand. In Canada, as is revealed in Table 1.1, union memberships remained relatively steady for much of the period under investigation. The country's economy is highly regionalized and provincial governments play the primary role in regulating the labour market. The effect of this political-economic fragmentation within Canada has been uneven deregulation of labour markets and the dismantling of the existing industrial relations system. Only recently have governments in several jurisdictions undertaken a sustained legislative and ideological assault on unions modelled on American practice, one effect of which has been the recent decline in union memberships. Australia stands out as the one country where deregulation of labour markets and devolution of the industrial relations system to encourage flexibility and responsiveness to the competitiveness of enterprise was achieved initially through consent from central labour bodies. Under the Hawke Labor government, elected in 1993, centralized protection for unions was maintained, giving unions some time to develop strategies to meet the economic challenges that were becoming apparent. Unfortunately, most unions were unsuccessful in adapting to new conditions and membership levels continued to decline. When the Keating Labor government (1991–6) introduced legislative changes that encouraged enterprise bargaining and flexibility, this added momentum to a process of union decline already in train. Once this door was opened, the subsequent conservative coalition (Liberal and National parties) government accelerated changes to the industrial relations system and union recognition, measures that were unsuccessfully opposed by the labour movement. The outcome has been a precipitous decline in union membership throughout the 1990s.

Employers in these five countries have also been emboldened by changes in the political and ideological climate to increase their efforts either to contain or eliminate union influence in their workplaces. Although employers in the USA have gained the greatest notoriety for their union-avoidance tactics, similar tactics have been increasingly evident in the other four countries. A converging discourse and strategy of opposition to unions amongst employers across these countries is arguably aided by the championing of the US model of labour market deregulation by various supranational bodies such as the Organization for Economic Co-operation and Development (OECD, 1994), the exponential growth in English-language management literature on how to avoid unions and the emergence of American-based multinational law firms consulting with employers on union avoidance and union busting. Disputes from the mid-1990s onwards, ranging from the waterfront struggles in Australia through the Liverpool dock workers' strike and the British Airways air attendants' dispute in the UK, the Caterpillar and Yellowknife gold-mine strikes in Canada to the dispute at the New Zealand ports over casualization, point to the growing employer hostility encountered by labour movements in these countries.

Although union memberships across the five countries have declined in part as a result of government actions and employer offensives, they have also been undercut by structural changes in the economy, and in particular labour markets. Employment in traditional areas of union strength, namely manufacturing, resource extraction, transportation and the public sector, has declined while employment in the private service sector, where unions across the five countries are weak, has increased (OECD, 2000). The drive for labour flexibility and just-in-time production has meant changes to the employment contract, whereby full-time work is declining, and part-time, casual and contract work is on the increase (O'Connor et al., 1999: 72; OECD, 1994; Campbell and Burgess, 2001). Again, these changes cut into traditional sources of union membership, which have been concentrated amongst full-time permanent workers.

The example of the steel industry underscores the effects of labour-market changes on unions across the countries. The steel industry, because of rapid technological change, the shifting of production to non-union mini-mills and growing international competition, has shed thousands of workers from its employment rolls. This has severely weakened unions in this industry, reducing their memberships and their strategic capacity to negotiate with management from a position of strength. Interestingly, in a number of countries, notably Canada, the USA and Britain, union responses to these conditions have been similar, aimed at recruiting membership outside their traditional economic base (for example, see Chapter 11).

Declining union memberships in traditional strongholds have combined in several countries with ongoing changes in the labour force, most notably continued increases in labour force participation by women and ethnic and racial minorities, to question the basis of unionism. Unions are confronted with the need to expand their organizational focus to include these groups and change symbolic representations of unions so that they better mirror the changing composition of the workforce (on women, see Briskin and McDermott, 1993; Cobble, 1991). Interestingly, women and ethnic and racial minorities have been found in Britain, the USA, Canada and Australia to be more likely to join unions than Anglo-Saxon men. In Australia, where this has long been the case, workers from non-English-speaking backgrounds have traditionally been more highly unionized than Australian-born workers or workers from English-speaking backgrounds. Yet, union leadership and established structures and practices in all the five countries have still tended to favour Anglo-Saxon men, a situation that some unions and labour movements are trying to change.

The cumulative effect of structural and political-legislative changes to labour markets is seen in declining union memberships, which has led to a sense of crisis within unions. In the context of this crisis, unions have focused on organizing, and in many cases the organizing model, as a key part of their strategic response to membership declines. Yet, despite the common problem of declining memberships and converging labour market conditions, national industrial relations institutions and morphologies of national labour movements play a decisive role in how organizing is understood and strategically pursued. In essence, the particular strategic response by unions and labour federations across the five countries continues to be path dependent, arising from the historical legacy of each union movement.

Ideas and strategies across borders: organizing – a common solution

While union adaptation in response to crisis is not new, the current moment raises important new questions about the boundaries of unionism. In earlier periods, national trade union movements were assaulted and threatened, but were able to rebuild, often with the tacit support of governments. For example, in the 1890s unions in Australia all but disappeared but slowly re-established themselves with government support. The Great Depression of the 1930s, followed by World War II provided an impetus to union organizing in all the countries. In the case of the trade union movements covered by this study, the post-World War II period was one of consolidation and expansion, resulting in the building of more powerful and prominent union movements. Nonetheless, the trajectories of union growth were different between countries, with union density peaking in the USA as early as 1946 compared to peaks in 1979 in Britain and even later for the Canadian labour movement. At present, and under more hostile political and economic conditions, it is impossible to predict whether contemporary union adaptation will be similarly effective in restoring the influence of unions and national labour movements. Nonetheless, an emerging debate on union renewal through organizing makes the present period a critical one for assessing the future of unions in these five countries.

For much of the post-World War II period, up until the 1980s, unions focused their energies on bargaining with employers, with periodic spurts of political activism around election times. Industrial relations were highly institutionalized, whether through state arbitration systems, such as in Australia and New Zealand, or through workplace-based employer-union relations, as developed in the USA, UK and Canada. Unions paid little strategic attention to, and invested few resources in, actively organizing the unorganized. Even in the USA, where union membership decline was evident in the 1960s, much earlier than in the other countries, organizing was not a priority for unions.

The election of Margaret Thatcher in the UK in 1979 and Ronald Reagan in the USA in 1980 marked a radical shift in government orientations towards unions in these countries. These elections symbolized, more broadly across the Anglo-American countries, a regime change in industrial relations marked by active, although not universal, employer hostility to unions, and rapid labour market deregulation, with particular emphasis on restricting the scope of union influence. Declining union memberships (see Table 1.1) combined with the growing popularity of neo-liberal market solutions to economic crisis opened up space in the political discourse for a growing cacophony of criticism of unions. Responsibility for union membership decline was laid squarely at the feet of unions themselves, with many analysts and popular pundits arguing that unions had outlived their usefulness. As Fiorito, Jarley and Delaney wrote, unions were blamed for a host of 'sins':

[from] undemocratic practices, inadequate or excessive centralization, insufficient rationalization, unwillingness to innovate, overly narrow goals, insufficient or poorly focused organizing effort, and reliance on a 'service model' of unions that fails to activate rank-and-file workers ... Although many of the criticisms are complementary, some are potentially in conflict: too little versus too much centralization, for example, or a need for greater rationalization – operating in a more 'business-like manner' – versus a need for more democracy. (1995: 614)

After a period of disarray and retrenchment, unions have begun to regroup, looking for new ways to rebuild their memberships and restore their political-economic legitimacy and influence.

The quest for organization

One response to these challenges has been to organize the unorganized and to reorganize the organized. In rather uneven ways, and after experiments with other approaches, such as union consolidation through mergers or expanding services offered to union members, organizing emerged as the strategy for union revitalization. Such an approach was pursued by many unions and national labour movements across the five Anglo-American countries covered by this study. Very quickly, debate over how this was to be done centred on US proponents and critics of competing, and sometimes interlocking strategies for union renewal through new organizing initiatives and the organizing model. These ideas filtered through American unions in the early 1990s, via informal discussions amongst 'activist-oriented' officials from unions such as the Service Employees International Union (SEIU), Amalgamated Clothing and Textile Workers Union (ACTWU and now the Union of Needletrades, Industrial and Textile Employees, UNITE), Teamsters and Communications Workers of America (CWA) as well as via the journal *Labor Research Review* (see various issues). These new organizing initiatives and models spread rapidly out from the USA in the early 1990s, receiving further impetus after the 1995 election of a new leadership to the American Federation of Labor – Congress of Industrial Organizations (AFL-CIO).

Debate over organizing strategies has distinguished two models of union development: the 'service' model versus the 'organizing' model.

- *Service model:* Unions should organize to service the membership more effectively and efficiently. Union paid union staff and full-time officials solve problems for workers, relying upon expertise and central union resources. They channel union-management problems through formal labour-management institutions and legalistic grievance and arbitration processes. This model relies heavily upon union staff who service the membership on the assumption that this secures membership support by representing individual member's interests. This form of trade unionism is seen by commentators as the prevailing model, and increasingly in need of revision as unions grapple with reduced resources.

- *Organizing model:* Members are active participants in the way unions organize and operate, thereby contributing to the collective focus and practice of the union. Members are encouraged and 'trained' to take responsibility for solving their own and the collective's problems and to take an active role in extending union membership through organizing. The emphasis in training is on collective problem solving and self-sufficiency, with the intention of taking pressure off full-time officials. Problems are often solved in 'creative' fashions, circumventing established institutions, and placing direct pressure on employers through community and workplace activism. (Grabelsky and Hurd, 1994; Fletcher and Hurd, 1998; Oxenbridge, 1997; Schenck in Chapter 12)

Between these two models, debates over union renewal focus on the relationship between forms of organizing and effective recruitment, including shifting more resources into organizing, building community-based organizing coalitions with non-government organizations, and utilizing more grassroots, bottom-up union-building strategies during organizing campaigns. The articulation of these strategies by the AFL-CIO and some affiliates, combined with research by Kate Bronfenbrenner demonstrating the positive effect on organizing outcomes of rank-and-file intensive organizing strategies (Bronfenbrenner and Juravich, 1998), had a catalytic effect on debates over the future of unions and the strategies employed by unions in their organizing efforts.

These organizing initiatives came rapidly to be seen as the solution to American labour movement problems, and to those of other countries. In the USA, the Justice for Janitors campaign in California symbolized for union activists and commentators alike the potential of the community-based organizing strategy for rebuilding union memberships. This multi-year campaign began in 1990 when more than 8000 janitors in California joined the SEIU and signed a contract. The campaign's success relied upon massive rank-and-file activism, community coalitions, creative 'guerrilla'-like tactics and an organizational renewal of the union itself which included shifting resources into organizing. By 1997, 45 per cent of the SEIU's total US budget was devoted to organizing (Waldinger *et al.*, 1998; Fletcher and Hurd, 1998). Creative organizing by other unions, such as the CWA and Hotel and Restaurant Employees Union (HERE), several unions in the building trades, and UNITE, confirmed the importance of new approaches to organizing for rebuilding the fortunes of the American labour movement (Bronfenbrenner *et al.*, 1998; Cobble, 1993; Grabelsky and Hurd, 1994). Additionally, the community union organizing strategies advocated as part of the organizing model were designed with the express intent of reaching outwards to new communities of workers amongst which unions had weak or non-existent networks and contacts thereby further contributing to this process of renewal (Banks, 1991; Milkman, 2000).

As labour movements across the Anglo-American world became increasingly concerned about their future in the face of membership decline and organizational atrophy, unions and labour federations looked across borders to each other for example and inspiration (Oxenbridge, 1997; Pocock, 1998; Heery, 1999; Carter, 2000). The cross-fertilization of ideas and union practices between countries was facilitated by the historical-cultural links between Anglo-American countries, underpinned by a common language, as well as the increasing ease of communication and social exchange. Delegations of visiting union leaders to the USA learned about the organizing model and other organizing initiatives such as the AFL-CIO's Organizing Institute and community-based organizing. At the same time key union leaders and experts from the USA travelled throughout the Anglo-American world. The distinctions and differences in emphasis in US organizing strategies notwithstanding, these strategies were regarded collectively as parts of the organizing model by the trade union movement internationally.

The Australian and New Zealand union movements were two of the earliest to begin experimenting with the 'organizing model' in 1993–4, although less so in New Zealand than Australia. The servicing relationship between members and leaders and the professionalization and bureaucratization of union activities, both of which are at the heart of the organizing model's critique, resonated with unions in Australia and New Zealand. Having in many cases tried and failed to bolster union memberships in the 1980s and 1990s initially through offering a wide range of new services to members, many unions in Australia and New Zealand learned the limits of servicing as a strategy for rebuilding membership. Moreover, the enterprise-based model for organizing workers, which was implicit in the American organizing model, increasingly made sense in Australia and New Zealand where governments insisted that the key to economic competitiveness lay in micro-economic reform, at the enterprise level. It is therefore not surprising that the organizing model was embraced by some unions in these countries. For the ACTU, arguably it was a response to the continued decline in aggregate union membership, despite several strategic initiatives in the late 1980s and early 1990s to restore union membership, especially in promoting union mergers (see Chapter 4). For New Zealand unions, as both the Walsh and Crawford (Chapter 6) and the Oxenbridge (Chapter 7) chapters demon-strate, the organizing model came to New Zealand after years of steep membership decline and an organizational crisis that wiped out several unions and left many others beleaguered. But whether this model was embraced, how it was interpreted and how it changed union strategy was mediated through the enduring legacy of unions that had grown up under the protection of an industrial relations system of conciliation and arbitration.

Moreover, the fact that labour governments still rely upon unions for electoral support and periodically gain power tempers the extent to which many unions in Australia and New Zealand are willing to engage in militant confrontational strategies that could undermine future promises of social partnerships. In New Zealand, for example, there was a dual face to the union response. On the one hand, as both Oxenbridge (Chapter 7) and Walsh and Crawford (Chapter 6) show, for many unions one response to massive membership defection was to strengthen and develop workplace representation. On the other hand, unions also began to embrace partner-ship models, whereby unions sought to contribute to corporate efficiency and performance (known as 'strategic unionism', see Chapter 6). Thus while many unions became convinced that hitherto cooperative strategies had played into the hands of employers, rather than bolstering the presence of unions, there was in both Australia and New Zealand caution about a com-prehensive take-up of the organizing model.

In the UK, union membership decline and increased political and eco-nomic isolation forced the TUC to begin looking to organizational solutions to these problems as well as reconsidering policy stances. During the 1980s, the TUC and leading unions embarked on a reconsideration of the focus of trade unionism in the UK, which laid the foundation for the partnership policies and organizational strategies of the 1990s (Taylor, 2000). During this period, the TUC adopted a more positive outlook on the European Union and began a consideration of social partnership approaches familiar in a number of other European countries. At the same time, unions, supported by the TUC, began to experiment with the British version of the US organizing model, as a means to recruit new members and extend the membership base (Taylor, 2000: 255–7). Further, the senior leadership worked closely in the 1980s with the Labour Party in opposition, giving some grounds for optimism that with the future election of a Labour government the trade union movement, and particularly the TUC, would have a positive role to play. However, when the resulting organizational strategies apparently failed, the TUC, in particular, looked again at US developments as well as conducting a more sustained examination of Australian union strategies and the partnership models evident in mainland Europe (Chapter 8). Consistent with this history, the TUC remained equivocal about wholesale adoption of the organizing model, and incorporated elements of this model alongside a continued desire for partnership and compromise. Critical to this approach was the re-election of a Labour government in 1997 and the promotion of a more benign approach towards trade unionism by the state, although in practice the relationship with the government has proved fraught and somewhat dissatisfying for individual trade unions and the TUC. A number of unions, supported by the TUC, pursued a twin strategy of organizing as principally concerned with membership recruitment and retention and a partnership strategy, focused on securing union-employer agreements on union rights (see Chapter 8 and Heery, 1999). Yet few individual unions identified with the organizing strategy in any committed and comprehensive way (Carter, 2000).

Attempts to embrace the organizing model in Canada were equally prob-lematic. This was due to the relative stability of union membership throughout the 1980s and 1990s as well as heightened political-ideological debate and splits within the labour movements, which pitted more militant nationalist and public sector unions, against American-based international unions. With their main operations, including their headquarters in the USA, international unions represent approximately 30 per cent of unionized workers in Canada and were the major conveyor of ideas and strategies centred on the organizing model. Many other unions, however, resisted these ideas, in part due to suspicions that American lessons about union renewal could and should not be imported into Canada. These unions often devel-oped their own organizing strategies, embracing a diverse range of com-munity organizing strategies that built upon years of alliances between community groups and unions. A series of tensions emerged within and between unions over proactive and defensive strategies and partnership and mobilizing strategies, which in many cases fuelled splits and ideological differ-ences within the labour movement (Chapters 10 and 11). One result of this growing competition between unions and the debate over the best way forward has been the decline in influence of central labour federations, which are caught in the crossfire of inter-union rivalry and political-ideological differences. Hence, while the organizing model has made its way into many unions' strategic development, it has not become a dominant model for union renewal.

In some ways, the Canadian case stands out as exceptional when compared with the other four countries, in that trade union membership levels were maintained for a far longer time than elsewhere. Nonetheless, Canadian union leaderships were aware of the impending difficulties they faced as provincial and the national governments promoted neo-liberal reforms (see Chapter 10). The Canadian case also highlights the ways in which the development of localized organizing strategies redefined the boundaries of union organization and activity in the 1980s. Yet, the Canadian case (Chapters 10 and 11) as well as the case studies found in chapters by Ewer and Probert (Chapter 5), Oxenbridge (Chapter 7) and Carter (Chapter 9) highlight an emergent debate in all the countries over the adequacy and transferability of the organizing model. A discussion of critiques of this model underscores the strategic debate and realignment taking place within individual unions and entire national labour movements around issues of membership and organizational renewal.

Many unions and labour federations latched on to new organizing initiatives as the answer to their problems of membership decline, organizational sclerosis and inadequate resources. Several unions, using the lexicon of the organizing model, tried to impose new organizing initiatives and strategies on to union branches and activists. Yet, as the chapters by Carter (Chapter 9), Oxenbridge (Chapter 7) and Voss and Sherman (Chapter 3) show, any simple imposition of this model was fraught with problems, most notably membership, staff and leadership resistance. In some places, the result has been adaptation of the model to fit varying union and national historical and institutional legacies. Elsewhere, in other unions, the organizing model has failed to take root at all or has been adopted in a piecemeal fashion. As Bronfenbrenner has also found in her series of studies of US union organizing campaigns (Chapter 2), many unions saw these new models of organizing as simply an effective means to mobilize both organized and unorganized workers as dues payers for the *status quo* rather than a sincere effort to build real membership participation and ownership of their union.

One of the particular concerns of many unions was the juxtaposition of servicing versus organizing contained in the organizing model (see Chapters 5, 9, 10 and 11). Organizing was central to the idea of expanding union memberships, but many unions rejected the view of servicing as essentially passive and detrimental to union revitalization. Many industrial unions in Canada, for instance, have seen servicing as central to securing the long-term support of union members and a means of adapting hitherto centralized industrial institutions to the service sector in an effort to take wages out of competition and find creative ways of delivering benefits (Chapter 11). Tensions in other unions (see Chapters 5 and 9) caused debates about the possibility for servicing to be done in a manner that subsequently encouraged membership activism and support for the union. In yet other countries, the UK and to a lesser extent New Zealand, servicing versus organizing was supplanted by organizing versus partnership (Chapter 8).

A more broad-ranging critique of the 'organizing model' centres on its political and strategic inadequacy as an end in itself. Although the 'organizing model' is built on practices involving greater internal union democracy, membership activism and broader-based community alliances and coalitions, critics have argued that it lacks or side-steps a coherent political project aimed at rebuilding the strength of the working class (Fletcher and Hurd, 1998: 52). The absence of an explicitly articulated political strategy within the organizing model has led to two different solutions to this dilemma. In Canada and the USA, where unions are enterprise based and lack concerted political representation through governing labour or social democratric parties, an argument has been made about the need to combine the ideas in the organizing model with a broader political agenda of democratization to encourage the growth of social movement unionism (see Chapter 12). According to Kim Moody, social movement unionism asserts 'the centrality of union democracy as a source of power and broader social vision, and outreach as a means of enhancing that power' (1997: 4).

The argument is that the organizing model tends to address elements of the crisis of labour unionism rather than its source. It is an appropriate tactic to breathe life into local unions that have relied too heavily on bureaucratic methods but it is not a sufficient antidote to the broader deficiencies of business unionism. Thus, there is a need to build the links between organizing for self-interest and organizing for social justice and a transformation of the broader 'regime politique' based on a new mobilized and oppositional working class (Gindin, 1995: 268; also see Beynon in Chapter 13).

In contrast, in the UK, with its social democratic or Labour Party governance, debate has focused on 'social partnership' versus the rebuilding of an oppositional politics (Heery, 1999; and Chapter 8). By partnership is meant an accommodative, cooperative and engaged form of unionism prepared to work with employers, government and other relevant agencies at workplace, regional and national levels (Martinez Lucio and Stuart, 2000). The notion of partnership unionism established a tension between a more social democratic, *qua* European form of participation, with its focus on tripartite-type arrangements, and one where the focus is on promoting employer-trade union agreements through membership activism. In the latter case, the emphasis is on representation, mobilization and bargaining procedures. Recently, Heery has proposed an argument that seeks to resolve this dilemma. For him, 'organizing' builds a form of representation that is a pre-condition for effective partnership between employers and trade unions (Heery, 1999). Heery's attempted resolution notwithstanding, increasingly in the UK the emphasis is on accommodative forms of unionism, rather than a trade unionism concerned with renewal and resistance (see Chapter 8).

One final distinguishing feature in relation to the adoption of organizing or partnership models by these five trade union movements lies in the role played by labour federations in their respective countries. In none of the countries did the labour union federations achieve the degree of national influence over economic policy and national labour market development experienced in many mainland European and especially social democratic countries. Yet, in three of these countries, the USA, Australia and the UK, labour federations have played a pivotal role in advancing a renewal strategy based on organizing. These federations played a decisive role in coordinating organizing initiatives, training organizers and providing strategic leadership to their respective national labour movements. Nonetheless, the actual work of organizing on the ground remains the responsibility of individual unions. In New Zealand and Canada, with the exception of the province of British Columbia, labour federations have been unable to play a leadership or coordinating role in organizing. Such initiatives have instead been driven by individual unions, the result of which has been a less coordinated, more diffuse approach and strategy. In Canada, in particular, this localization of responsibility for organizing has led to growing rivalry and competition between unions, a situation that although not apparently detrimental to organizing success has further eroded the strategic capacity of labour federations, most notably the Canadian Labour Congress (CLC). In New Zealand, a new leadership was elected to the Council of Trade Unions (CTU) in 1999. They promoted an emphasis on grassroots organizing within the federation and at an individual union level, which contributed to a major change in union organization and operation. These developments included a change in resource allocation within unions, union style and an increase in the level of union protest and campaigning among the general public (see Chapter 7).

Although the role played by the labour federations in organizing has had no apparent decisive impact on the success of membership recruitment and union renewal, it does change the dynamics of organizing. In New Zealand and Canada where labour federations play a weak role in organizing, the process of union renewal was not centrally coordinated but relied upon individual unions and local union branches. Although this may result in a duplication of resources and competition between unions, there is no clear reason why this should have a negative effect on organizing outcomes given the structural importance of local union branches rebuilding union support amongst individual workers. Conversely, while central coordination of organizing through labour federations, as exists in the USA, Australia and the UK, reduces waste of resources through duplication and inter-union competition, without strong workplace connections and commitments from local activists, it is extremely unlikely that labour federations can themselves rebuild union memberships. The workplace remains the primary site of union activity. It is here that class relations are forged, surplus produced, members recruited, organized and potentially involved in discussions about union strategies and tactics.

What these debates and differences underline is the contested nature of the concept of 'organizing' and its elasticity. In some contexts, particularly the UK, the term is synonymous with recruiting and more moderate institutional change; in others, such as the USA, Australia, and Canada, it is counterposed to the idea of the union as an external, servicing organization to indicate a model of more active and participative unionism in which unions mobilize against employers. The stance taken here is that the concept of organizing should be understood to encompass those attempts to promote worker self-organization, albeit not restricted simply to the workplace.

In many countries, unions have initially been attracted to organizing the unorganized rather than examining and reinforcing the effectiveness of the organization of existing members. In the UK, for instance, there has been relatively little concern with what has become termed internal organizing. For particular reasons, namely the nature of battles over collective agreements, the beleaguered position of trade unions and the threat of decertification, internal organizing has received increasing attention in the USA. Moreover, there is much evidence that the effectiveness of recruitment is intimately linked to the organizing tactics adopted, which prefigure democratic and representative forms of workplace organization (Bronfenbrenner *et al.*, 1998).

With reference to the USA, Fletcher and Hurd (1998) argue that organizing should focus on external organizing by debating the scope and scale of organizing, the resource base for the organizing programme, the focus of organizing (jurisdiction and demographics) and the strategy to be pursued. This emphasis on membership expansion through organizing the unorganized developed initially out of the US and Canadian experiences with workplace campaigns for certification and encouraged a host of new organizing strategies and debates over how best to build majority support for unions in previously non-union workplaces. This external organizing corresponds most closely in Britain, Australia and New Zealand to notions of membership recruitment and retention, which are differently articulated in light of distinct national institutional legacies and the absence of requirements for majority support for unions desiring to represent workers.

Recently, there has emerged a way of bridging the gap between internal and external organizing focused on comprehensive union building (Chapters 2 and 3). Here the emphasis is on promoting external and internal organizing, focusing on building leadership amongst the rank-and-file workers, engaging in direct pressure on employers in the workplace and community, focusing on justice issues, as well as bread and butter issues. Despite the different emphases suggested by the term 'organizing', there are similarities across these five countries. The critical dimension of a comprehensive union-building strategy is one where the focus of organizing is on building local forms of activism, experimenting with ways of redefining the boundaries of traditional forms of unions, as well as refocusing and identifying new subjects with which unions deal and around which they organize. In this way the term 'organizing' provides a unifying focus across these different union movements.

Overall, these debates point to a recognition that the circumstances and conditions for bargaining and negotiation, as well as worker representation, are in the process of transformation. Yet, despite this open-endedness to the meaning of organizing and the organizing model, this is still a debate that has more resonance within the Anglo-American countries than, for example, European countries. As argued above, the transference of ideas across countries with a common language and more dialogue between unions across countries, owing to increased ease of travel and communication in part explain this greater resonance of debates over the organizing model amongst these five countries. A second, but no less important reason for this convergence lies in the many shared experiences of labour movements in Anglo-American countries.

Final comment

The labour movements across the five countries of this study have responded to the current union crisis with renewed emphasis on organizing both members and non-members. In many cases they have adopted the American-based organizing model as a guide if not an archetype of reform. Yet, the legacy of past industrial relations, and the roles played by labour federations in organizing, help us to understand the different interpretations and problems encountered by unions and centrals across these countries in rebuilding memberships. Moreover they provide clues to the future shape, if not success, of unions and national labour movements as they rebuild themselves from the ashes left behind in the wake of neo-liberal policies and ideologies. It is to these concerns that we now turn.

The themes addressed in this chapter are taken up in a variety of ways by the contributors to the book. Each country is examined, first in a general overview chapter, identifying some of the central issues that define the recent history of these different trade union movements. In some cases the emphasis is on the role of the central labour federations, in others the focus is on aspects of the trade union movement as a whole (Chapters 2, 4, 6, 8 and 10). These chapters are each followed by more focused studies, of individual unions, tracing out the ways in which particular unions, or clusters of unions, have addressed the threats and challenges of the last two decades (Chapters 3, 5, 7, 9 and 11). These country-focused chapters are followed by two concluding chapters, in which the analytic and political questions raised by the earlier chapters are examined. In the first of these chapters (12) the question of social movement unionism is interrogated and in the last chapter (13) the possible futures for trade unions are presented. The result is a comprehensive assessment of trade unionism in these five countries at the end of the last millennium and the beginning of the new one.

Note

[1]   This chapter has been drafted by the two editors, but has benefited from the input of all the other contributors to the book. It has gone through three major revisions, as well as other lesser revisions and alterations. The contributors come from a range of disciplines and approach questions relating to trade unionism differently, but they are also bound together by a number of common understandings about the history of trade unionism in the five countries as well as a shared view of the

problems unions face and the possible range of solutions on offer. The result is that this chapter is a collective statement of the focus and scope of the book, indicating a general approach to questions relating to trade unions in the current political economy. Readers will tell the contributors if they have succeeded.

References

Australian Bureau of Statistics, *Trade Union Statistics Australia*, Catalogue No. 6323.0 (1960–80).

Australian Bureau of Statistics, *Trade Union Members Australia*, Catalogue No. 6325.0 (1990).

Australian Bureau of Statistics, *Employee Earnings, Benefits and Trade Union Membership Australia*, Catalogue No. 6310.0 (1998–9).

Banks, A. (1991) 'The Power and Promise of Community Unionism', *Labour Research Review*, 18 (2): 17–31.

Bornstein, S. and Gourevitch, P. (1984) 'Unions in a Declining Economy: The Case of the British TUC', in Gourevitch P., Martin A., Ross G., Allen C., Bornstein S. and Markovits A. (eds) *Unions and Economic Crisis: Britain, West Germany and Sweden*, London: George Allen & Unwin, pp. 13–88.

Briskin, L. and McDermott, P. (eds) (1993) *Women Challenging Unions: Feminism, Democracy and Militancy*, Toronto: University of Toronto Press.

Bronfenbrenner, K. and Juravich, T. (1998) 'It Takes More Than House Calls: Organizing to Win with a Comprehensive Union-Building Strategy', in Bronfenbrenner, K., Friedman, S., Hurd, R., Oswald, R. and Seeter, R. (eds) *Organizing to Win: New Research on Union Strategies*, Ithaca and London: ILR Press.

Bronfenbrenner, K., Friedman, S., Hurd, R., Oswald, R. and Seeber, R. (eds) (1998) *Organizing to Win: New Research on Union Strategies*, Ithaca and London: ILR Press.

Campbell, I. and Burgess, J. (2001) 'Casual Employment in Australia and Temporary Employment in Europe: Developing a Cross-National Comparison', *Work, Employment and Society*, 15 (1): 171–84.

Card, D. and Freeman, R. (eds) *Small Differences That Matter: Labour Markets and Income Maintenance in Canada and the United States*, Chicago: University of Chicago Press.

Carter, B. (2000) 'Adoption of the Organising Model in British Trade Unions: Some Evidence from Manufacturing, Science and Finance (MSF)', *Work, Employment and Society*, 14 (1): 117–36.

Carter, B. and Fairbrother, P. (1999) 'The Transformation of British Public Sector Industrial Relations', *Historical Studies in Industrial Relations*, 7: 119–46.

Cobble, D. (1991) 'Organizing the Postindustrial Work Force: Lessons from the History of Waitress Unionism', *Industrial and Labor Relations Review*, 44 (3): 419–36.

Cobble, D. (1993) *Women and Unions: Forging a Partnership*, Ithaca, NY: ILR Press.

Cornish, M. and Spink, L. (1994) *Organizing Unions*, Toronto: Second Story Press.

Crawford, A., Harbridge, R. and Walsh, P. (1999) 'Unions and Union Membership in New Zealand: Annual Review for 1998', *New Zealand Journal of Industrial Relations*, 24(3): 383–96.

Esping-Andersen, G. (1990) *The Three Worlds of Welfare Capitalism*, Princeton, NJ: Princeton University Press.

Ewer, P., Hampson, S., Lloyd, C., Rainford, J., Rix S. and Smith M. (1991) *The Politics of the Accord*, Sydney: Pluto Press.

Fairbrother, P. (2000a) 'British Trade Unions Facing the Future', *Capital and Class*, 71: 47–78.

Fairbrother, P. (2000b) *Trade Unions at the Crossroads*, London: Mansell.

Fiorito, J., Jarley, P. and Delaney, J. (1995) 'National Union Effectiveness in Organizing: Measures and Influences', *Industrial and Labor Relations Review (Ithaca)*, 48 (4): 613–34.

Fletcher, B. and Hurd, R. (1998) 'Beyond the Organizing Model: The Transformation Process in Local Unions', in Bronfenbrenner, K., Friedman, S., Hurd, R., Oswald, R. and Seeber, R. (eds) *Organizing to Win: New Research on Union Strategies*, Ithaca: Cornell University Press, pp. 37–53.

Gindin, S. (1995) *The Canadian Auto Workers: The Birth and Transformation of a Union*, Toronto: James Lorimer & Co.

Goldfield, M. (1987) *The Decline of Organized Labor in the United States*, Chicago: University of Chicago Press.

Grabelsky, J. and Hurd, R. (1994) 'Reinventing an Organizing Union: Strategies for Change', *Proceedings of the Industrial Relations Research Association 46th Annual Meeting*, January 3–5, Boston, pp. 95–104.

Harbridge, R. and Honeybone, A. (1995) 'External Legitimacy of Unions: Trends in New Zealand', paper presented to Second International Conference on Emerging Union Structures, Stockholm, Sweden, 11–14 June.

Heery, E. (1999) 'Social Movement or Social Partner? Strategies for the Revitalisation of British Trade Unionism', European Community Studies Association Annual Conference, June 2–6, Pittsburgh, USA.

Hill, J., William H. and Lansbury, R. (1984) *Industrial Relations: An Australian Introduction*, Melbourne: Longman Cheshire.

Hince, K. (1993) 'Is Euro-American Union Theory Universally Applicable? An Australasian Perspective', in Adams, R. and Meltz, N. (eds) *Industrial Relations Theory: Its Nature, Scope and Pedagogy*, London: IMLR Press/Rutgers University: Scarecrow Press, pp. 81–102.

Howard, W. (1977) 'Australian Trade Unions in the Context of Union Theory', *Journal of Industrial Relations*, 19 (3): 255–73.

Jamieson, S. (1973) *Industrial Relations in Canada*, second edition, New York: St. Martin's Press.

Martinez-Lucio, M. and Stuart, M. (2000) 'Swimming Against the Tide: Social Partnership, Mutual Gains and the Renewal of "Tired" HRM', Centre for Industrial Relations and Human Resource Management, Discussion Paper Series, IH00/03 University of Leeds.

McIlroy, J. (1997) 'Still under Siege: British Trade Unions at the Turn of the Century', *Historical Studies in Industrial Relations*, 3 (March): 93–122.

McIlroy, J. (2000) 'New Labour, New Unions, New Left', *Capital and Class*, No. 71: 11–45.

Milkman, R. (ed.) (2000) *Organizing Immigrants: The Challenge for Unions in Contemporary California*, Ithaca: Cornell University Press.

Moody, K. (1997) *Workers in a Lean World: Unions in the International Economy*, London, New York: Verso.

New Zealand Department of Labour (1991) *Annual Reports*, Wellington: Government Printer.

O'Connor, J., Orloff, A. and Shaver, S. (1999) *States, Markets, Families*, Cambridge: Cambridge University Press.

OECD (1994) *The OECD Jobs Study: Facts, Analysis, Strategies – Unemployment in the OECD Area, 1950–1995*, Paris: OECD.

OECD (2000) *OECD Employment Outlook*, Paris: OECD.

Oxenbridge, S. (1997) 'Organizing Strategies and Organizing Reform in New Zealand Service Sector Unions', *Labor Studies Journal*, 22 (3): 3–27.

Peetz, D. (1998) *Unions in a Contrary World: The Future of the Australian Trade Union Movement*, Cambridge: Cambridge University Press.

Pocock, B. (1998) 'Institutional Sclerosis: Prospects for Trade Union Transformation', *Labour and Industry*, 9 (1): 17–36.

Royal Commission on Trade Unions and Employers' Associations, 1965–68 (1968) *Report* (Donovan Commission), Cmnd. 3623, London: Her Majesty's Stationery Office.

Statistics Canada (1960–99) *Labour Force Survey*, Catalogue No. 75.001.

Taylor, R. (2000) *The TUC: From General Strike to New Unionism*, Basingstoke: Palgrave.

Tomlins, C. (1985). *The State and the Unions: Labor Relations, Law and the Organized Labor Movement in America, 1880–1960*, Cambridge: Cambridge University Press.

Towers, B. (1997) *The Representation Gap: Change and Reform in British and American Industrial Relations*, Oxford: Oxford University Press.

U.S. Department of Labor (1960–99) *Bureau of Labor Statistics, Employment and Earnings*, Washington DC: Government Printing Office.

Waddington, J. (2000) 'United Kingdom: Recovering from the Neo-Liberal Assault', in J. Waddington and R. Hoffmann (eds) *Trade Unions in Europe: Facing Challenges and Searching for Solutions*, Brussels: European Trade Union Institute, pp. 575–626.

Waldinger, R., Erickson, C., Milkman, R., Mitchell, D., Valenzuela, A., Wong, K. and Zeitlin, M. (1998) 'Helots No More: A Case Study of the Justice for Janitors Campaign in Los Angeles', in K. Bronfenbrenner, S. Friedman, R. Hurd, R. Oswald and R. Seeber (eds) *Organizing to Win: New Research on Union Strategies*, Cornell: ILR Press, pp. 102–19.

Walsh, P. (1997) 'From Arbitration to Bargaining: Changing State Strategies in Industrial Relations', in C. Rudd and B. Roper (eds) *The Political Economy of New Zealand*, Auckland: Oxford University Press, pp. 183–201.

Wooden, M. (2000) *The Transformation of Australian Industrial Relations*, Sydney: Federation Press.

2 THE AMERICAN LABOUR MOVEMENT AND THE RESURGENCE IN UNION ORGANIZING

Kate Bronfenbrenner

In the last two decades, unions around the globe have watched in dismay as employers and governments have hastened to replicate US economic policies, labour laws, and union avoidance strategies. The result has been a race to the bottom for every aspect of the employment relationship – whether safety and health, contract enforcement, job security, pension benefits, or the right to organize.

In all of these areas, US employers have led the descent. Union density in the USA has dropped to 14 per cent for the first time in more than 60 years. For the last two decades, unions have been able to gain representation for fewer than 100,000 workers each year, far fewer than the 400,000 union jobs that are lost each year from plant closings, lay-offs, corporate restructuring, decertifications, and contracting out. Instead of the union-friendly labour law reform that unions hoped to achieve under a Democratic administration, they now watch as conservatives at all levels of government pursue an aggressive campaign to undercut severely all protective labour legislation. Deregulation, privatization, and liberalized trade policies threaten the security of workers throughout the economy.

Yet, at the dawn of a new century, the American labour movement shows signs of resurgence that make it as much a model for renewal as a prototype for decline. This resurgence is evident on the political front, where, through grassroots education and mobilization of their members and community allies, American unions have recently won victories in Congress on issues such as the minimum wage and maintaining restrictions on company unions. It is also evident in a series of recent bargaining victories at Verizon, Boeing, Kaiser Aluminum, United Parcel Service, and Continental Tire, where, through the use of creative and aggressive strategic campaigns, unions have successfully challenged some of the world's most powerful corporations.

We also see evidence of labour's revival in the new wave of student activism that has swept across American college campuses with a focus on anti-sweatshop campaigns and support for unionized campus service-workers. And we have witnessed a sea change in media attention to labour issues, with union victories and concerns making front-page news for the first time in decades.

But it is in organizing that the US labour movement's efforts at renewal have been most dramatic. Despite a rapidly deteriorating economic, political, and legal climate, for the last several years the AFL-CIO (the US national trade union federation), along with national and local unions, have together been engaged in an aggressive effort to improve significantly their organizing capacity and success. This has included shifting staff and financial resources into organizing, mobilizing leaders and members to support organizing campaigns, and developing and implementing more effective organizing strategies and tactics.

Recent victories such as the 74,000 homecare workers organized by the Service Employees International Union (SEIU) in Los Angeles, California; the nearly 10,000 workers organized by the Hotel and Restaurant Employees (HERE) at the MGM and Bellagio hotels in Las Vegas; the more than 26,000 airline reservation agents organized by the Communication Workers of America (CWA) at USAIRWAYS and the Machinists at United Airlines; or the recent Union of Needletrades, Industrial and Textile Employees (UNITE) victory for 5000 textile workers at Fieldcrest Cannon in North Carolina prove that some unions are winning, and winning big, even when faced with extremely aggressive employer opposition. More than that, we have seen a national commitment at the highest levels of the AFL-CIO and many of its largest affiliates to commit more resources to organizing and to 'organize at an unprecedented pace and scale' (Sweeney, Trumka, and Chavez-Thompson, 1995).

Slowly but surely these changes and initiatives are beginning to bear fruit. In 1998, for the first time in decades, American unions organized as many new workers as were lost from lay-offs, plant closings, decertifications, and contracting out. Unions won 1653 private sector representation elections involving 105,624 eligible voters. This is a 31 per cent increase from the 80,421 workers involved in National Labour Relations Board (NLRB) elections won by unions in 1996 and a 58 per cent increase in the number involved in winning elections in 1995. After a twenty-year decline, private sector first contract rates also increased to 68 per cent in 1998 from a low of 60 per cent in 1995 (BNA Plus, 1999). Unions also continue actively to organize state and local government workers in the American public sector while tens of thousands of US private sector workers are now seeking to organize outside of the traditional government supervised and regulated election process through community-based and industry-based direct pressure campaigns calling on employers to recognize the union and bargain a first agreement without going through a lengthy election process.

Many of these organizing gains were with new workers in new industries. More than half of the new workers organized are in health care, social services, hotel, entertainment, and other service sector units where women and people of colour predominate. Non-traditional community-based campaigns have been particularly effective among leased and contract employees such as janitors and home-health aides, construction workers, and low-wage workers in the hospitality industry. Not only are the majority of these workers women and people of colour, but many are new immigrants from Asia, Latin America, and the Carribean (BNA Plus, 1999).

By 1999, the combination of organizing victories and employment expansion in unionized industries resulted in a net gain of 265,000 in union membership, the first such gain in more than twenty years (AFL-CIO, 2000). The great American decline in union organizing may have finally bottomed out. Yet, in order to reverse the decline in organizing and regain their power at the bargaining table and in the broader community, American unions are going to have to organize millions, not hundreds of thousands, of workers each year. We can only hope that other nations learn both from our mistakes and our belated attempts at revitalization, so that they can stem their own decline before it reaches the same depths as in the USA.

The legal framework for organizing in the USA

The legal right to organize and to collective bargaining was first extended to the majority of private sector workers in the USA with the passage of the National Labour Relations Act (NLRA) in 1935. Today the NLRA covers the right to organize and collectively bargain for all private sector workers with the exception of railway and airline employees, who are covered under the Railway Labor Act; and domestic workers, agricultural workers, independent contractors, supervisors and managerial employees, who are excluded from all private sector collective bargaining legislation. Workers in federal, state, and local government did not gain legal protection for the right to organize until the 1960s and 1970s, and only then on a state-by-state basis. Today there are 43 different public sector labour relations laws and agencies in 37 states outlining the right to organize for government workers in those states. In thirteen states, mostly in the south and south-west, there are no collective bargaining laws covering public sector workers.

Private sector labour laws in the USA are administered by the NLRB and enforced by federal courts, whereas state labour laws are administered by state labour relations agencies and enforced by state courts. Most state labour laws mimic federal labour law in the procedures and regulations relating to organizing. These laws grant workers the right to organize and to bargain collectively through representatives of their own choosing and outline union and employer 'unfair labour practices', which are actions by either the union or the company that interfere with, threaten, penalize, or coerce workers in the exercise of these rights. When workers or unions believe the employer has committed unfair labour practices they file charges with the NLRB. However, because penalties for most employer violations are fairly minimal and include neither criminal penalties nor punitive damages, the law provides little disincentive for those employers determined to remain non-union.

The primary route to union representation in the USA is through the NLRB certification election process. Under this procedure a minimum of 30 per cent of workers in a specified bargaining unit (a group of workers which the NLRB believes have sufficient community of interest to bargain collectively for a single contract with the employer) petition the NLRB, either through individual signed authorization cards or multiple signatures on petition, to hold a secret ballot election to determine whether a majority of employees seek to be represented by the union.

Because of high turnover and inevitable loss of support for the union in response to aggressive employer anti-union campaigns, most unions wait until they have at least 70 per cent of the workers signed up prior to petitioning the NLRB. If the union can prove that the majority of the bargaining unit has signed a petition (or cards) authorizing the union to represent them in collective bargaining, then, prior to petitioning the NLRB, the union can go directly to the employer to demand that the employer voluntarily recognize the union as the exclusive representative for the workers in that bargaining unit and commence bargaining a first agreement, without first going through an election. Although in the public sector voluntary recognitions are quite common, in the private sector they are extremely rare and only happen in the context of extraordinary efforts by the union to leverage the employer to agree to recognize the union without first going through the certification election process.

In most cases, the employer refuses to recognize the union voluntarily and the union petitions the NLRB for a certification election. The NLRB then schedules a secret ballot election, on average, 30 to 50 days after the petition is filed. However, the election can be delayed by weeks, or even years, in those cases where the employer contests the appropriateness of the bargaining unit petitioned for by the union.

If the union wins a majority of the votes in the election (50 per cent plus one), or if the employer voluntarily recognizes the union, the NLRB certifies the union as the exclusive representative for the purposes of collective bargaining for that unit. That means that for at least one year after the unit is certified, or for as long as any collective bargaining agreement is in effect, no other union may bargain with the employer on behalf of workers in this unit. Once the union is certified the employer is required under the law to bargain in good faith in an attempt to reach an agreement. There is no requirement to reach an agreement and the only penalty for employers who refuse to bargain in good faith is a court order ordering them to go back to the bargaining table to attempt to reach an agreement.

The roots of the decline in US organizing

Many in the US labour movement mistakenly believe that their organizing problems began with President Reagan's anti-union initiatives in the 1980s. However, unlike other industrial countries, where free market economic policies and the recent dismantling of protective labour legislation have, in just a few short years, devastated union organizing efforts, the decline in US union density and organizing success began decades before the Reagan era. As long as US companies and their employees were reaping the benefits of an expanding world economy in the 1950s and 1960s, union leaders were able to keep their heads in the sand, ignoring the devastating long-term implications of a deteriorating legal, economic, and political climate. The full force of these environmental changes was not felt until the 1980s, too late easily to institute the serious strategic and structural changes necessary to reverse the decline.

In the 1930s and early 1940s US unions greatly increased their membership and power through aggressive organizing in the context of an expanding economy and a favourable political and social climate. In the decades that followed, actual union membership remained fairly stable, but overall density declined because unions failed to keep up with a rapidly expanding workforce. Some of this decline can be attributed to a series of structural changes in the US economy and workforce, including increased capital mobility, technological change, and changes in work organization, which have resulted in both significant job losses in unionized industries and dramatic growth in the largely unorganized service sector. These pressures on unionized industries were further exacerbated by government economic initiatives such as deregulation and free-trade policies (Bronfenbrenner *et al.*, 1998).

The changing labour law climate has also contributed to the decline. Union density peaked in the late 1940s, just before the enactment of the Taft–Hartley amendments to the National Labour Relations Act, which codified into law the pro-business decisions of a much more conservative, post-New Deal judiciary. Taft–Hartley expanded employer rights to oppose unions at the same time as it removed one of labour's most effective organizing tools: the secondary boycott. Reflecting the Cold War hysteria of the time, Taft-Hartley also included a clause requiring unions to sign 'non-communist' affidavits if they wanted to be covered under the Act. In the years that followed an entire generation of the industrial labour movement's best organizers were purged from their unions for being communists, socialists, or 'fellow travellers'. With them went a wealth of strategic knowledge and organizing experience that is only now being regained, more than two generations later (Green, 1980: 195–205).

Although the decline in union density started in the years after Taft–Hartley, the true effect of these labour law changes was masked by the expanding economy. During the 1950s and 1960s unions focused their efforts on servicing their existing members rather than organizing industries and sectors that had been untouched by the wave of industrial organizing in the 1930s. It was not until the US post-war economic boom first faltered in the 1970s, and unions first began to lose significant numbers through lay-offs, plant closings, and capital flight, that they felt the full force of their weakened labour rights. For now when they tried to organize they found employers committed to containing unionization to already-organized industries and aggressively opposing all union efforts to organize the unorganized.

Unions were ill prepared for the employers' onslaught. Earlier in the century in the textile mills in Lawrence, Massachusetts, or in the auto-plants in Flint, Michigan, organizers understood that their success depended on running slow, underground, community-based campaigns. Faced with employers who readily spied on, beat up, fired, blacklisted, and evicted workers for the slightest evidence of union sympathy, these organizers went house to house, neighbourhood to neighbourhood, building leaders, capitalizing on community networks and allies, and steadily preparing for more aggressive action (Kraus, 1947: 1–87; Cameron 1993: 117–69). For most industrial unions in the 1950s and 1960s, however, organizing involved no more than handing out authorization cards outside the plant gate, followed by a few large meetings and some mass mailings. For other unions, particularly the building trades and the Teamsters, most organizing was accomplished top down, through visits by union officers to non-union employers. These strategies worked as long as unions controlled the market share of the industry and employer opposition was minimal. But once employers became more aggressive in their opposition to unions in the 1970s and 1980s, both union organizing activity and union organizing success plummeted (Chaison and Rose, 1991: 26).

As unions grew weaker, employers became more emboldened and sophisticated in their union-avoidance strategies. An entire industry of management consultants sprang up, feeding off employers eager to spare no expense to keep their workplaces 'union-free'. By the mid-1980s employers used anti-union consultants in 71 per cent of private sector union organizing campaigns (Bronfenbrenner and Juravich, 1995). By 1995 the number had increased to 90 per cent (Bronfenbrenner, 1997b).

Illegal anti-union activity also increased. According to Richard Freeman:

> From 1960 to 1980 the number of all employer unfair labour practice charges rose fourfold; the number of charges involving a firing for union activity rose threefold; and the number of workers awarded back pay or reinstated into their jobs rose fivefold. (Freeman, 1985: 53)

By 1980, the overwhelming majority of employers aggressively opposed union organizing efforts through a combination of delays, harassment, discharges, misinformation, interrogation, threats, promises, bribes, and surveillance (Bronfenbrenner, 1994). Emboldened by President Reagan's unequivocal support for their anti-union agenda, as demonstrated by his discharge and replacement of striking air-traffic controllers, many openly flaunted labour law, secure in the knowledge that the penalties for even the most egregious violations were little more than a slap on the wrist.

Today, more than one-third of US employers discharge workers for union activity during organizing campaigns, more than half threaten a full or partial shutdown of their company if the union succeeds in organizing the facility, and between 15 and 40 per cent make illegal changes in wages, benefits and working conditions, give bribes to those who oppose the union, or use electronic surveillance of union activists during the organizing campaign (Bronfenbrenner, 1997b). In short, US employers faced with organizing campaigns, stop at nothing to create a climate so fraught with fear, conflict, suspicion, and intimidation, that workers long for the time before the union drive began.

Employers in the USA engage in these aggressive actions with little fear of any significant legal penalties from the NLRB or the courts. Even in the most serious cases, such as the CWA's 1994 campaign at Sprint's Hispanic marketing division in San Francisco – where the NLRB and the courts found Sprint guilty of more than 50 egregious labour law violations during the organizing campaigns, including fabricating evidence, bribes, threats, surveillance, discharges, and ultimately shutting down and transferring work in direct response to the union campaign – the only penalty was an order to refrain from engaging in similar violations if they were ever to open again.

Not surprisingly, the intensity of these employer campaigns has had a devastating impact on union organizing success. Research has consistently found that most individual anti-union employer tactics are associated with union win rates 10 to 20 per cent lower than in units where they are not utilized. In addition, when included in a regression equation controlling for the influence of election background, bargaining-unit demographics, and union tactic variables, these individual employer actions decrease the probability that the union will win the election by between 3 per cent and 22 per cent, whereas each additional aggressive anti-union tactic the employer uses reduces the probability of the union winning the election by 7 per cent (Bronfenbrenner, 1994, 1997b; Bronfenbrenner and Juravich, 1998).

Given the evidence, it is not surprising that many researchers have concluded that employer opposition and weak and poorly enforced labour laws are the primary causes of the declining organizing success of US unions. Yet, unions in the USA cannot simply blame external factors for their failure to organize. They themselves must take a significant share of the blame. In the 1950s and 1960s, when unions had the resources and power to launch massive organizing campaigns, taking on entire industries, they failed to do so. Equally damaging, they completely ignored, and in many cases consciously neglected, whole sectors of the economy because they were dominated by low-wage women and people of colour (Bronfenbrenner et al., 1998). In part this was due to prejudice but it was also due to the mistaken belief that these workers were less interested in unions and these industries were more difficult to organize. Many unions have held on to this belief in the 1990s, despite the fact that research has consistently shown that women workers, low-wage service workers, and people of colour are just as likely, if not more likely, to organize (Bronfenbrenner, 1993).

For decades US unions also neglected to organize professional, technical, and clerical workers in white-collar occupations, once again convinced that these workers were less interested in unions than their blue-collar counterparts. This changed somewhat in the 1960s and 1970s, when, with the advent of public sector collective bargaining, public sector teachers, office workers, and administrators began to flock to unions in droves. Although by the

1990s, only 16 per cent of the total US workforce was employed by state, local, and federal government entities, a third of the workers represented by AFL-CIO affiliates were employed in the public sector and public sector union density stabilized above 35 per cent. These public sector workers were able to organize into unions and bargain first agreements largely free of the aggressive employer opposition that is so prevalent in the private sector, which explains why public sector white-collar workers have been so much more likely to organize than their private sector counterparts (Juravich and Bronfenbrenner, 1998).

In the 1970s, with the elimination of the healthcare worker exclusion from the National Labour Relations Act, there was a burst of organizing activity among private sector hospital and nursing home employees. Similarly in the 1980s, unions such as District 65 of the United Auto Workers (UAW) won several major campaigns among university clerical workers. Coupled with victories in the public sector, these efforts brought thousands of women and people of colour into the labour movement. Yet even these gains were not enough to stop the haemorrhaging of union membership in labours' former strongholds in auto, steel, construction, electronics, and textiles (Bronfenbrenner et al., 1988).

Even by the 1980s, when it was difficult for any union leader in the USA to ignore the hard numbers of labour's decline, few unions were willing or able to rise to the organizing challenge. Instead, most concentrated their resources on servicing and bargaining for a shrinking membership. The majority of those that did organize ran very weak top-down organizing campaigns, which were no match for most employers. Some unions were organizing and winning despite employer opposition, however, and despite the deteriorating organizing climate. The challenge for the US labour movement was to determine why these unions were more successful and which tactics and strategies contributed most to their success.

Factors contributing to union organizing success

Although there has been extensive research on factors contributing to the decline in union organizing in the USA, very few studies have examined the role played by union tactics in the organizing process. In part this is because many industrial relations researchers are not convinced that union tactics play a significant role in determining election outcomes. Some, like Dickens (1983), believe that union tactics are entirely reactive, determined solely by management tactics, and therefore should not and do not need to be included in organizing research models. Others may believe that union tactics matter, but are unable to include them in their research models, both because they have limited understanding of the tactics that unions have available to them in organizing drives, and because they lack access to union campaign data. Thus most industrial relations research on private sector organizing in the USA continues to focus primarily on the election, unit, and employer variables easily accessible in NLRB databases.

In 1988, in cooperation with the Organizing Department of the AFL-CIO, I launched the first of a series of studies specifically designed to expand the body of knowledge available to the labour movement and scholars of the labour movement regarding factors contributing to union success or failure in certification election campaigns. Through surveys of leading organizers in private and public sector organizing campaigns, we have been able to determine which union tactics have the most positive impact on union organizing success while controlling for the impact of election environment, organizer background, bargaining unit demographics, and employer characteristics and tactics (Bronfenbrenner, 1993, 1997a, 1997b, 1997c; Bronfenbrenner and Juravich 1998; Juravich and Bronfenbrenner, 1998).

The findings from these studies have been consistent and clear. Unions that win elections in the context of aggressive employer opposition, tend to run very different campaigns from those that lose. In fact, union strategies and tactics were found as a group to matter just as much, if not more, in determining election outcomes than other groups of variables including bargaining unit demographics, employer characteristics and tactics, and the broader organizing climate. This is one of the most striking findings of the research because this means that the one element of the election process that US unions control, namely their own organizing strategy and tactics, can make a significant difference in determining whether they win or lose elections, even in a hostile organizing climate.

What we found is that unions are most likely to win certification election campaigns when they run aggressive and creative campaigns utilizing a grassroots, rank-and-file intensive strategy, building a union and acting like a union from the very beginning of the campaign. Thus, campaigns where the union focused on person-to-person contact, house calls, and small-group meetings to develop leadership and union consciousness and inoculate workers against the employer's anti-union strategy were associated with significantly higher win rates than traditional campaigns, which primarily utilized gate leafleting, mass meetings, and glossy mailings to contact unorganized workers.

This is not to say that there is something inherently wrong with leaflets and mailings during organizing campaigns. Rather, what our research shows is that these leaflets and mailings act as a proxy for traditional campaigns where the union's energy is focused on indirect means of communication rather than on the personal contact and leadership development necessary to build the union and counteract the employer campaign. Unlike leaflets and mailings, person-to-person contact through house calls and small group meetings is an essential and effective means for organizers to listen to workers' concerns, allay their fears, and mobilize them around the justice and dignity issues that matter enough to them to challenge the employer and win, regardless of the brutality and intensity of the employer campaign.

Unions were also more successful when they encouraged rank-and-file participation in and responsibility for the organizing campaign. More than any other single variable, having a large, active, rank-and-file committee representative of all the different interest groups in the bargaining unit was found to be critical to union organizing success, increasing the probability of the union winning the election by as much as 20 per cent. With employers aggressively campaigning against the union eight hours a day in the workplace, these committees are the most effective vehicles for generating the worker participation and commitment necessary to counteract the fears and misinformation created by the employer campaign. Representative rank-and-file committees are also essential in order for the union to keep in touch with the issues and concerns of the workers they are attempting to organize. But perhaps most important of all, these committees give workers a sense of ownership of the union and the organizing campaign and a sense that they are part of a democratic and inclusive organization. Rank-and-file leadership and ownership of the union campaign also make it much more difficult for the employer to paint the union as an outside third party.

Escalating pressure tactics in the workplace and the community such as petitions, mass grievances, T-shirt or button days, rallies, public forums, or leveraging the employer through suppliers, investors, stockholders or customers, were also found to have a significant positive impact on union organizing success. These actions are important because they build worker solidarity, develop leadership, reinforce commitment among pro-union workers and help to convince undecided voters that they can safely support the union. These tactics also actively demonstrate support for the union among the workers and the broader community and can therefore compel the employer to scale back its anti-union campaign.

According to our findings, union success also depends on developing a long-range campaign strategy that incorporates building for the first contract into the original organizing process. Union win rates were significantly higher in campaigns where the union started preparing for the first contract before the election by conducting bargaining surveys, selecting the bargaining committee, and involving the workers in researching and preparing proposals. These tactics are important because they build worker confidence that the union is going to win the election and successfully bargain a first agreement and because they demonstrate to the workers that they are going to play an active role in the collective bargaining process.

Unions are also more successful in organizing when there is an emphasis on developing a culture of organizing that permeates everything that the union does. This includes a serious commitment of staff and financial resources to organizing at both the local and international levels. Organizing costs money – for staff, training, cars, gas, hotels, literature, computers, and phones. In a time of declining members and dues, most unions are struggling with how best to allocate increasingly scarce resources. Thus, unions will only be successful in transferring sufficient resources into organizing if they are able to convince union leaders and their members that the future of their union depends on organizing, and organizing depends on transferring resources from servicing to organizing.

One of the most effective ways to mobilize membership support for organizing is through the recruitment, training, and utilization of member organizers from already-organized units. These volunteers are not only important because they can inexpensively supplement scarce organizing staff resources. Their most important contribution is in their ability to speak sincerely and powerfully from their own experiences of organizing and winning a first contract. Much more than paid professional organizers, these volunteers can credibly convince unorganized workers that not only is it possible to organize and win but it is also worth the risk, fear, and conflict that it takes to do so.

Lastly, union organizing success depends on strategic research and targeting that carefully assesses whether the workers are really ready to organize; whether the union has the expertise, experience, and resources to organize workers in this industry; and perhaps most important of all, whether the union has the leverage to gain a first contract for the workers once the election is won.

At a time when private sector union density has dropped down to 9 per cent and most union organizing campaigns barely get off the ground, unions can ill afford to waste precious time and resources on campaigns they are doomed to lose. They need to focus their energies on the workers and units where they are most likely to win, and on the units that, once won, will have the greatest impact on strengthening their bargaining power in their existing units. Unions that attempt to organize any type of worker in any industry, with no regard to the workers' experience or bargaining leverage in the enterprise, community, or industry, risk seriously diluting their power, and the power of other unions, at a time when they most need to concentrate their power in any way they can.

In the late 1980s, when the first of these organizing studies was conducted, we found many of the individual components of the comprehensive strategy described above to be associated with win rates 10 to 30 per cent higher than win rates in campaigns that did not use those tactics (Bronfenbrenner 1997a). The tactics associated with the highest win rates included having a representative committee; house calling the majority of the unit; using escalating pressure tactics such as solidarity days; establishing a rank-and-file bargaining committee before the election; using member volunteer organizers; and focusing on issues of dignity and justice rather than just bread-and-butter issues. We also found that when union building tactics were included in a regression equation controlling for the influence of other election campaign variables, most were associated with as much as a 3 per cent increase in the percentage of votes received by the union and as much as a 10 per cent increase in the probability of the union winning the elections. The probability of the union winning the election also increased by 10 per cent for each additional union building tactic used by the union during the organizing campaign (Bronfenbrenner and Juravich, 1998).

Unfortunately, the study also found that, in the late 1980s, only a very small number of unions were using a comprehensive union building strategy in their certification election campaigns. Fewer than a third of the unions surveyed had representative committees, house called the majority of the members of the unit, held ten or more small-group meetings, or focused on dignity and fairness as the primary issues. Even fewer started preparing for the first contract before the election or used escalating pressure tactics such as solidarity days, community coalitions, rallies, job actions or media campaigns.

Unions were able to win every election in the extremely small number of campaigns (3 per cent) where the union ran a comprehensive campaign using five or more of the union building tactics described above. However the win rate was only 41 per cent in campaigns where they used fewer than five union-building tactics.

Since that time, we have conducted two follow-up studies of NLRB election campaigns, one of elections that took place in 1994 and one of elections that took place between 1993 and 1995 (Bronfenbrenner, 1997b, 1997c; Bronfenbrenner and Juravich, 1998). Although overall the results from these studies are consistent with the findings from the 1980s study there are two important differences. First, although employer campaigns have dramatically increased in intensity and effectiveness, the nature and intensity of union campaigns have increased to a much smaller extent. It is true that more unions are committing more staff and financial resources to organizing, and more are also using representative committees, person-to-person contact, and escalating pressure tactics, and preparing for the first contract during the organizing campaign. However, although the percentage of employers that run aggressive campaigns increased from 21 per cent to 64 per cent, the percentage of unions that run aggressive campaigns increased from 3 per cent to only 30 per cent.

Second, in the 1990s individual union tactics variables were found to be associated with win rates only 2 per cent to 16 per cent higher than campaigns in which the tactics were not used. A few tactics, when measured individually, such as house calling the majority of the unit, were now associated with lower win rates than campaigns where they were not used. In the 30 per cent of the campaigns where the union did use five or more union building tactics the win rate was 50 per cent, compared to 36 per cent where they used fewer than five tactics and 27 per cent where no union building tactics were used. More important, for the 6 per cent of the campaigns where the union ran a true multifaceted comprehensive campaign, using ten or more union building tactics, the win rate increased to 72 per cent (Bronfenbrenner, 1997c). When a variable measuring the number of union tactics used was included in a regression equation controlling for the influence of other election campaign variables, including employer tactics, the probability of the union winning the election increased by 9 per cent for each additional union building tactic used. At the same time the probability of the union winning the election declined by 7 per cent for each additional anti-union tactic the employer used (Bronfenbrenner and Juravich, 1998).

The results of the 1990s data show that, in the USA today, when employer campaigns are dramatically increasing in their intensity and the broader economic, social and political climate is becoming more and more hostile to organizing, the strategies and tactics that unions use matter now, more than ever. However, there are no silver bullets; there is no single tactic that guarantees union victory. Instead union success depends on utilizing a multifaceted comprehensive strategy incorporating as many rank-and-file intensive union building strategies as possible, including person-to-person contact, rank-and-file leadership development, escalating pressure tactics, and building for the first contract during the organizing campaign. The more comprehensive and multifaceted the union strategy is during an organizing campaign, the more union building strategies it uses, the more likely it is to win the election.

The data also show that in the last ten years more and more organizers are beginning to try to run more aggressive organizing campaigns. However, their approach to organizing has been piecemeal. They have been adding one or two new tactics to their traditional organizing practice without incorporating them into a more cohesive and comprehensive strategy. Thus more unions may be house calling the majority of the unit, but if they are using only professional staff to conduct the house calls, without building an effective rank-and-file committee and without using volunteer organizers from other units, those house calls are much less effective. More unions are also using representative committees, but because they are not always actively involving them in an aggressive and creative campaign, their positive impact is greatly muted. We also see more unions resorting to external pressure tactics targeted at investors, suppliers, or customers, both in voluntary recognition and first contract campaigns.

We found evidence in our research that in the past few years the shortage of skilled, experienced organizers, particularly women and people of colour, has reached crisis proportions. Today, just as ten years ago, just over half of the campaigns had the needed ratio of one full-time organizer per 100 eligible voters. Even more disturbing, where ten years ago 12 per cent of lead organizers were women and 15 per cent were people of colour, today the percentage of women lead organizers has only increased to 16 per cent and the percentage of lead organizers who are people of colour has actually dropped to 9 per cent. Even in campaigns with a majority of women, only 23 per cent have a woman lead organizer, while in campaigns with a majority of workers of colour, only 16 per cent have a person of colour as the lead organizer. This occurs despite the fact that win rates are significantly higher in units with a majority of women with a woman lead organizer (50 per cent versus 39 per cent for a male lead organizer) and in units with a majority of workers of colour for a lead organizer of colour (64 per cent versus 35 per cent).

Significant gains have been made in recruiting more women and people of colour to staff organizing campaigns. Today more than 40 per cent of all NLRB campaigns and 58 per cent of campaigns in primarily female units have at least one woman organizer staffing or leading the campaign, whereas a third of all campaigns and 58 per cent of campaigns with a majority of workers of colour have at least one person of colour on staff or leading the campaign. Most of these organizers are African-American or Hispanic, whereas fewer than 2 per cent are Asian, despite the large numbers of Asian workers currently participating in organizing campaigns.

Conclusion

Our research on organizing campaigns clearly demonstrates that, in the 1990s, more unions in the USA were consistently adopting the more comprehensive approach that is required to win elections in the current organizing climate. Not surprisingly, it is these unions that have won the lion's share of the union victories in recent years. These are also the unions that are committing the most resources to organizing, recruiting the most women and people of colour to their organizing staff, running the most election campaigns, winning the largest units, and are contributing the most to the recent upturn in union organizing numbers. Unfortunately they still represent the minority, which is why the US labour movement remains so far from organizing the millions of new workers it needs to regain its bargaining and political power.

There is no question that free market economic policies, liberalized trade practices, and the elimination or weakening of protective labour legislation have greatly increased the costs and risks to workers and unions attempting to organize in every nation. But the findings from our organizing contract research also hold out the promise and possibility that unions can organize and win, even in the most hostile organizing climate, if they are willing to commit to a much more costly and comprehensive organizing strategy.

But they cannot delay. For too many decades unions in the USA failed to accept responsibility for their declining numbers and power. Not only did they continue to blame external forces for their organizing difficulties, but they also continued to seek to be rescued by their political allies, blinded by the belief that any organizing renewal was entirely dependent on first achieving significant labour law reform. In doing so they failed to understand that the deteriorating legal climate for organizing has always been a direct result of their declining numbers and political power. In fact, only through organizing massive numbers of new members in every sector of the economy, will US unions once again have the political leverage to ensure more progressive and more effective labour legislation.

This organizing will need to be achieved through massive numbers of NLRB elections in larger and larger units but increasingly it will also need to go beyond the traditional board certification election process to organize workers in industries and occupations that are either too large, too diffuse, or too contingent, to be successfully organized under the certification election model. For these employers, many of whom are the richest and most powerful multinational corporations in the world, what is required is a comprehensive campaign simultaneously organizing the rank-and-file workers in the workplace and the community from the bottom up, while leveraging the employer through its investors, suppliers, customers, owners, and subsidiaries from the top down.

As difficult as it is to achieve, a certification election victory is just the first step in the organizing process. For, without a first agreement, there are no new members, no contract gains, and the union often ends up being decertified or withdrawing in a few years. Despite progress on the organizing front, today the overall private sector first contract rate is only 60 per cent. This means that fewer than a quarter of the private sector workers who attempt to organize under the NLRB are able to gain representation under a union contract.

This high failure rate occurs both because the majority of employers continue their anti-union campaign after the election is won and because the majority of unions fail to continue an aggressive, rank-and-file intensive strategy after the election campaign. What our research has found is that unions' success in winning first agreements and staying organized after the first contract is reached depends on continuing and intensifying the same kind of multifaceted, rank-and-file intensive campaign that is so essential to the initial organizing campaign. The organizing never stops.

But unions engaging in such organizing cannot and should not assume that they are simply mobilizing new workers to become dues payers for the *status quo*. Workers who organize today are not going to be willing to take on the risks or put in the hard work of organizing if they are not going to be given a voice and a seat at the table once the union has won. These new workers will come into the labour movement with new issues and new demands and with the expectation that the union will continue to be the same activist and democratic organization it was during the organizing campaign through the first contract and beyond.

Nor can we assume that there is some other, less difficult and less adversarial, model that would more gently convince employers to grant union recognition and utilize new, more collaborative, industrial relations strategies for the new millennium. The evidence from the last decade is very clear. Employers in the USA today, whether foreign-based multinationals or US-based family businesses, manufacturing or healthcare, high tech or low wage, will not and do not voluntarily recognize unions in the absence of the expression of union power in the workplace and broader community.

For many years labour's declining political power in the USA was cushioned by the post-World War II economic boom. By the time most of the US labour movement woke up and recognized that they were in a crisis, they faced a hostile President and a global market economy. For other industrial nations the crisis has developed much later and much more quickly. But today, whether in Great Britain, Brazil, Korea, or New Zealand, it is no less acute.

Unions in the USA are learning that, even in the most hostile organizing climate, workers do organize and unions can win, if they are willing to commit to a more aggressive and comprehensive organizing strategy which slowly but steadily builds the union from the bottom up. This is how unions everywhere have always had to organize in the absence of strong enforceable protective labour legislation and this is how more and more unions around the world will have to organize in an era of free markets, free trade, deregulation, and multinational corporate restructuring. It is a great challenge, but it is also a great opportunity, to build a stronger, and more united labour movement around the globe.

References

AFL-CIO (2000) 'Union Membership Shows Biggest Growth in Over 20 Years, According to New Government Data', AFL-CIO Press Release, 19 January 2000.

BNA Plus (1999) *NLRB Representation and Decertification Elections Statistics*, Washington DC: Bureau of National Affairs.

Bronfenbrenner, K. (1993) *Seeds of Resurgence: Successful Union Strategies for Winning Certification Elections and First Contracts in the 1980s and Beyond*, PhD Dissertation, Cornell University.

Bronfenbrenner, K. (1994) 'Employer Behavior in Certification Elections and First-Contract Campaigns: Implications for Labor Law Reform', in S. Friedman, R. Hurd, R. Seeber, and R. Oswald (eds) *Restoring the Promise of American Labor Law*, Ithaca NY: ILR Press, pp. 75–89.

Bronfenbrenner, K. (1997a) 'The Role of Union Strategies in NLRB Certification Elections', *Industrial and Labor Relations Review*, 50 (2): 195–221.

Bronfenbrenner, K. (1997b) 'The Effects of Plant Closing or Threat of Plant Closing on the Right of Workers to Organize', supplement to *Plant Closings and Workers Rights: A Report to the Council of Ministers by the Secretariat of the Commission for Labor Cooperation*, Dallas TX: Bernan Press.

Bronfenbrenner, K. (1997c) 'Organizing in the NAFTA Environment', *New Labor Forum*, 1 (1): 50–60.

Bronfenbrenner, K. and Friedman, S., Hurd R., Seeber R. and Oswald, R. (eds) (1998) *Organizing to Win: New Research on Union Strategies*, Ithaca NY: ILR Press.

Bronfenbrenner, K. and Juravich, T. (1995) *The Impact of Employer Opposition on Union Certification Win Rates: A Private/Public Sector Comparison*, Washington DC: Economic Policy Institute Working Paper No. 113.

Bronfenbrenner, K. and Juravich, T. (1998) 'It Takes More Than House Calls: Organizing to Win with a Comprehensive Union-Building Strategy', in K. Bronfenbrenner, S. Friedman, R. Hurd, R. Seeber, and R. Oswald (eds) *Organizing to Win: New Research on Union Strategies*, Ithaca NY: ILR Press, pp. 19–36.

Cameron, A. (1993) *Radicals of the Worst Sort*, Urbana IL: University of Illinois Press.

Chaison, G. N. and Rose, J. B. (1991) 'The Macro Determinants of Union Growth and Decline', in G. Strauss, D. Gallagher, and J. Fiorito (eds) *The State of the Unions*. Madison WI: IRRA, pp. 3–46.

Dickens, W. T. (1983) 'The Effect of Company Campaigns on Certification Elections: Law and Reality Once Again', *Industrial Relations*, 36: 323–34.

Freeman, R. (1985) 'Why Are Unions Faring Poorly in NLRB Representation Elections?' in Kochan, T. A. (ed.) *Challenges and Choices Facing American Labor*, Cambridge MA: MIT Press, pp. 45–64.

Green, J. (1980) *World of the Worker: Labor in Twentieth Century America*, New York NY: Hill & Wong.

Juravich, T. and Bronfenbrenner, K. (1998) 'Preparing for the Worst: Organizing and Staying Organized in the Public Sector', in Bronfenbrenner, K., Friedman, S., Hurd, R., Seeber, R. and Oswald, R. (eds) *Organizing to Win: New Research on Union Strategies*, Ithaca NY: ILR Press, pp. 262–82.

Kraus, H. (1947) *The Many and the Few*, Los Angeles CA: Plantin Press.

Sweeney, J., Trumka, R. and Chavez-Thompson, L. (1995) *A New Voice for American Workers: Rebuilding the American Movement – A Summary of Proposals from the Unions Supporting John J. Sweeney, Richard Trumka, and Linda Chavez-Thompson*, Washington DC: New Voice for American Workers.

3 You Just Can't Do It Automatically: The Transition to Social Movement Unionism in the United States

Kim Voss and Rachel Sherman

Introduction

After years of decline, a few American unions began to experiment with a new model of unionism in the late 1980s. Rejecting business unionism, with its emphasis on servicing current union members and partnership with employers, activists started to push for 'social movement' unionism. This model emphasized organizing the unorganized, direct-action tactics, active rank-and-file participation in union affairs, and the pursuit of a broad agenda of social change. This new model gained additional currency when the new leadership of the AFL-CIO endorsed it in 1995.

Social movement unionism has yielded dramatic victories for American workers. In the late 1980s and early 1990s, tens of thousands of low-wage building service workers were organized in the Justice for Janitors campaigns, carried out in several cities by the Service Workers International Union (SEIU). This union also achieved a historic victory in February 1999 by organizing a single unit of 74,000 minimum-wage homecare workers in Southern California – the largest successful unionization drive in the USA since the United Auto Workers (UAW) organized General Motors in 1937. The Hotel and Restaurant Workers Union (HERE) has also organized significant numbers of poorly paid hotel workers, most notably in the huge casinos of Las Vegas, where in recent years, over 9000 workers have unionized. Beyond these high-profile victories, researchers have found that organizing campaigns that utilize a social movement approach are significantly more successful than those that are run along traditional business union lines (Bronfenbrenner and Juravich, 1994, 1998).

These successes and the promise they hold for revitalizing the American labour movement have attracted attention internationally. Unions in many countries have experienced steep declines during the 1990s and activists are looking outside their national borders for ways to rebuild union power. Most notably, labour confederations in Britain and Australia have borrowed some aspects of new organizing methods from the USA (Carter and Fairbrother, 1998).

Despite the achievements of the new approach, a majority of American unions remain unchanged. By one estimate, only ten of the 66 national unions affiliated with the AFL-CIO are devoting significant attention to organizing new members (Meyerson, 2000a). Even within these ten unions, large numbers of locals remain oriented toward business unionism: their staffs continue to spend their time servicing current members rather than using innovative tactics to organize new members. Why should this be?

In this chapter, we investigate the sources of transformation and resistance in local unions by comparing those that have substantially altered their goals and tactics with those that have changed little. Using in-depth interviews with local union organizers and staff in northern California, as well as information on particular organizing campaigns, we ask: what is the process by which social movement unionism occurs? Why have some locals adopted this new model of unionism and not others? We argue that three conditions characterize the locals that have been transformed. First, some local unions experienced internal political crises that fostered the entry of new leadership, either through intervention by the international union or local electoral upheaval. Second, these new leaders had activist experience in other social movements, which led them to interpret labour's decline as a mandate to organize, and gave them the skills and vision to implement new organizing programmes using innovative tactics. Finally, international unions with leaders committed to organizing in new ways facilitated the entry of these activists into locals and provided them with the resources and legitimacy to make changes that facilitated the process of organizational transformation.

Research design

In the American labour movement, which has a federated structure, local unions are responsible for conducting organizing campaigns and for the day-to-day servicing of members. Although international unions have, in the last decade or so, undertaken their own organizing campaigns, these campaigns occur with much less frequency than those conducted primarily by local unions. Thus, we took local unions as our unit of analysis. Locals vary greatly in size, with some representing a single occupation in one workplace and others representing workers in multiple workplaces and occupations.

Typically, however, locals cover a delimited geographical area. Our research strategy was to study both locals that have been revitalized and those that have not. Through comparisons we could identify what differentiates more and less transformed locals.

In selecting our cases, we first identified the international unions that had affiliated locals doing significant amounts of organizing in Northern California: SEIU, HERE and the UFCW (United Food and Commercial Workers). We then focused on the local affiliates of these international unions, first making sure that each international had both more and less innovative locals.

This approach of selecting our cases by initially identifying the relevant international unions had the advantage of allowing us to compare locals both within and among internationals, so that we could better distinguish the features common to revitalized locals. Our design also reduced some potentially confounding variation. All our internationals organize in the same sector of the economy and the same region of the country; industry and regional variation cannot account for the differences we observed between more and less revitalized locals.

Although our study is confined to one region of the USA, it is important to note that the unions we examine are ones that are generally doing the most innovative and aggressive organizing in the USA as a whole. In particular, SEIU and HERE are at the top of every list of 'organizing unions' (Meyerson, 2000a, b). All are decentralized unions operating in the service sector. This is true of many successful 'organizing unions' in the USA. Piore (1994) suggests that decentralization allows union leaders a great deal of latitude, sometimes resulting in corruption but sometimes encouraging radical leadership and innovative organizational experiments – things that never would be tolerated in more centralized unions. Decentralization, however, might also account for some of the specific problems our locals faced.

We conducted interviews, each of approximately two hours, with 29 union staffers and organizers in a total of fourteen locals. The interviews were conducted in 1996–7 and followed up with telephone interviews during late 1997 and early 1998. Questions focused on the current situation in the local at the time of the interview, as well as on the local's history. We also reviewed the local and labour press, as well as international and local union publications, for information on organizing drives. To protect the confidentiality of our informants, we have identified them by pseudonyms; union locals are identified by letters rather than by numbers.

To measure revitalization, we assessed two types of changes: first, the extent to which locals had shifted from servicing to organizing, and, second,

Table 3.1 *Union organizational structure*

Locals	Ratio of org/rep 1:2 or more	Researchers on staff (full time)	Bilingual organizers	Member education[1]	Member training (external)[3]	Member training (internal)[4]	Overcome staff resistance	Articulated programme[2]
Full								
HERE A	Y	Y	Y	Y	Y	Y	Y	Y (1989)
HERE B	Y	Y	Y	Y	Y	Y	Y	Y (1994)
SEIU F	Y	Y	Y	Y	Y	Y	Y	Y (1989)
SEIU G	Y	Y	Y	Y	Y	Y	Y	Y (1992)
SEIU H	Y	Y	Y	Y	Y	Y	Y	Y (1994)
Partial								
SEIU J	Y	N	Y	Y	Y	Y	Y	Y (1996)
HERE E	Y	Y	Y	N	Y	Y	Y	Y (1997)
SEIU K	N	N	Y	N	N	N	N	Y (1997)
SEIU L	N	N	Y	N	N	N	N	Y (1997)
UFCW X	N	N	N	N	Y[5]	N	N	Y (1996)
UFCW Y	N	N	Y	N	Y[5]	N	N	Y (1995)
UFCW Z	N	N	N	N	Y[5]	N	N	N

| HERE D | N | N | N | N | N | N |
| HERE C | N | N | N | N | N | N |

[1] We define formal educational efforts as attempts systematically to educate members about the need for new organizing, usually consisting of membership conferences or shop-floor educational workshops.

[2] The articulated programme variable measures whether respondents articulated a comprehensive, strategic understanding of organizing that was supported by the local's staff, including the following elements: the need for strategic planning of campaigns, the need to shift resources to these campaigns, and familiarity with the tactical possibilities of the campaigns and the resources these would entail.

[3] This variable refers to whether members were specifically trained to assist on organizing campaigns and used in such campaigns.

[4] This variable refers to whether members were trained to handle their own grievances and shop-floor problems.

[5] The UFCW locals all used members participating in the Special Projects Union Representative (SPUR) programme, in which they were taken off their jobs to help with organizing campaigns. This effort was funded primarily by the UFCW International Union.

Table 3.2 *Union locals and new tactics*

Locals	Confrontational non-NLRB[1]	Strategic targeting[2]	Corporate campaign[3]	Mobilization of workers being organized	Disruptive direct action[4]	Sustained community alliances
				Tactics used		
Full						
HERE A	Y	2	2	Y	2	Y
HERE B	Y	2	2	Y	2	Y
SEIU F	Y	2	2	Y	2	Y
SEIU G	Y	2	2	Y	2	Y
SEIU H	Y	2	2	Y	2	Y
Partial						
SEIU J	N	2	1	Y	0	Y
HERE E	Y	1	1	Y	1	N
SEIU K	N	1	0	Y	0	Y
SEIU L	N	1	0	N	0	Y
UFCW X	Y	0	0	Y	1	N

UFCW Y	N	1	0	N	1	Y
UFCW Z	N	1	2	N	0	Y
HERE D	N	1	0	N	0	N
HERE C	N	0	0	N	0	N

[1] By 'confrontational non-NLRB', we mean the local's refusal to go to an NLRB election against the opposition of the employer, rather than a top-down agreement for a card check.

[2] By 'strategic targeting', we mean that the local has both targeted an industry and chosen strategic employers to organize within the industry. Locals that have done both are rated '2', and locals that have done one or done both to a lesser extent or inconsistently are rated '1'.

[3] The range of possible corporate campaign tactics includes: pressure on the company's subsidiaries, clients, lenders, and stock-holders; interference with development opportunities; and pressure on state officials in their capacity as regulators or clients. Locals that used several of these tactics are rated '2', and those that used only one or two are rated '1'.

[4] Elements included in the range of disruptive direct action are: civil disobedience, large demonstrations, arrest actions, and regular picketing. Locals that have used all four are rated '2' while locals that have used some or used them infrequently are rated '1'.

the degree to which locals used labour's new social movement repertoire in their organizing campaigns. We gauged the first with several indicators of the extent to which each local had directed resources away from servicing and toward organizing, including the ratio of organizing to servicing staff, the presence of full-time researchers and bilingual organizers; and the existence of formal educational programmes in the local to persuade members about the need for new organizing and train them to do some of the work in organizing new members (see Table 3.1).

To assess tactical revitalization, we measured the extent to which locals had used labour's new tactical repertoire in their organizing campaigns, including non-NLRB recognition (see Chapter 2), strategic targeting, corporate campaigns, mobilization of workers being organized, disruptive direct action, and community alliances (see Table 3.2). In general, locals were identified as fully revitalized if they had an articulated organizing programme, made corresponding organizational shifts, and used the tactics in labour's new tactical repertoire. Locals that had used only a few of the new tactics and made fewer organizational changes were identified as partially revitalized locals.

Revitalized and partially revitalized unions

Five of the fourteen locals were fully revitalized. They include HERE locals A and B, and SEIU locals F, G, and H. These locals had all established major organizing programmes, beginning between 1989 and 1994. Organizers understood the strategic organizing model, articulated it clearly, and had used it more than once. All had made significant organizational changes in order to be able to pursue aggressive organizing (see Table 3.1) and all had used labour's social movement repertoire in their organizing campaigns (see Table 3.2). As a result, these unions ran more successful campaigns to organize the unorganized than did the partially revitalized locals and they achieved more active member participation in these campaigns.

The second group, the partially revitalized, had made fewer tactical and organizational changes. While all the locals in this group reported doing more organizing than they had done previously, none had initiated and carried out a social-movement-type organizing campaign. Nor had they made the necessary organizational shifts to be able to put into practice their rhetorical commitment to organizing. They had smaller organizing departments than the fully revitalized locals, and smaller ratios of organizing to servicing staff. Several locals lacked bilingual organizing staff even when most of their potential organizing targets employed many immigrants. Few of these locals hired researchers. For the most part, these locals had made few efforts to mobilize their members in support of organizing, either in terms of helping with membership drives or in resolving more of their own grievances. The few that trained shop stewards had much less developed programmes than those of the more innovative locals. In terms of tactics, these locals had adopted a few of the new techniques and combined these with more traditional strategies. Few had attempted to avoid the NLRB process or use corporate campaigns; some failed to involve workers in campaigns; many eschewed disruptive direct action. Nine of the locals were in this group: HERE locals C, D, and E, UFCW locals X, Y, and Z, and SEIU locals J, K, and L.

The process of change: overcoming member and staff resistance

In order to comprehend how transformation occurs, it is important first to understand why union members and staff resist change. Informants indicated that traditional servicing-model unionism was convenient, and that members and staff in both fully and partially revitalized locals resisted change. Union culture was frequently identified as the biggest obstacle to transforming the priorities and practices of the local. Fully revitalized locals dealt with this by designing educational programmes for members and staff that challenged their interpretation of the situation and helped them see the need for new organizing. These locals also sometimes dismissed field staff who could not make the transition to an organizing mentality. Partially revitalized locals made fewer such efforts and did not exert the political will necessary to make staffing changes and overcome other institutional obstacles.

One organizer in a fully revitalized local, for example, said that the local's 'single biggest problem' in implementing the shift to organizing was member resistance to becoming more active on and off the shop floor. Another told us:

> There's a lot of resistance and a lot of pressure from the membership to do things the old way. They don't want to get involved, in large part, they don't want to have to take responsibility, they'd much rather have someone that comes in and takes care of their problems for them. And if that's their experience, and that's how they're used to having things done, if someone new comes in and says 'no, you have to do it, no, you pay your dues, yeah, but you have to stand up to the boss, that's not my job,' their initial reaction is 'geez, service has just gone down the hill, now we have a union rep that

has no backbone or that's a wimp or that won't stand up for us or take care of my problems, what do I pay my dues for.' So it's not just sort of laziness or complacency or conservatism on the part of the union staff, there is a real resistance that you have to fight through. (Mike: HERE Local B)

Staff resistance is another major obstacle to implementing organizational change, largely because staff tasks are redefined with the shift to organizing. An AFL-CIO organizing leader called local staff 'the major cause of resistance to institutional change' (George: AFL-CIO). Longtime staff members fear losing power, or even losing their jobs. They also resist having to perform unfamiliar and daunting tasks; organizing means working harder and being more confrontational than usual. As one organizing director said about her staff:

For most field reps, it scares them 'cause it means they have to give up a little power. ... I've had comments from local staff [who] say, 'Well, if we train our shop stewards to be able to process grievances, what are we gonna do'? ... [I]t means working differently. It also means ... longer hours 'cause to build up an internal structure at a worksite, that's a lot of one on ones [meetings with workers]. You've really gotta know what your unit is like and know who the leaders are. And it's also doing a fight. Taking on the boss, where you may have kind of a decent relationship with the boss, right? So I think it's a real challenge. (Rosa: SEIU Local H)

An informant in a partially revitalized local invoked oligarchical reasoning for staff resistance:

In these small locals, you get elected to this job, and it's every three years, and after a while you don't feel like going back and tending bar any more. Well, you start bringing in real sharp, young people [the stewards]. And [the officers] say, 'wait a minute, they might want my job'. (Peter: HERE Local C)

Other organizers pointed out the rewards union staff gained from resolving people's problems for them. For example:

There's also kind of a natural resistance from people who are doing the field staff kind of stuff. They want to help people. They want to do for people. It's a lot easier to take care of someone's problem than it is to train them how to take care of their own problem. (Josh: SEIU Local J)

Clearly both members and staff had become attached to the servicing model and had difficulty understanding the need for change. The fully revitalized locals approached this resistance primarily through major educational efforts, including membership conventions and training, to demonstrate to members the importance of organizing to their own contracts and standard of living. These efforts included the active participation of the members in role-plays and small-group discussions. They involved communicating to members the idea that the labour movement is facing a crisis and that without augmenting the membership and the shop-floor strength of local unions, they will cease to exist. In cases when the local itself was in decline, leaders illustrated the need for change with local examples; when it was not, educators spoke of the decline of the movement as a whole and the eventual effects of that decline on the members themselves.

These efforts have largely been successful. In some cases, members have defined their self-interest as new organizing and prioritized organizing over traditional concerns such as increasing their own wages or benefits, or augmenting their strike fund. In 1996, for instance, HERE Local A members voted overwhelmingly to put the $2 each member paid every month for a strike fund into an organizing fund instead, despite the fact that they had recently experienced a major strike. In HERE Local B, for instance, workers at one restaurant chain temporarily gave up their employer's contribution to the pension fund in exchange for his guarantee of neutrality in organizing drives at his future restaurants. At the same local's membership convention in 1997, members signed pledges to spend at least two hours a month participating in union activities outside their own workplaces.

The fully revitalized locals have dealt with staff resistance much as they have dealt with member resistance: with education and retraining. However, when retraining has not worked, resistant staff have been let go or encouraged to quit. Significantly, these locals have not faced as much staff resistance as have partially revitalized locals because they have experienced more leadership turnover of a particular kind, which we will discuss below.

Partially revitalized locals, in contrast, had made fewer systematic efforts to counter member and staff resistance. Except for Local J, these locals did not have fully functioning member or staff education programmes. Nor had they brought in new organizers to replace intransigent business agents. The organizers we interviewed in these locals were often in the minority in their commitment to organizing, and they lacked the expertise and the institutional support to implement strategies for changing organizational culture. As an organizer in one partially revitalized local commented:

> In reality, [the amount of resources devoted to organizing] is so low it's almost embarrassing. I'm constantly on them here about it because, you know, the mandate [from the AFL-CIO] is 30% and we're lucky if we're doing three. But then again three years ago, five years ago there was nothing ... I mean even though [the local's president] professes an interest in organizing, it's still not something to go into the red because of. That's something, if that's gonna make us go into the red we're not gonna do it. (Milo: UFCW Local X)

In addition to problems of explicit staff and member resistance, these organizers described deeply entrenched cultural and practical obstacles to organizing. For example, one organizer noted:

> We plan to activate our stewards and get them to be doing more stuff but I don't see them handling grievances. That is not our philosophy. I mean, it is mine ... I've been pushing it for years, but the predominant feeling at least in California locals [of this union] is that business agents handle grievances, not the members ... So the stewards that we have, their job is pretty much to disseminate information and maybe observe if there's contract violations, and so on. (Bob: UFCW Local Y)

This informant and another UFCW organizer also saw contract provisions as an obstacle to increasing member participation, as contract language fails to protect stewards, which makes them reluctant to become active on the shop-floor.

Other informants cited lack of time and resources as a barrier to change:

> You just can't do it automatically. We don't have the money to just go out and hire three people and say, let's go organize. So we are trying to get the situation where everybody would say, okay, two days a week you'll do nothing but organizing. [But] grievances come up seven days a week, twenty-four hours a day, and you can't tell a guy, 'well, I can't talk to you for three days because it's my organizing day'. (Peter: HERE Local C)

Organizers in fully revitalized locals did not identify such entrenched cultural obstacles, largely because they had already resolved these problems. Because leaders in these locals were committed to changing to organize, they had overcome institutional impediments and surmounted resistance to transformation. They had changed the culture of the union. Organizers in partially revitalized locals lacked knowledge and institutional power to make these shifts. What explains the difference, then, between these two types of locals?

Causes of transformation: political crisis, outside activists, and centralized pressure

Our data show that three factors in conjunction distinguish the fully revitalized locals from the others. These are: the experience of an internal political crisis, which facilitated the entrance of new leaders into the local, either through international union (IU) intervention or local elections; the presence in the local of staff with social movement experience outside the labour movement; and support from the international union. Any one of these factors alone was not enough to spur full revitalization: only in combination do they explain why fully revitalized locals had staff committed to making changes and were successful in making those changes, while others did not (see Table 3.3).

Political crisis

First, fully revitalized locals had all experienced political crises, ranging from disastrous strikes to mismanagement of the local. These crises were important primarily because they resulted in a change in leadership. Sometimes locals were temporarily taken over by the international union (placed under 'trusteeship'), while in other cases electoral shake-ups occurred.

As one organizer described the events that led to the trusteeship:

> There was a lot of concession bargaining and just general chaos, things just not being together, having no administrative systems, contracts lapsing for not being re-opened ... One [problem] was mismanagement of the union, cronyism, you know, different stuff like that. (Phil: SEIU Local F)

Another organizer described how a series of strike defeats meant that a new slate of elected leaders committed to organizing came into power:

> In 1984, there was rather a disastrous turn, in that we had a strike in the restaurants and clubs, which the union lost ... And it really demonstrated a lot of other organizational problems in the union ... [Before that] organizing existed in a vacuum, primarily. So, that kind of non-broader-organizing

Table 3.3 *Factors explaining full revitalization*

Locals	Explanatory factors		
	Political crisis within local	Leaders and staff with experience in other movements prior to revitalization	Sustained IU intervention during revitalization
Full			
HERE A	Y	Y	Y
HERE B	Y	Y	Y
SEIU F	Y	Y	Y
SEIU G	Y	Y	Y[1]
SEIU H	Y	Y	Y
Partial			
SEIU J	N	Y	Y
HERE E	N	N	Y
SEIU K	N	N	Y
SEIU L	N	N	Y
UFCW X	N	N	N
UFCW Y	N	N	N
UFCW Z	N	N	N
HERE D	Y	N	Y
HERE C	N	N	Y[2]

[1] As noted in the text, Local G's innovation arose in response to conflict with the international in the wake of the trusteeship.

[2] We have coded this variable 'Y' because at the time of the interview the HERE IU was attempting to foster local organizing by sending IU organizers to run a campaign out of the local. Their focus on organizing had some impact on the local respondent's rhetoric about organizing, but the local clearly had not made its own organizing a priority. The IU organizers worked out of a different office and eventually the campaign was dropped and the organizers were relocated.

mentality came home to roost in 1984 [in the strike], which the union lost, and in the worst case, in certain restaurants and private clubs the union not only lost the strike, they broke the union. So out of that, in 1985 there were elections for leadership of the union, and [new people] became the elected leadership of Local A. And ... the important thing was [the new president] understood organizing. Not just organizing in the non-union sense, but organizing for union power. (Paul: HERE Local A)

Similar political upheaval occurred in Local B:

> [The challenging president] had actually been brought on staff with the old group, and was really just sort of discouraged and put off by how they did things. How they didn't do things, basically. So she ran a campaign against the current leadership at that time and was successful. And then asked the International to come in and assist in rebuilding the local. (Mike: HERE Local B)

The partially revitalized locals had not experienced the same kinds of political turmoil. None of the informants in this group described major political crises leading to innovative leadership. Only one of the partially revitalized locals was placed under trusteeship and in this case the trustee was not interested in new organizing programmes using disruptive tactics. When electoral turnover occurred in these locals, new leaders were not committed to organizing.

Individual innovators and outside experience

The political crisis, then, facilitated the presence of new leaders in the local. These were not just any new leaders – they were people with a particular interpretation of the situation of the movement: that it required organizing in order to survive. These individuals had the knowledge, vision, and sense of urgency required to use confrontational strategies and take organizational chances. One AFL-CIO Organizing Department leader suggested: 'I think that it's people who have a vision and who are willing to take political risks ... when most union leaders haven't been' (George: AFL-CIO). We found that these individuals understood and supported alternative models largely because they had worked in other social movements. In all the locals we identified as full revitalizers, at least half the organizing staff had been hired from outside the rank and file, and almost all arrived with prior experience in other movements. Many leaders over 40 had experience in community or welfare rights organizing, or the United Farm Workers (UFW), a labour group that always rejected the service model of unionism. Younger informants (in their twenties and early thirties) had also participated in community organizing or in student activism, particularly in Central American solidarity groups and anti-apartheid struggles on college campuses. Thus there are two types of experience, related to age: the organizers who came out of the 1960s and 1970s organizing and political activism, and those who were trained in campus activism and identity politics in the 1980s and 1990s.

Informants from all fully revitalized locals saw outside activism as an important force for change. One HERE organizer, asked what differentiated unions that had innovated fully from those that had not, replied:

> I would say a big part of it is a lot of activists from the '60s ... Similar to John Lewis saying 'let's bring in the Communists 'cause they know how to organize' ... I think SEIU realized that let's bring in these activists who were involved in the civil rights movement, the anti-war movement ... some sort of political organization, some sort of socialist organization, even, who are actively committed to building the union movement, and have some new ideas about how to do that, and will use the strategies developed in the civil rights movement, and the welfare rights organizations, the women's rights movement, all these different organizations, and get them plugged in and involved ... And where unions have done that, there's been more militancy. (Mike: HERE Local B)

These experiences contributed in several ways to these individuals' developing and embracing a revitalized vision of the labour movement. First, the experience gave them a broader perspective on social injustice and helped them see beyond the universe of unionized workers, thus leading them to consider organizing crucial to the movement's survival. One International staff member described the world-view of people from outside the movement:

> [They] don't have a world vision that everything's okay. We haven't been encapsulated in the rather safe union world, we've been out in the rest of the completely non-unionized world. And bringing in people I think with that kind of vision and energy has really driven some of our [growth] ... [For example, one organizer] is really driven to organize, and it's not because he was a bellman or a dishwasher somewhere, he just got a certain world view of poverty and power, and he worked for [a community organizing group], I mean, he has not been out talking to unionized workers! He's out talking to people on the threshold of total disaster. So his world vision is really different than a UFCW retail clerk investing in his vacation home for fifteen years ... And that's how he came into this and said 'we gotta organize, man.' (Pamela: HERE IU)

Second, these organizers were less caught up in traditional models of unionism and were familiar with alternative models of mobilization. They were not accustomed to the servicing model prevalent in the labour movement, but saw organizing people as the way to build union power. One organizer described the worker-centred approach to organizing he and several colleagues implemented at HERE Local A:

> We didn't know any different. We all came out of the Farmworkers [with] a lot of experience ... So the idea of, like, 'if you're gonna win, you're gonna involve workers' ... we never thought there was any other way to do it. (Paul: HERE Local A)

Third, these activities gave organizers the skills they need to mobilize workers. One HERE organizer said of his community organizing background:

> Yeah, that's where I learned to build committees, and what a committee does and how it functions ... It really came from that training ... you have to have committees because you don't have money. You can't pay staff ... So getting people to do it themselves. Also, it's the philosophy of empowering people. That comes more from the community organizing than the labor movement, unfortunately. (Mark: HERE Local B)

Another organizer described a similar dynamic:

> So [community organizing] was an experience that was very formative ... Just getting exposure to role-playing, raps, door-knocking, going door to door, trying to agitate people around issues, identifying people who had some leadership, pushing people to do things, you know, all the sort of skills that you need in union organizing are very similar in community organizing. (Mike: HERE Local B)

Fourth, union staff said that outside experience had influenced how they thought about tactics. One organizer said that because there was less to lose in community organizing, 'there was more creativity, more pushing the limits', which she and others imported into their union organizing (Brenda: SEIU Local G). One labour lawyer renowned for using creative tactics attributed his understanding of the need for non-routine approaches to his experience in the anti-war movement:

> The entire labor movement was like that, it followed proper channels. Just exactly what we learned during the Vietnam war does not work. That the

proper channels are laid down to defuse energy that's directed at the ruling class, not to impair that class's interests. And that's one of the ways that working in the anti-war movement was so helpful to me, because I realized as a result of the experiences there that reason and proper channels are only for defusing energy, not for channeling it. And you have to act outside those structures if you intend to get anything done.

Speaking specifically of the use of corporate campaign tactics, which target employers' corporate structure and particular corporate leaders, in the pioneering J. P. Stevens organizing campaign of the 1970s and 1980s, he said:

I can't minimize the influence of the Vietnam War on [the corporate campaign]. One of the things that we did during the anti-war struggle was to start understanding how corporations were making a huge amount of money off the war ... And that was a part of the war that the teach-ins were all about. The teach-ins weren't just to tell about the atrocities being committed, but to explain the economics behind the war. And remember the Berrigans ... They didn't just go to the headquarters, they would go to the directors too. So they were doing the same type of corporate structure analysis.

Finally, organizers described more tangible benefits to outside activism in terms of making alliances and bringing new kinds of resources into the local. An SEIU organizer said that outside activists were important 'just in terms of building community ties' (Rosa: SEIU Local H). One HERE organizer described staff participation in other movements as:

Totally crucial. Absolutely crucial. Because you bring that with you. The union completely benefits by having people that work with it that have their own base, their own community, and that have their own networks. Because if you run the kind of program that we're running, those networks need to be tapped into. (Michelle: HERE Local B)

In contrast, the partially revitalized locals hired few organizers from outside the labour movement, or even from outside the union. As a consequence, leaders in these locals did not interpret their situation as requiring a shift to organizing. Instead, in the face of employer attacks, they decided to try to protect the members they still represented. The UFCW representatives, despite having lost almost all their power in the retail sector, still spoke of 'not having to worry about market share' because they had simply decided only to think of themselves as representing grocery workers. One leader of a HERE partially revitalized local described a typical approach to declining power in the 1980s:

> We probably made an unconscious decision, which was to [say], 'look, let's batten down the hatches, circle the wagons, see what we got here, let's try [to] keep what we got inside the fold, by the time this tornado is through maybe we'll not have lost half our membership.' And so that was probably an unconscious decision from the mid-80s 'til early in the '90s to try to do that. And even as a result of that, we dropped a thousand members. Just circling the wagons. (Maurice: HERE Local E)

Moreover, leaders in these locals were clearly not as committed to the idea of mobilizing workers, or as familiar with tactics and strategies of doing so. One local leader described the local's relation to the worker committee in an organizing drive as 'keeping them updated' and 'utilizing' them in public events, rather than empowering them on the job (Scott: UFCW Local Z).

In sum, activists with experience outside the labour movement brought broad visions, knowledge of alternative organizational models and practice in disruptive tactics to the locals that became fully revitalized. These individuals interpreted the local's political crisis as a mandate to change, and they had the know-how and vision to develop new programmes to organize aggressively the unorganized.

International union influence

A third major factor in full revitalization, which we have already touched on, is the activity of the international union. In the cases of the fully revitalized locals, IU activity came together with the situation of crisis in the local to facilitate innovation. The IU helped ameliorate local oligarchical tendencies by placing people with a commitment to organizing in locals that were under trusteeship or had new leadership. The IU also gave IU-trained organizers and/or financial resources to these locals, and thus provided them with the know-how and the capability to carry out innovative organizing. In the partially revitalized locals, IU influence was not as great.

The three international unions relevant to this study differ in how much and how consistently they press locals to organize. The SEIU is the most institutionally committed to organizing, and has now mandated locals develop an organizing programme. The international mandated locals devote 10 per cent of their budgets to organizing in 1996, 15 per cent in 1997, and 20 per cent in 1998. Locals that did not comply with this mandate were threatened with the removal of IU subsidies and support. The IU itself is currently directing more than 30 per cent of its resources to organizing, and has been actively promoting a model of militant organizing longer than most other unions. For many years, the international regularly sent its own organizers to locals to lead organizing drives, and now directs national campaigns. The renewed commitment to organizing came during the presidency of John Sweeney, and was further institutionalized under Andy Stern, the former organizing director who became president when Sweeney moved to the AFL-CIO.

Organizing has not become as fully institutionalized in HERE, which has not undertaken significant nationwide campaigns, nor has the IU mandated organizing officially. However, the IU is directing increasing resources to locals that organize, and provided major support to intensive organizing campaigns in Las Vegas in the 1990s, which it hopes will provide a model for future HERE campaigns. As in SEIU, the rise through the IU hierarchy of individual leaders committed to organizing has contributed to its growing importance. Particularly notable in this respect is the 1998 ascension to the union's presidency of John Wilhelm, the architect of the union's organizing programme in Las Vegas.

The UFCW organizers did not relate as clear a narrative as SEIU and HERE organizers about their IU's stance on organizing. But it seems that in the wake of major loss of market share in the Midwest in the mid-1980s, the IU began to pay more attention to organizing. In 1994 the IU instituted the SPUR (Special Projects Union Representative) programme, in which the IU pays the expenses of member organizers temporarily taken off their regular jobs. Furthermore, the former organizing director became the IU president, which at least two interviewees saw as favourable to organizing. Yet the initiative seems to rest primarily with the locals: one organizer characterized his IU's attitude as 'if you show me you're gonna do something, I'll match you' (Milo: UFCW Local X). This programme appears less comprehensive than SEIU's, and interviewees did not mention particular leaders who strongly influenced organizing (at least not in the Bay Area) as there were in HERE. Other labour movement informants were also sceptical about the depths of the UFCW IU's commitment to organizing.

The fully revitalized locals have clearly been connected to the organizing efforts of their Internationals. Two of the three SEIU fully revitalized locals were trusteed. In the case of Local F, new leaders were brought in as a result of the trusteeship, which allowed the organizing model to be implemented:

> [Before the trusteeship], those were ... much more a kind of old school locals, you know, just entrenched leadership that didn't represent the work force, that couldn't speak Spanish, that was just holding onto this dying thing. So there was a real housecleaning when [the new local president, who had experience in other movements] came in ... he came in first as a trustee and then was elected president. That laid the ground work for doing this kind of organizing ... [He] is very strategic and has a clear understanding of this industry and what that takes and he saw that this was the way to go. He had tried to make some of these changes earlier on and been unsuccessful. So he was really important in that and also having the International support for what was at that time a pretty small local. I don't think the campaign, the organizing could have happened, without those things. (Julie: SEIU Local F)

Another organizer from the local said that the drive to organize was, 'in a lot of ways, coming from the International staff who were embedded in the local ... There were certain people in place that were driving the program ... [The IU] hired people based on their compatibility with the program' (Phil: SEIU Local F). Another former IU staffer described how this process worked:

> I [used to work] for the International ... [At one local], I worked with them to develop and organize; [at another local], I worked with them to get up an organizing program, to get involved. So there was a big emphasis and we would go back and have our meetings and talk about which locals had our program, how to get them on the program and what we could do to help. Part of it was just going in and doing campaigns and winning and saying it can be done, and part of it was engaging in the political conversations. (Josh: SEIU Local J)

Local F continues to receive large subsidies from the international as well as some staff. Local H also received major support from the International, including organizing directors and organizing staff, as well as assistance from the IU president on how to target their organizing strategically.

In SEIU Local G, IU influence was less direct but still crucial. As in the other fully revitalized locals, organizing began as a result of the opening generated by a trusteeship. In this case, however, the local split with the international over conflicts arising from the take-over, so innovation continued in the absence of the international rather than as a result of extended international involvement. However, even here the IU's commitment to innovative organizing spurred local innovation. Local leaders were determined to reestablish their independence and beat the IU at its own game.

Fully revitalized Locals A and B of HERE benefited from their contact with the pro-organizing sector of the international, in a process that was similar to what happened in SEIU Locals F and H. Vincent Sirabella, an organizing pioneer in the international, worked with staff at Local A in the early 1980s, learned from his organizing focus and experience. Later in the decade, international organizers again came to the aid of the local after it had developed its organizing focus and was facing difficult contract negotiations. Several times, the international provided funds to the local for organizing. At Local B, when internal crisis led to a change in the elected leadership, the IU furnished an organizer, now president of the local. This organizer had himself worked previously with several of the more experienced IU organizers, and went on to become the trustee of a nearby local that was merged into Local B. The international has continued to support the local with organizers and resources.

In the partially revitalized locals, the IU was less influential. As we have seen, the IU did not intervene significantly in these locals, in part because they had not experienced local political crisis that paved the way for change. Only one of the eight locals was trustee. In the one that was partially revitalized – HERE D – the trustee was not committed to innovative strategies. Although the local has added members, this has occurred primarily through negotiated recognition agreements with employers rather than through the use of disruptive tactics. In other HERE locals the IU did attempt to spur change but local resistance and/or lack of consistency on the part of the international prevented comprehensive change. For example, international organizers in one of the HERE partially revitalized locals remained marginalized, because no one in the local was part of the sector of the IU committed to militant organizing. A leader of a third partially revitalized local, asked how the organizing emphasis had begun there, described the IU's influence in terms of changing his interpretation of the situation:

> I'd say probably in the early '90s the awareness came from leaders within our international union, who came to visit us. We had an industry-wide negotiation in 1989 and the employers here, who used to negotiate as one group, broke up individually. And so we had negotiations that were going to be going on with 12 hotels at the same time. And so we had help from the international, and during that time I was able to see a different side of what needs to be implemented within the local in order to turn around

some of the stuff that we had been experiencing during the '80s. (Maurice: HERE Local E)

However, the presence of the IU in this local diminished after the contract negotiations. The local did not implement a real organizing programme until 1997, after sustained IU support re-emerged.

The SEIU partially revitalized locals did not experience sustained IU intervention until recently. Yet leaders explicitly attribute their increasing revitalization to IU influence; these locals were responding to the SEIU international's aforementioned mandate. In SEIU Local J, this process is more advanced than it is in the other locals because of the local leader's participation in SEIU's Committee on the Future, an IU-coordinated effort to discuss and disseminate organizing, which led to the union-wide mandate. The other two locals have begun more recently to respond to the mandate. As one organizer described her local's situation:

In terms of organizing, our local is just starting to get a statewide program off the ground ... there's never been any statewide-run program throughout the entire local. And there's never been a lot of money dedicated to organizing. And this past year, the international union ... has set some standards, and [is] requiring locals to spend a certain percentage of our per capita. So we were actually spending closer to 5 per cent in 1996, and we're taking a leap to 15 per cent in '97. And so we're taking a huge jump in terms of the amount of money that we're putting into organizing, and we're absolutely starting from scratch, pretty much. (Donna: SEIU Local K)

The UFCW locals had not been particularly influenced by their international. No UFCW organizer mentioned a major influx of IU personnel or philosophical influence. Nor had the IU taken advantage of opportunities to intervene in these locals at moments of organizational change. The IU sometimes supported these locals by subsidizing the SPUR programme. However, this support clearly followed initiatives taken by the local, rather than the IU's actively promoting change.

Overall, international union leadership was crucial in leading to full revitalization. The international initiated or supported much of the change in local unions; this process was not one of 'bottom-up,' local innovation that later reached the top echelons of the bureaucracy. Rather, progressive sectors of the international exerted varying degrees of influence over locals in crisis, which led to full revitalization. Furthermore, IU influence helps explain the differences among the partially revitalized locals; those that have made more changes, in particular HERE Local E and SEIU Local J, acknowledge significant influence by the IU, as do the other SEIU locals, which are responding to the SEIU mandate. The UFCW locals did not experience major IU intervention, and the other HERE partially revitalized locals were either not receptive to the organizing emphasis of the IU or did not experience IU intervention that attempted to promulgate an organizing focus.

Summary

The three factors we have identified – crisis, outside activists, and international union influence – are related in complicated ways. In most cases, the pattern seems to have been that the local was opened up to outside influence by a political crisis, which allowed particular elements of the international to encourage innovation through trustees, other staff, training, and/or material resources. Leaders with new interpretations of the situation of the labour movement and new strategies for increasing union power, who had often developed these views in other social movements, came to wield influence through these openings. In some cases, although not all, the outside activists within the local arrived there because of this opening to the international. In any event, these factors in combination were crucial to transformation; locals that did not have crisis, sustained IU intervention, and outside activists did not revitalize fully.

Conclusion

Recent developments in the American labour movement suggest that even servicing unions can sometimes radicalize their goals and tactics. This process, however, never happens automatically or easily. Our analysis of local unions that have 'changed to organize' highlights the role of three factors: the occurrence of a localized political crisis leading to new leadership, the presence of leaders with activist experience outside the labour movement who interpret the decline of labour's power as a mandate for change, and the influence of the international union in favour of innovation.

Resistance to change was widespread, on the part of both union members and union staff. Often, scholars and reformers identify union leaders and staff as the primary obstacles to change (Michels, 1962; Piven and Cloward,

1979; Slaughter, 1999). In the locals we looked at, we certainly found leaders who were reluctant to risk their own positions, thus illustrating this view of oligarchical resistance. Beyond these narrow interests of individual leaders, however, we also found that union culture stood in the way of transformation, as both staff and members had developed and defended symbiotic understandings of their roles as business agents and consumers of services. Revitalized locals had to transform this organizational culture, which they did through participatory education and by emphasizing a new, more expansive model of membership. This new model stresses the development of political skills and a sense of efficacy on the part of members, along with greater rank-and-file activism in the labour movement. The salience of this cultural dimension suggests both that members can grow as habituated to oligarchy as leaders, and that changing organizational culture is an important key to radical transformation

These findings suggest that crisis played an important role in undermining union leaders' commitment to the servicing model of unionism. Under conditions of crisis, organizational survival is no longer necessarily best pursued by aiming small and adhering to conventional tactics, as is demonstrated by the locals that tried to do this and continued to decline. Indeed, contra Michels, labour activists in some locals argued that survival could only be achieved by the radical transformation of union goals and tactics. Those are the locals that revitalized and grew.

However, while the general crisis of the labour movement was important as a background condition, it by itself was not enough to prompt revitalization. The locals we studied had all, by the 1980s, become heavily invested in the service model of unionism; it took a localized political crisis, activists with experience outside the labour movement, and resources from the international to make transformation happen.

What are the implications of these findings for unions in other countries that are trying to 'change to organize?' First, they reinforce Carter and Fairbrother's (1998) assertion that 'changing to organize' entails more than simply borrowing a few tactical and organizational innovations piecemeal from the USA. Second, they suggest that central labour confederations can play a crucial role in diffusing social movement unionism. Centralized pressure was key to transformation in our fully revitalized locals. The fact that the impetus to change came in part from the IU may seem counterintuitive; we tend to think of 'progressive' change as originating with small, local-level organizations and making its way up to the entrenched bureaucracy at the top (Rosenthal and Schwartz, 1989). Nonetheless, in our study, the bureaucratic power of the international was an important factor in both initiating change (by promoting new leaders) and supporting continued revitalization (by providing continuing resources and legitimacy to locals). Furthermore, it appears likely that the IU bureaucracy will play a major role in widely diffusing the revitalized model to other local unions. Third, the role crisis played in undermining union leaders' commitment to the servicing model of unionism suggests that it might be harder to garner the political will to transform when labour movement decline is less serious than it is in the USA.

Acknowledgements

We gratefully acknowledge the financial support of the Institute of Industrial Relations at the University of California, Berkeley. Research material for this chapter was previously published in an article by the two authors in the *American Journal of Sociology* (September 2000).

References

Bronfenbrenner, K. and Juravich, T. (1994) 'Seeds of Resurgence: The Promise of Organizing in the Public and Private Sectors', working paper, Institute for the Study of Labor Organizations, Washington DC.

Bronfenbrenner, K., and Juravich, T. (1998) 'It Takes More Than Housecalls: Organizing to Win with a Comprehensive Union-building Strategy', in K. Bronfenbrenner, S. Friedman, R. Hurd, R. Seeber, and R. Oswald (eds) *Organizing to Win: New Research on Union Strategies*, Ithaca: ILR Press, pp. 19–36.

Carter, B. and Fairbrother, P. (1998) 'Coherence or Contradiction: The TUC's "New Unionism" Project', paper given to *Work, Employment and Society* Conference, Cambridge, September.

Meyerson, H. (2000a) 'Rolling the Union on: John Sweeney's Movement Four Years Later', *Dissent* (Winter): 47–55.

Meyerson, H. (2000b) 'A Clean Sweep: The SEIU's Organizing Drive for Janitors Shows How Unionization Can Raise Wages', *American Prospect* 11 (15): 24–9.

Michels, R. (1962) *Political Parties: A Sociological Study of the Oligarchical Tendencies of Modern Democracy*, New York: Dover.

Piore, M. (1994) 'Unions: A Reorientation to Survive', in C. Kerr and P. D. Staudohar, *Labor Economics and Industrial Relations: Markets and Institutions*, Cambridge MA: Harvard University Press, pp. 512–41.

Piven, F. F. and Cloward, R. (1977) *Poor People's Movements: Why They Succeed, How They Fail*, New York: Vintage.

Rosenthal, N. and Schwartz, M. (1989) 'Spontaneity and Democracy in Social Movements', in B. Klandermans, *Organizing for Change*, Greenwich CT: JAI Press, pp. 33–59.

Slaughter, J. (1999) 'The New AFL-CIO: No Salvation from on High for the Working Stiff', in R. M. Tilman and M. S. Cummings, *The Transformation of US Unions*, Boulder CO: Lynne Rienner, pp. 49–60.

4 TRADE UNION INNOVATION, ADAPTATION AND RENEWAL IN AUSTRALIA: STILL SEARCHING FOR THE HOLY MEMBERSHIP GRAIL

Gerard Griffin, Rai Small and Stuart Svensen

Introduction

Trade unionism flourished in Australia throughout most of the twentieth century. Between 1920 and 1980 membership density was greater than 50 per cent for all but a handful of years, wages were relatively high by international standards and, generally, members exercised a significant degree of control over working conditions. Much of this power and status was derived from the centralized conciliation and arbitration system introduced in 1904. Practically destroyed during a series of major strikes in the 1890s, the remnants of the union movement eagerly accepted this new industrial relations system. The new system promised significant benefits such as legally mandated employer recognition, exclusive jurisdiction over a segment of the workforce and legally enforceable minimum wages and working conditions, all highly attractive prizes to a very weak union movement. Over time, practical union officials increasingly utilized this 'arbitral strategy' to achieve their goals. Thus, Australian unions increasingly followed a hierarchy of, in descending order, arbitral, political and industrial strategies rather than the industrial strategy, complemented by a political strategy, found more traditionally in other countries.

The outcome was that in many cases, wage increases were won not on the industrial battleground but rather through tactics such as National Wage Cases or applying, on the grounds of traditional relativities, to the Australian Industrial Relations Commission (AIRC) for flow-ons of increases granted to other groups of workers. Equally, rather than visit the workplaces and sign up non-organized employees, membership was achieved and retained through strategies such as *de facto* closed shops, government policies, employer support and the insertion of preference clauses – clauses granting preference in a wide area of employment conditions to unionists over non-unionists – into legally binding decisions of the AIRC. In practice, a centralized, arbitral model of industrial relations that, arguably, necessitated and required an organized and representative union movement, offered a range of inducements to Australian unions to operate within this centralized system.

This reliance of Australian unions on various organs of the state has led a number of commentators, principally Howard (1977), to argue that they are not worthy of the title 'union'. The argument goes that organizations so dependent on the state for, among other things, membership and wage increases are not trade unions in the accepted sense of the word. The degree of dependence has been vigorously debated (see Gahan, 1996), but there can be little doubt that Australian unions have derived significant succour from the state. This chapter examines the response of unions to rapidly declining membership when, commencing in the mid-to-late 1980s, this succour was increasingly withdrawn. We argue that the traditional hierarchy of union strategies was unable to stem the decline of membership. Consequently, after some years of uncertainty, unions have attempted to reposition these strategies and, in particular, during the 1990s attempted to follow a more industrial strategy. Two key elements of this repositioning – restructuring the union movement to create twenty large 'super-unions' and an attempt to develop an organizing culture through a flagship programme named Organising Works – are the focus of this chapter. We commence with a discussion on the decline of Australian unionism in the 1990s and its probable causes.

Membership decline

The decline of Australian union membership is detailed in Table 4.1. Absolute membership held up during the 1980s, but density fell. During the 1990s absolute membership has fallen rapidly; density even more rapidly. Currently, union density is at its lowest level since before World War I.

Both Peetz (1998) and Drago and Wooden (1998) attribute the decline to two main factors: first, increased government and employer opposition to unions that resulted in a substantial reduction in the incidence of closed shops and compulsory unionism; secondly, structural changes in the economy. According to Peetz, structural changes were the dominant factor in the decline of union density in the 1980s, whereas the reduction of compulsory unionism was the chief factor in the 1990s. Drago and Wooden attribute some of the 1990s decline to structural factors, but agree with Peetz that the reduction of compulsory unionism was a more important reason.

Table 4.1 *Australian trade union membership, 1982–99*

	Number of members ('000)	Total members as percentage of employees	Male members as percentage of male employees	Female members as percentage of female employees
1982	2568	49	53	43
1986	2594	46	50	39
1988	2536	42	46	35
1990	2660	41	45	35
1992	2509	40	43	35
1993	2377	38	41	34
1994	2283	35	38	31
1995	2252	33	37	30
1996	2194	31	34	28
1997	2110	30	33	27
1998	2037	28	30	26
1999	1878	26	28	23

Note: These data are based on household surveys conducted by the Australian Bureau of Statistics (ABS) in 1976 and 1982, biennially between 1986 and 1992, and annually since 1992. The traditional source of membership data was the annual series of data collected directly from trade unions by the ABS, but this was discontinued in the mid-1990s.

Source: Australian Bureau of Statistics, *Trade Union Members Australia*, Cat. No. 6325, and *Employee Earnings, Benefits and Trade Union Membership Australia*, Cat. No. 6310.

The effect of governments and legislation on union density is controversial. In Australia this effect is complicated by a number of factors including the coexistence of state and federal governments of different political hues and the adoption by Labor governments of neo-liberal policies. What these contradictory patterns may indicate is that, while industrial relations legislation and the ways in which it is applied are important to the unionization process, a simple Labor/non-Labor distinction may be irrelevant. In brief, if policies that adversely affect unionization are implemented, union density will fall, irrespective of which party is in power. The role played by employers in declining union density has received little attention. There can be little doubt, however, that, commencing in the mid-1980s and influenced by 'new right' economic philosophies, a growing number of employers have sought to introduce anti-union measures. As the legal options and policy choices available to employers expanded, increasing numbers sought to achieve an individualistic employment relationship. Other suggested reasons for the decline of Australian unionism include the corporatist-style Accord between the ACTU and Labor governments between 1983 and 1996, membership dissatisfaction with the way union mergers were handled and the move to an enterprise bargaining system (Kenyon and Lewis, 1992, 1996; Peetz, 1998).

Cooper (1997) points out that there is a lacuna in the Australian literature regarding the role of unions themselves in membership growth and decline; the focus has been on the external variables that affect unions, rather than union strategy. She argues that, in contrast, the international literature has examined this issue and that its absence in the Australian case does not indicate complete impotence on the part of unions. The inadequacy of current union strategies could conceivably be the 'something' referred to above that is discouraging Australians from joining unions.

Such developments have long been a concern within unions and subject to debate. The ACTU has made sporadic and often unsuccessful efforts over the years to introduce new services for members (Norington, 1998). Nonetheless, responses to union decline are not confined to the ACTU. Each state and many regions within each state have trades and labour councils – inter-union councils that draw together the various unions operating in these states or regions – and officials in the largest of these, the New South Wales Labor Council, have been active participants in the debate on the future of unionism and how best to respond to the membership crisis. As well as being vocal critics of the ACTU amalgamation strategy (Costa and Duffy, 1991; Costa and Hearn, 1997) these officials have set up a comprehensive website and recently launched an on-line newspaper, *Workers Online*. In addition, many individual unions have initiated campaigns and devoted significant resources to boosting membership.

While these initiatives are important, we focus on those actions that, linked to the centralized wage system and the related dominant role of the ACTU (see Griffin, 1994), were the main strategic responses of the union movement. The first is union restructuring through mergers. The second element has been an attempt to invigorate the movement by the development of a more organizing-based culture.

Union amalgamations

The issue of trade union amalgamations has a long pedigree in academic literature. It has been argued for some time that there were too many trade unions with small memberships, leading to gross diseconomies of scale. The argument that nothing would change so long as the arbitral model protected such unions has an equally long pedigree, as has the recognition that change would have to emerge from within the union movement. Declining membership in the mid-1980s provided the spur.

The first formal union recommendation for mergers followed a joint ACTU/Trade Development Council fact-finding mission to Western Europe. Two resultant strategy documents (ACTU, 1987; ACTU/TDC, 1987) advocated the adoption of a model of 'strategic unionism', to be achieved chiefly by transferring most of the members of the then existing 326 mainly occupationally based unions into twenty mainly industry-based 'super-unions'. This, it was hoped, would produce larger and more efficient unions capable of responding to the challenges of downward pressures on unionization that had already become apparent (ACTU, 1987: 14). The 1987 ACTU Biennial Conference adopted a formal policy titled *Future Strategies for the Trade Union Movement* that strongly recommended a series of union mergers. This policy had no immediate formal impact. Inevitably, many unions were resistant to change with a number pointing out that, while the trend in density was worrying, absolute membership had actually increased slightly between 1982 and 1986. The 1988 membership data changed this attitude: density had dropped from 46 per cent in 1986 to 42 per cent in 1988. A publication authored by union officials, *Can Unions Survive?* (Berry and Kitchener, 1989) reflected this growing concern. At the 1989 ACTU Congress the mood had changed with a strong majority of unions now favouring a restructured union movement. This attitude was reinforced by the actions of the federal Labor government that facilitated the amalgamation process by changes to legislation that included the effective removal of a requirement that amalgamations could not take place without 25 per cent membership approval. The minimum size of a registered union was raised to 1000 and subsequently 10,000, although this was later reversed after employer complaints that it amounted to an infringement of the rights of freedom of association (Hawke and Wooden, 1998).

The restructuring drive from the ACTU, allied with the actions of the government, proved irresistible. During the five-year period 1990–4, some 130 mergers occurred. Nothing remotely approaching this number of mergers has occurred previously in Australia (Griffin and Scarcebrook, 1989) or indeed in most other industrialized countries. Over this time period the total number of unions decreased from 295 to 157 while, more importantly, the number of federally registered unions – the larger unions that operate in two or more states – dropped from 134 to 52. In 1994, these 52 unions accounted for 85 per cent of total union membership. In effect, a complete restructuring of Australian trade unionism had occurred within half a decade, a startling change given the inactivity of the previous decades.

Inevitably, a number of the amalgamated unions were marriages of factional, political convenience rather than true industry unions (Yates and Ewer, 1997) while some unions were amalgamated in name only, retaining duplicated executives and infrastructure (Richardson, 1994). Equally, the amalgamations had their share of tensions and problems (Dabscheck, 1995) but, overall, they were effected about as smoothly as could reasonably have been expected. The amalgamations largely had rank-and-file support. Only six merger proposals were defeated in membership ballots and in each case the defeat was attributable to opposition from key power bases within one of the proposed partners. Most ballots resulted in large majority membership support. Some critics have argued that the amalgamation process was designed not so much for the purpose of resisting deunionization, but to centralize power, and to increase the union movement's domination by the ACTU and its senior officials (Costa and Duffy, 1991; Thompson, 1990). While such a motive cannot be totally discounted, the weight of evidence points to declining membership as the predominant rationale for the merger boom.

Table 4.1 indicates that amalgamations were not effective in boosting membership. Indeed, on the contrary, union membership went into its steepest decline since the great depression of the 1930s. There has been an attempt by critics of the merger process to link mergers with declining membership. This correlation does not, however, imply causation. Bodman (1998) claimed to have found a significant causal relationship between amalgamations and membership decline, but his data and methodology are unconvincing (Duy and Thomas, 1998; Griffin and Svensen, 1996).

Equally, data from the 1995 Australian Industrial Relations Survey (AWIRS) provide no evidence that union amalgamations at the aggregate level were associated with union exit (Drago and Wooden, 1998; Griffin and Svensen, 1998; Peetz, 1998). Data limitations mean that it is not possible to say what impact amalgamations may have had on unionization in particular unions. It may well be the case that, in some unions, amalgamations have produced high levels of member dissatisfaction and exit. The then ACTU general secretary, Bill Kelty, conceded that some amalgamations had not gone well, nominating the Australian Workers Union (AWU) and the Federation of Industrial Manufacturing and Engineering Employees (FIMEE) as one example (Carney and Johnston, 1995). At the same time, there may have been cases where amalgamation had a positive impact on unionization by, for example, reducing inter-union conflict (Penn and Scattergood, 1996).

What is clear, though, is that amalgamations did not prove to be the hoped-for mechanism to reverse declining unionization. While the ACTU 'top-down' approach was effective at effecting a large number of amalgamations in a relatively short span of time, the process must be judged unsuccessful on the membership criterion. As the merger boom was drawing to an end, the search commenced for the replacement grail.

Organizing

The recognition that amalgamations were not, of themselves, the answer to declining union membership led to some rethinking within the ACTU and a number of key individual unions. Two interrelated problems were identified. The first was the changing industrial environment within which the mergers were taking place. Commencing in 1987, a new workplace bargaining-oriented system was starting to replace the traditional centralized system. The ACTU agreement in 1990 to embrace enterprise bargaining was promoted as a means of increasing unions' workplace relevance and presence. What instead seems to have occurred is that many union officials and delegates became mired in never-ending bargaining negotiations, leaving fewer resources available for members' servicing and organizing. Unions had planned to funnel expected financial gains from merger-related economies of scale into membership recruitment and retention activities. The reality was that even where economies were gained they were swallowed up in negotiating new enterprise agreements.

The second problem was the lack of a workplace-based union delegate structure. Traditionally, unions had achieved wage increases and improved conditions through the AIRC, a process that inhibited the development of strong shop-floor union organization, except in a small number of industries (Benson, 1988; Rimmer and Sutcliffe, 1981). This union vacuum at the workplace level caused major problems for unions in the enterprise bargaining process. At the same time, the level of workplace activity was being recognized as a key factor influencing trends in membership levels. Intuitively, and fairly basically, the decreasing influence of closed shops, preference clauses and the broad influence of the centralized system on levels of membership needed to be replaced with a workplace delegate system. Subsequently, data from the two Australian Workplace Industrial Relations Surveys indicated the key role of delegates. The panel data showed that, between 1990 and 1995, the rate of deunionization was 2 per cent in workplaces that had union delegates as compared to 21 per cent in workplaces that did not (Peetz, 1998: 121). Over the same time period the percentage of workplaces with no union presence increased from 20 per cent to 26 per cent overall, and from 28 per cent to 36 per cent in the private sector (Morehead *et al.*, 1997: 140).

Given this context, in July 1993 the ACTU led a delegation of union officials to the USA in search of ideas for building membership levels, with a specific brief to examine recruiting methods and techniques. The rationale was that American unions were operating in an extremely difficult legal and political environment, and that lessons could, accordingly, be drawn from their experiences. The delegation's subsequent report argued that the low USA unionization levels stemmed not only from the climate, but also from the failure of the trade union movement to build on the position of relative strength it had achieved in the 1950s and 1960s (Stuart, 1993). In the late 1980s and early 1990s, American trade unions were finding it difficult to build from their weakened position. The obvious lesson for Australian trade unions was not to let membership levels slide to the point where they had neither a presence nor legitimacy in the workplace. A second theme of the report was organizing. In the mid-to-late 1980s, influential sections of the American trade union movement argued for a more strategic and innovative approach to organizing. One aspect of this new focus was the creation of the Organizing Institute by large unions and the AFL-CIO, the US peak union council, in 1989. The Institute was directed towards addressing the lack of outstanding organizers in the movement. The brief of the Institute is to recruit, train and place field organizers so as to increase both the quality and quantity of union organizers. Training involved both formal and on-the-job aspects (Stuart, 1993).

The Australian delegation was evidently impressed with the operations of the Institute, as indeed was the ACTU Executive. In August 1993, the Executive determined on a programme to:

- select and train young persons for recruitment and organizing;
- devote more resources to recruitment and organizing activities more generally;
- ensure that organizers appropriately reflect union membership and potential membership in terms of gender, age and ethnicity.

The philosophy underlying this programme became known as the organizing model. Adherents and supporters of this model contrasted it with the servicing model, which they characterized as an approach that situates the union as a reactive third party that attempts to solve problems and can be blamed when results are unsatisfactory. In contrast, the organizing model was viewed as a more inclusive, empowering approach, where members see themselves as the union and establish their own agendas (ACTU, 1995b). Organizers employed by the union will provide assistance as required, especially in specialized areas, but the focus is on members becoming active, organizing themselves, and establishing a culture of unionization in the workplace. Adherents also argued that an organizing approach will give rise to more sustainable improvements in the position of unions and their members (O'Sullivan, interview 1999; Larsen, interview 1999; Daley, interview 1999).

It was in this context that Organising Works was established by the ACTU in 1994. It was developed as an avenue for recruiting, training and supporting new union recruiter/organizers, who would each be attached to a participating union. The Organising Works programme lasted for twelve months, was a registered traineeship and received subsidies under a federal government labour market programme. The mentoring union provided most of the remainder of the trainees' $17,410 salary, with assistance from the ACTU for training and support. The low salary level was designed to discourage applicants with low levels of commitment to the union movement (O'Sullivan, interview 1999).

Initially, and perhaps not unexpectedly, some tensions emerged between adherents of the two models. Chris Walton, Executive Officer of Organising Works, acknowledges: 'our own tone about it was probably too zealous, that it potentially got people in their corners a little bit' (Walton, 1999). However, he argues that the point was never to eliminate servicing but rather make workplaces more self-reliant and find other ways to service members that would free the organizer to play a more strategic role.

Over time, the dichotomy between organizing and servicing has been eroded, at least to some extent. For example, Walton now holds the view that:

> They're [organizing and servicing] both theoretical models. In the real world you can't be one or the other. Of course you have to still service. It's about your approach to things. So, if you have an issue or a grievance, is this an opportunity to organize around it or is it our pure role to fix it? (Walton, interview 1999)

Officials have also recognized that, whatever the prescription for change, institutional resistance within the union movement (Pocock, 1998) and individual resistance from members who expect a servicing relationship with their union (Larsen, interview, 1999) will be encountered.

The organizing approach to trade unionism places workplace activity and membership involvement at its core. The role of workplace delegates is, therefore, central to the success of the strategy. Although there was little change in delegate presence in unionized workplaces between 1990 and 1995, this is not necessarily indicative of lack of effort by unions. Drago and Wooden (1998) contend that deunionization itself retards delegate presence while greater responsibilities of delegates may have reduced willingness to nominate. Alexander *et al.* (1998) reject this interpretation of the data, arguing that it is delegate presence that influences unionization.

The first intake of 58 trainees from New South Wales and Victoria was inducted in March 1994 into the Organising Works programme, 55 trainees graduated from the programme and 54 obtained ongoing jobs. The programme was expanded in 1995 with two drafts of 86 and 52 trainees respectively, and was also extended to Queensland. The initial focus of the programme was recruitment, especially in industries where union presence was weak (Bagnall, 1994). Changes were made to the second training programme, which, in 1995, included two residential courses and approximately 30 days of other training, delivered on average two days per fortnight (ACTU, 1998; Cooper and Walton, 1996).

In total, from 1994 to 1998 some 310 trainees commenced the traineeships within Organising Works. Approximately 55 per cent were female, their average age was 26, they were highly likely to have a degree or be studying, and likely to have previous union experience and to have been nominated by a union (see Table 4.2).

What effect has the programme had on union membership and on trade unionism in Australia in its five years of operation? Initial reports of progress were encouraging and it received generally favourable media coverage (Bagnall, 1994; Davis, 1995a). The ACTU claimed considerable success, stating that over 10,000 new members were recruited as a direct result of the efforts of the 1994 intake. The first intake of 1995 was said to have recruited 13,800 members representing an income of $2.7 million per annum, or an average of 174 members and $34,000 per trainee, meaning that the programme more than paid for itself. However, the provision of this information was somewhat problematic. The premis of the organizing model was not that organizers personally sign up all members. Rather, they aim to organize a workplace in such a way that the union has an identity independent of paid

Table 4.2 *Characteristics of Organising Works trainees*

	1994		1995 (1)		1995 (2)		1996	
	No.	%	No.	%	No.	%	No.	%
Total number	58		86		52		38	
Number mid-course	n/a		n/a		49		41	
Average age	24.5		24.1		26.7		28.4	
Below 26 years	38	66	66	77	25	51	18	44
Women	35	60	53	62	27	55	20	49
Degree	30	52	43	50	21	43	19	46
Higher degree	4	7	8	9	1	2	3	7
Current student	19	33	33	38	11	22	10	24
Second language	17	29	10	12	15	30	10	24
Previously union member	49	85	76	88	39	79	38	93
Previously held union position	17	29	35	41	15	30	30	73
Nominated by union	38	66	37	43	35	71	27	66
State								
NSW			25				8	
Victoria			32				7	
Queensland			25				5	
South Australia							15	
Western Australia							5	
Tasmania							1	
Graduated	55	95	79	92	42	81	36	95

Source: Organising Works (1994–9) *Reports to Annual General Meetings of the Committee o*

union employees and thus a culture of unionization is developed that boosts membership numbers. In the context of this approach, the number of members recruited by an individual organizer is misleading and may not reflect his or her success. However, initially it was politically important to argue that Organising Works was a good investment for unions and a simple way of doing this was to point to the numbers of new members recruited (Walton, interview 1999; O'Sullivan, interview 1999). Since the first two intakes, the ACTU has stopped publicly releasing data on the numbers of union members recruited by the trainees, although it continues to collect the data for its own purposes.

The numbers of trainees passing though the programme were reduced after the first two intakes, raising some questions about the effectiveness of the programme. Although the programme was extended to other states, there has been a steady reduction in the number of trainees inducted, with 38 entrants in the fourth intake in 1996, 27 in 1997 and 23 in 1998. Numbers increased slightly to 26 in 1999. Union officials interviewed argue that a range of factors contributed to the decline in the number of trainees, including:

- The two large intakes in 1995 were found to be unmanageable and a conscious decision was taken to scale back the programme.
- Individual unions have faced increasingly hostile environments and their capacity to devote resources to programmes such as Organising Works has been stretched.
- The resources available for training generally have been affected by the withdrawal of federal government funding for the Trade Union Training Authority.
- There were organizational difficulties associated with gathering together enough trainees outside Sydney and Melbourne to support formal training programmes.
- Finally, one union official involved with the programme since its inception noted that, in 1994, there was a large group of committed activists seeking an opportunity to become involved in the union movement so there was a large pool of excellent candidates from which to choose. Since the programme started, unions have become less the 'flavour of the month' (O'Sullivan, interview 1999).

In attempting to evaluate the impact of Organising Works, it is necessary to take account of four confounding factors. First, the aspirations of the ACTU and the union movement with respect to the programme must be kept in perspective. Organising Works was not intended to be the complete answer to the membership decline in Australian unions. Rather, it is only one element, albeit a key element, of a wider strategy to promote recruitment, organizing and workplace activity, and make unions more relevant to Australian workers. In a complementary initiative the ACTU decided, in 1995, to create a $10-million recruitment fund to finance a series of initiatives including: Organising Works; Jobshop; marketing of union/ACTU associated services; provision of services and discounts relating to home loans, travel, insurance and other products; traineeship programmes for advocates; assistance for promoting and encouraging workplace delegates; organizing large national conferences; and special recruiting activities (ACTU, 1995a). The programme involved hiring new union organizers, establishing telephone centres to handle inquiries from potential members, and targeting regional centres in recruitment campaigns (Davis, 1995b). Although some of these initiatives were short-lived or did not eventuate, the point to note is that Organising Works was just one part of the ACTU strategy.

Second, in common with this multifaceted ACTU approach, individual participating unions have generally treated Organising Works as only one element in a broader strategy to attack the decline in membership levels. Other strategies have involved reorganizing the internal workings of unions, establishing call centres, developing performance management and appraisal systems, enhancing technical resources to provide quality data and membership feedback, and extending an organizing approach to all layers of the organization (Daley, interview 1999; Larsen, interview 1999).

Third, from the early 1990s, there has been a renewed interest in unions delivering non-industrial services to their members. For example, the ACTU and trade unions developed a range of services for all members relating to financial advice, income protection insurance, home loans, special deals on credit cards, and access to a wine club. Other services, such as those relating to the Union Shopper programme, are available only to members of participating unions. There is evidence that consumer services, health and financial security services are valued by existing union members (Griffin *et al.*, 1997). However, it is unclear whether such services are relevant to potential members when they are contemplating membership or would affect the decisions of current members who are reconsidering their membership status. The delivery of such services is consistent with a servicing approach to union members and, to the extent that it distracts attention and draws resources away from organizing efforts, it is often seen as negative by proponents of the organizing model (Lewis, 1999). The provision of these services has become increasingly peripheral to the activities of some unions in recent years (Larsen, interview 1999), while others still market such services as a key feature of union membership (Donovan, interview 1999).

Fourth, it was quickly realized by the initiators of the Organising Works programme that trainee organizers entering a union at the most junior level would not be able to bring about cultural change. It was essential that the debate about directions for change reach officials and existing organizers. Therefore it was decided that a broader cross-section of the union movement should be exposed to an organizing approach. Thus, the focus of the programme has broadened since its inception. Organising Works, in conjunction with Trade Union Training Australia Inc. (TUTA), has developed a number of initiatives including:

- 'Organising in Everything We Do' – a one-day course and manual for union staff that aimed at developing an 'organizing culture'.
- 'Planning To Be Effective' – a two-day course that covers the principles of strategic planning and implemented organizing as a priority.
- A packaged course and handbook for union delegates or activists titled 'Winning in the Workplace'.
- A two- or three-day course, 'Skills of Recruitment and Organising' for organizers aimed at assisting unions in the development and implementation of recruitment plans and strategies.
- A two-week 'Craft of Organising' programme for experienced organizers (ACTU, 1998).

Accordingly, any assessment of the impact of Organising Works must proceed at two levels: a micro level and as part of an overall union attempt to arrest declining membership.

Focusing initially on the macro level, it is clear that Organising Works, along with all of the other initiatives of the ACTU and individual unions, has failed to stem the decline in membership density. To take one example, the goal set in 1995 of a net increase in national membership levels of 200,000 by 1997 was not even partially met; indeed, absolute membership decreased by over 100,000 between 1995 and 1997. A contributing factor to this failure is the fact that the ambitious, multifaceted programme of the ACTU largely went unrealized. Resources went towards Organising Works and TUTA but Jobshops did not eventuate and regional recruitment campaigns were very limited. And while there were some changing, explanatory circumstances – such as the hostile political and legislative environment following the election of the Liberal/National Coalition Government in 1996 – the outcome was a continuing significant decline in membership during the second half of the 1990s decade (see Table 4.1).

Moving to the micro level, this ACTU target of a net increase of 200,000 in the number of union members by 1997 was interlocked with the goal of employing an additional 300 recruiting officers through Organising Works within two years (Davis, 1995c). The reduction in trainees involved in the programme meant that this goal was not reached. Between 1994 and the end of 1997, 237 trainees graduated from the programme. Upon graduating the vast majority continued to work in the union movement, primarily in a recruitment capacity. Thus, while the goal of the ACTU and unions was not met, nevertheless a significant group of committed organizers has been absorbed into the union movement.

In keeping with its position on the importance of organizing, the ACTU argues that an assessment of Organising Works should not be looked at in financial terms alone. It argues that the programme has achieved recruitment success in workplaces and industries previously thought unorganizable, ranging from horse-racing to hairdressing. The ACTU contends that the aim was not merely recruitment, but also the establishment of sustainable workplace organization based on an organizing model of unionism. The ACTU also claims success in getting more women, young people, and workers from different ethnic and diverse backgrounds into the union movement. The trainees were a diverse range of people with experience in women's organizations, green and peace groups, student politics, socialist groups, Christian organizations, the Labor Party, gay and lesbian groups, ethnic communities organizations, independent struggles and animal liberationists, providing a base to build the vital links between the union movement and other social and community movements. The ACTU claims that a survey of graduates found that the overwhelming majority maintain an organizing/recruitment focus, and that a minority maintain dedicated recruitment roles (ACTU, 1998).

The peak council also links a recent successful initiative to Organising Works: it has employed four organizers directly, who are seconded to two unions per year to assist in organizing campaigns. The organizers are all graduates of Organising Works. The objective of these campaigns is to assist in the building of delegates' networks and training activists to be more self-sufficient in solving their own problems. The organizers attempt to engage workers in targeted industries outside the workplace, in pubs, cafés and even in their homes. Targeted industries to date include private bus and coach services, charities, hotels, retail outlets and film technicians. The ACTU claimed 300 new members from the film technician campaign (Lewis, 1999). The Executive Officer of Organising Works, Chris Walton, indicates that this approach has been an outstanding success. Positive reports have also come from trade unions that have used the programme. The Liquor, Hospitality and Miscellaneous Workers Union (LHMWU) has recruited approximately

1500 hotel workers across New South Wales and Victoria in less than a year through a drive led by the ACTU recruitment unit. The Victorian Branch of the Shop Assistants Association has improved its communication with members as a result of ideas introduced by the Organising Unit (Donovan, interview 1999). Walton (interview 1999) argues that the programme has given unions some practical assistance in the process of assessing their strategies and training in how to how to develop an organizing approach.

The process of developing Organising Works in recent years has had two further beneficial by-products for the union movement. First, it has allowed the ACTU to gain information on the internal workings of unions and barriers to change. Trainees report to the programme on how their union functions. These reports are likely to be more detailed and open than the public views of a trade union official. This information has provided the impetus for the development of training designed to reach officials at all levels. Second, extensive training packages have been developed for the Organising Works trainees and these packages can be modified for existing organizers with relative ease (Walton, interview 1999). Walton contends that these two by-products are of great significance to the movement as a whole.

Turning to the impact of Organising Works on individual unions, officials interviewed emphasize that it is only one aspect of their strategy and operations and that other factors, both external and internal to the union, have had a greater impact on the culture and position of the union. Such factors include the changing structure of the labour market, the approach of government to industrial relations, financial pressures, lessons from abroad, and the more active role of bodies such as TUTA in shaping the thinking of trade unions. Officials of trade unions that have had generally positive experiences of the programme and indicate that they would participate again in future programmes are low key about the prospects of Organising Works having a significant impact on the position of the union movement in Australia. They consider the programme to be well run and argue that generally it produces competent and effective organizers. However, the problems that beset the Australian union movement are such that no one programme or initiative can greatly improve the position of trade unions. Nevertheless, the organizing philosophy underpinning the Organising Works programme has challenged the way unions have traditionally operated and has created debate in the union movement and generated ideas about how to go forward. Thus, although the numbers are not evident in the membership data, a number of officials claim a philosophical success for Organising Works.

It is true that organizing campaigns can have benefits even in the absence of recruitment success. These claims have yet to be independently verified in the case of the Organising Works programme. American experience indicates that recruiting is expensive (Voos, 1984) and that most workers are not impressed much by the appeals of fresh-faced university graduates who lack local ties and much shop-floor or union experience (Early, 1998). Indeed, the demographics of Organising Works trainees have changed to some extent since the programme commenced. Trainees are older, on average, than they were (30.4 years of age in 1999 compared with 24.5 in 1994) and are more likely to have backgrounds as union activists (see Table 4.2). However, union officials who have been involved in the programme argue that a mix of backgrounds is important and that there is no one template for a successful union organizer.

Most of the information available on the impact of Organising Works on union membership is based on anecdotal evidence from union officials. Given the complex context in which unions operate it is difficult to attribute any particular change in the fortunes of a union to one strategy or programme. Gahan and Bell (1999) have attempted to isolate the effect of particular variables on union experiences. They used a questionnaire survey of union officials to explore relationships between union strategy, the membership orientation of unions, and union effectiveness, addressing factors ranging from union amalgamations and strikes to recruitment and Organising Works. They found that unions that reported a strong recruitment focus also reported a higher degree of organizational effectiveness. These unions also had a lower rate of decline in membership density but in this case the relationship was not statistically significant. The results were less promising in relation to Organising Works. The research found no significant relationship between attitudes to Organising Works and organizational effectiveness. However, a larger decline in membership density was reported by unions that relied heavily on Organising Works than by unions with a less heavy reliance. Less than half of all respondents indicated that Organising Works had been successful for their union. Gahan and Bell (1999) do not argue that these findings indicate that the programme is a failure. Rather, they emphasize two points: first, no causality can be suggested by their results, and, second, it is too early to evaluate the effectiveness of the Organising Works programme.

Nevertheless, some five years after the programme was initiated some assessment can be attempted. Relying on the crude, macro-instrument of overall union membership, Organising Works and all of the other union organizing initiatives aimed at halting the declining union membership have failed. At the micro level we would acknowledge some intangible beneficial spin offs, particularly the ongoing introduction of a new generation of trained activists committed to the organizing model. However, there is significant doubt about the effect of both the programme and its graduates on the attitudes of union officials and the entrenched servicing culture. Insofar as we could determine, approximately two-thirds of programme graduates were still working in the union movement. Walton estimates that only a minority would be operating in an organizing fashion; most would have adopted the dominant approach in their employing union. He argues that it is possible for these organizers to refocus on an organizing approach if the culture of their unions change and optimistically contends that the latest initiative, unions@work – discussed below – revitalized the organizing debate in the later months of 1999.

The key question for the organizing model is obviously the role union members and potential members are willing to play in a union. An active workplace is the central tenet of the organizing model. Given past union history, structures and location of power; given traditionally low levels of participation by members in their union; given the changing nature of work; and given the current legislation and changing attitudes of employers, it may simply be unrealistic to expect union members to be more active and dedicated. Perhaps all that can be expected is the involvement of the traditional small numbers of committed activists at the workplace. The Organising Works programme and TUTA have not ignored this issue. Walton (interview, 1999) acknowledges that it is 'dangerous' for unions to shift their approach and change the nature of their presence in the workplace. TUTA accepts that its training packages are asking delegates to work harder and to ask more of their work colleagues. However, Walton argues that delegates are responsive when the issues are put to them in an intelligent way. He indicates that delegates are generally very aware of the issues impacting on the workplace and the limitations of traditional union approaches in the current environment. Nevertheless, it is a cause for concern that the ACTU seems to have placed a great deal of faith in the possibilities of an organizing approach without adequately engaging members in the debate and determining whether they are prepared to embrace such a change. While anecdotal evidence suggests that delegates have been responsive, at least one union official interviewed indicated that there has been resistance amongst members to the new approach (Larsen, interview 1999). Regardless of the strength of the organizing model as a concept, it will fail in practice if members are not involved in broader debates about its implementation and implications.

Where to from here?

The latest ACTU initiative to reinvigorate the union movement, unions@ work, was again a result of an ACTU overseas delegation, this time to Britain, Ireland, Belgium, Canada and the USA, in April/May 1999. The key priorities contained in the report are:

- Boosting workplace organization and union education so delegates can play a greater role in bargaining, recruiting and grievances.
- Investing in the organization of non-union workplaces and making a commitment to expand into employment growth areas.
- The use of information technology and call centres, allied with the efficient use of funds and management of union operations.
- Enhancing union communications and campaigning, participating in public debate, setting industrial goals, and involving people in unions. (ACTU, 1999)

The report is in keeping with an organizing approach to unionism, with its emphasis on workplace activity and the need to release union resources for recruitment. As noted above, Walton argues that this report has revitalized the debate about the future of the union movement. Unions@work advocates the establishment of a new ACTU Organising Centre, which would incorporate New TUTA, Organising Works and the Organising Unit. The report emphasizes the need for delegate and activist education, the development of rights, resources and incentives for delegates, and the involvement of delegates in industrial and political campaigns (ACTU, 1999: 15–18).

Unions@work highlights the numerical challenge facing the union movement in Australia. The document estimated that around 210,000 new union members are recruited in Australia each year. It estimated that unions must recruit 348,000 members in 1999 to maintain union density at 28 per cent, and at least 420,000 new members are required each year to increase union density by 1 per cent to 29 per cent (ACTU, 1999: 25). These figures seem rather high, but they nevertheless highlight the significant gap between actual recruitment levels and those needed to maintain a steady state. The document notes that decentralization of the industrial relations system is also increasing the wage differential between unionized and non-unionized workplaces. The difference currently stands at 15 per cent and acts as a powerful incentive for employers to resist unionization. While in the current environment union membership assists employees in terms of their wages, it is potentially a threat in terms of job security. The organization of non-union workplaces is therefore important to the job security of unionized workers the document argues. The report advocates the allocation of significant organizational and financial resources to organizing non-union areas. These resources should be focused in areas of growing employment, such as call centres, computer services, hospitality and tourism (ACTU, 1999: 25).

Other developments advocated by the report relate to the effective use of information technology to link delegates and activists, and the provision of information through websites and e-mail. Call centre use by unions may also streamline member contact and release union resources for other purposes. Unions are also encouraged to scrutinize their management structures and ensure that resources are allocated efficiently and effectively (ACTU, 1999: 31–36). Unions@work argues also for a higher public profile for unions and a concerted attempt to build community and international links. Unions should continue to campaign around issues such as the Living Wages policy and develop the Employment Security and Working Hours campaign. Essentially, the report advocates the promotion of the industrial, political and social facets of unions (ACTU, 1999: 39–46).

Another recent development has been the resignation of the long-serving ACTU secretary, Bill Kelty, in early 2000. His successor, Greg Combet, is likely to adopt a higher media profile and to be more effective at promoting the ACTU, and is considered to have superior organizational skills to Kelty (Carney, 1998). If this proves to be the case, it can only be good for the peak council and the union movement generally. As part of the overseas delegation that produced unions@work, Combet is also likely to drive the recommendations contained in the report.

Conclusion

The ACTU and the union movement as a whole have devoted resources and energy to reshaping its outlook and structure in many areas. This chapter analysed two key strategic responses to declining membership density, mergers and Organising Works. Neither initiative has stemmed the haemorrhaging of membership. The dramatic restructuring of the union movement has not produced the hoped-for economies of scale; neither has it resulted in a well-integrated, internally cohesive set of 'super' unions. In practice, many unions operate as loosely connected conglomerates. We conclude that the ACTU needs to re-examine the question of union structure in Australia. While unions are independent entities and the ACTU is limited in what it can achieve, problem areas need to be identified and mechanisms put in place to help heal damaging internal divisions. More needs to be done to boost membership involvement in unions, to democratize unions and to encourage the growth of union structures at the workplace.

Turning specifically to organizing initiatives, the ACTU and individual unions have, in the last couple of years, followed a new, more member-oriented direction and launched some promising policy initiatives. So far, based on membership data, these initiatives have not succeeded. A key issue to be resolved is the willingness of members to respond to the organizing model. For the immediate future, there is little choice but to continue with this model with its focus on workplaces and its emphasis on recruiting.

Union movements make a number of strategic choices in the way they operate and organize, whether or not this is made explicit. We have argued in this chapter that a sometimes reluctant change in the ordering of strategic priorities is under way. With the move towards an industrial strategy, some decisions need to be made. One key decision is the degree to which unions adopt an adversarial or a cooperative orientation towards management. The Australian industrial relations system is often described as adversarial, but conflict has long been contained, confined and formalized by the arbitration system to the extent that unions, employer associations and other industrial relations actors have been said to belong to a 'club'. A major failing of the Australian union movement in recent times has been an unwillingness to articulate clearly what form labour-capital relationships should take now that this club-like atmosphere has broken down. Another strategic choice confronting the Australian union movement is its orientation to governments, especially Labor governments, given the current tendency of non-Labor governments to marginalize unions. Shortly after the fall of the Keating Labor government in 1996, the ACTU decided against entering into an Accord-type arrangement with a future Labor government. Many may consider this to be a good thing, but the decision was implemented with little discussion or consultation, or analysis of the costs and benefits of the Accord and similar social-partner-type arrangements.

Extensive discussion and debate within Australian trade unions on the reordering of strategic priorities, and its implications, is currently under way. Realistically, severe doubts exist that the membership crisis can be reversed in the short term. For the medium term, these debates and discussions are a necessary prerequisite for launching an effective attack on the causes of membership decline.

References

ACTU (1987) *Future Strategies for the Trade Union Movement*, Melbourne: ACTU.

ACTU/TDC (1987) *Australia Reconstructed*, Canberra: AGPS.

ACTU (1995a) Decisions of ACTU Council Meeting, 15–17 May, http://www.actu.asn.au/national/about/matters/mat95may.htm

ACTU (1995b) *Organising Works*, No. 2, Melbourne: Australian Council of Trade Unions.

ACTU (1997) ACTU Policies and Resolutions: Membership and Services Resolution, http://www.actu.asn/national/about/policy/97mbrshp.htm

ACTU (1998) Organising Works: Annual Report 1998, http://www.actu.asn.au/national/people/ow/owanrep.htm

ACTU (1999) Unions@work, Report of the ACTU Overseas Delegation, August.

Alexander, M., Green, R. and Wilson, A. (1998) 'Delegate Structures and Strategic Unionism: Analysis of Factors in Union Resilience', *Journal of Industrial Relations* 40 (4): 663–89.

Bagnall, D. (1994) 'The New Breed', *Bulletin*, 116: 28–32.

Benson, J. (1988) *Workplace Union Organisation in Australia*, working paper No. 40, Labour Studies Programme, University of Melbourne.

Berry, P. and Kitchener, G. (1989) *Can Unions Survive?* Canberra: Building Workers Industrial Union.

Bodman, P. (1998) 'Trade Union Amalgamation, Openness and the Decline in Australian Trade Union Membership', *Australian Bulletin of Labour*, 24 (1): 1–38.

Carney, S. (1998) 'Behind the Fury of the Docks, the Kelty Factor Plays Its Part', *Age*, 11 April, p. 13.

Carney, S. and Johnston, N. (1995) 'Kelty Warns Unions', *Age*, 14 March, p. 5.

Cooper, R. (1997) 'Union Membership Recruitment: What Is Being Done?', paper presented at 11th AIRAANZ Conference, Brisbane, mimeo.

Cooper, R. and Walton, C. (1996) 'Organising and Recruitment in Australia: The Response of Unions to the "Membership Crisis"', paper presented to AFL-CIO and ILR School, Cornell University 'Organizing for Success' Conference, March.

Costa, M. and Duffy, M. (1991) 'The Decline of Trade Unions and the Amalgamation Quick Fix', in Costa, M. and Duffy, M. *Labor, Prosperity and the Nineties: Beyond the Bonsai Economy*, Leichhardt NSW: Federation Press, pp. 100–32.

Costa, M. and Hearn, M. (1997) *Reforming Australia's Unions: Insights from Southland Magazine*, Annandale NSW: Federation Press.

Dabscheck, B. (1995) *The Struggle for Australian Industrial Relations*, Melbourne: Oxford University Press.

Davis, M. (1995a) 'Talent Injection Aims to Boost Trade Unions', *Australian Financial Review*, 20 January, p. 4.

Davis, M. (1995b) 'ACTU Pledges to Fund Drive for Members', *Australian Financial Review*, 29 September, p. 8.

Davis, M. (1995c) 'Kelty's $40m Punt to Stop the Bleeding', *Australian Financial Review*, 3 March, p. 10.

Drago, R. and Wooden, M. (1998) *The Changing Role of Trade Unions in Australian Workplace Industrial Relations*, Transformation of Australian Industrial Relations Project, Discussion Paper Series, No. 3, Adelaide: National Institute Labour Studies.

Duy, T. A. and Thoma, M. A. (1998) 'Modelling and Forecasting Cointegrated Variables: Some Practical Experience', *Journal of Economics and Business*, 50 (3): 291–307.

Early, S. (1998) 'Membership-based Organizing', in G. Mantsios (ed.) *A New Labor Movement for the New Century*, New York: Garland Publishing, pp. 95–119.

Gahan, P. (1996) 'Did Arbitration Make for Dependent Unionism? Evidence from Historical Case Studies', *Journal of Industrial Relations*, 38 (4): 648–98.

Gahan, P. and Bell, S. (1999) 'Union Strategy, Membership Orientation and Union Effectiveness: An Exploratory Analysis', *Labour and Industry*, 9 (3): 5–30.

Griffin, G. (1994) 'The Authority of the ACTU', *Economic and Labour Relations Review*, 5 (1): 81–103.

Griffin, G. and Scarcebrook, V. (1989) 'Trends in Mergers of Federally Registered Unions, 1904–1986', *Journal of Industrial Relations*, 31 (2): 257–62.

Griffin, G. and Svensen, S. (1996) 'The Decline of Australian Union Density – Survey of the Literature', *Journal of Industrial Relations*, 38 (4): 505–47.

Griffin, G. and Svensen, S. (1998) 'Determinants of Same-Workplace Union Exit: Evidence from AWIRS II', in Harbridge, R., Gadd, C. and Crawford, A. (eds) *Current Research in Industrial Relations: Proceedings of the 12th AIRAANZ Conference*, Wellington, 3–5 February, 1998, pp. 150–8.

Griffin, G., Svensen, S. and Teicher, J. (1997) 'Trade Union Non-industrial Services: Membership Attitudes', *Labour and Industry*, 7 (3): 31–41.

Hawke, A. and Wooden, M. (1998) 'The Changing Face of Australian Industrial Relations: Survey', *Economic Record*, 74 (224): 74–88.

Howard, W. A. (1977) 'Australian Trade Unions in the Context of Union Theory', *Journal of Industrial Relations*, 19: 255–73.

Kenyon, P. D. and Lewis, P. E. T. (1992) 'Trade Union Membership and the Accord', *Australian Economic Papers*, 31: 325–45.

Kenyon, P. D. and Lewis, P. E. T. (1996) 'The Decline in Trade Union Membership: What Role Did the Accord Play' Discussion Paper 96/8, Centre for Labour Market Research, Murdoch University.

Lewis, P. (1999) 'Interview: How Organising Works', Workers Online, No. 3, 5 March, http://www.labor.net.au/workers/magazine/3/a_interview_sarah.html

Morehead, A., Steele, M., Alexander, M., Stephen, K. and Duffin, L. (1997) *Changes at Work: The 1995 Australian Workplace Industrial Relations Survey*, South Melbourne: Addison Wesley Longman.

Norington, B. (1998) 'Back to the 1850s: The Future of Unionism', *Sydney Morning Herald*, 4 December.

Organising Works (1994–9) *Reports to Annual General Meetings of the Committee of Management of Organising Works 1994–1999*, mimeo.

Peetz, D. (1998) 'Why Join? Why Stay? Instrumentality, Beliefs, Satisfaction and Individual Decisions on Union Membership', *Economic and Labour Relations Review*, 9 (1): 123–47.

Penn, R. and Scattergood, H. (1996) 'The Experience of Trade Unions in Rochdale during the 1980s', in D. Gallie, R. Penn and M. Rose (eds) *Trade Unionism in Recession*, New York: Oxford University Press, pp. 244–85.

Pocock, B. (1998) 'Institutional Sclerosis: Prospects for Trade Union Transformation', *Labour and Industry*, 9 (1): 17–36.

Richardson, N. (1994) 'Big Is Beautiful', *Bulletin*, 116: 32.

Rimmer, M. and Sutcliffe, P. (1981) 'The Origins of Australian Workshop Organisation, 1918 to 1950', *Journal of Industrial Relations*, 23: 216–39.

Stuart, M. (1993) *United States Mission on Recruitment and Organisation: Summary Report*, Melbourne: Australian Council of Trade Unions.

Thompson, J. (1990) 'Union Amalgamations: The ACTU's Grab for Power', *IPA Review*, 43 (3): 26–9.

Voos, P. B. (1984) 'Does It Pay to Organize? Estimating the Cost to Unions', *Monthly Labor Review*, 107 (6): 43–4.

Yates. C. and Ewer, P. (1997) 'Changing Strategic Capacities: Union Amalgamations in Canada and Australia', in Sverke, M. (ed) *The Future of Trade Unionism: International Perspectives on Emerging Union Structures*, Aldershot: Ashgate, pp. 131–48.

Interviews

Brian Daley, Victorian Branch Secretary, Miscellaneous Workers' Division, Australian Liquor, Hospitality and Miscellaneous Workers' Union (LHMU), 1 November 1999.

Michael Donovan, Victorian Branch Secretary, Shop, Distributive and Allied Employees' Association (SDA), 9 November 1999.

Malcolm Larsen, New South Wales Branch Secretary, PSU Group, Community and Public Sector Union (CPSU), 1 November 1999.

Michael O'Sullivan, National Executive President, Australian Services Union (ASU), 29 October 1999.

Chris Walton, Executive Officer, Organising Works, Australian Council of Trade Unions (ACTU), 5 November 1999, 9 November 1999.

5 A NEAR DEATH EXPERIENCE: ONE UNION FIGHTS FOR LIFE

Belinda Probert and Peter Ewer

Introduction

The debates swirling around the crisis of unionism suggest that it is possible to 'organize to win' (Bronfenbrenner *et al.* 1998). To what extent can a union, buffeted by industry restructuring and more generally by the ascendancy of neo-liberal public policy, actually control its own destiny? This chapter tackles this question through a case study of one union fighting for life in Australia – the Victorian Branch of the Technical and Services Group, Communications Division, Communications Electrical and Plumbing Union (hereafter T & S Group, and for the broader union, CEPU).

The membership of the T & S Group comprises mostly trades and technical workers, and phone operators, in the telecommunications industry. Certainly the union is engaged in a very real life-or-death struggle to reconfirm its identity and regain its memebrship numbers. How has the union arrived at this parlous state, and what is it doing about it? The particular circumstances facing the T & S Group are outlined later in this article, but it is first necessary to locate the fate of this individual union in the wider crisis of Australian unionism. The point of this analysis is to emphasize the extent to which organized labour in Australia is facing not just a prolonged period of hardship, but the collapse of organizing practices built up over the course of a century.

Australian unionism in crisis

The Australian union movement as a whole is traumatized by a crisis of declining membership. According to official statistics, the proportion of working people who are members of a union has declined from 51 per cent in 1976 to 30 per cent in 1997, with private sector coverage down to as low as 23 per cent (Peetz, 1998).

In long-run historical terms, this crisis is related to the unravelling of a social settlement forged in the first years of the twentieth century. This settlement was designed to promote 'wage earner security' (Castles, 1985, 1988) for male, full-time workers, partly through a judicial-based system of arbitration and conciliation. This system of industrial relations provided unions with legal recognition and helps explain the historically high levels of union membership in Australia.

With the globalization of the Australian economy, the highly centralized industrial relations system has lost many of its powers to legislative reforms designed to encourage 'flexibility' in workplace bargaining and individual employment contracts. This marginalization of the state institution that regulated and encouraged collective bargaining is partly responsible for the crisis of Australian unionism.

As Griffin explains elsewhere (Chapter 4), the national leadership of the Australian union movement has not been slow to develop innovative strategies to combat this crisis, both structurally in the shape of union mergers, and culturally through programmes designed to disseminate an 'organizing culture'. However what distinguishes the T & S Group is its reticence to embrace these official prescriptions for union renewal, including the ACTU Organising Works programme. The T & S Group have preferred instead to fashion an independent renewal strategy, which they believe is more suitable to the organizing environment they face. Their strategy complements workplace bargaining with a somewhat forgotten tradition in Australian union practice – that of craft or occupational organizing.

True, the T & S Group merged with a number of other unions in the early 1990s, covering postal workers, electricians and plumbers. The resulting organization, however, is essentially an umbrella confederation, with each of the different occupational and industry groups retaining significant autonomy through a divisional and branch structure.

Background to a union – structures and identities

The ancestry of the T & S Group can be found in two unions, the Australian Telecommunications Employees Association (ATEA) and the Australian Telephone and Phonogram Officers' Association (ATPOA), which amalgamated in 1992. Both these organizations were originally established to organize workers in the government department that operated both postal and telephone services – the Post Master

Generals Department (PMG). This was a nation-building agency in the classic Australian sense. Not only did it provide universal access to communications services throughout Australia, with all the difficulties that vast geography and dispersed population implied, but it used its purchasing powers to foster and maintain a domestic electronics manufacturing industry (Houghton and Paltridge, 1991). In the 1970s, the PMG was split into two statutory authorities – what is now Telstra, to provide telecommunications services, and Australia Post, to operate the postal service.

Within this industry, the union has two quite different constituencies. The ATEA was essentially a craft union, covering mostly male technicians and trades. For its part, ATPOA covered workers employed as telephone operators, and its members have traditionally been overwhelmingly female.

The craft or occupational unions which have come together as the Communications Division operated a strict system of job control unionism. Technicians within the industry have been traditionally trained in a complex system of structured training, one run for many years by PMG/Telstra. Like all craft unions, the ATEA used this system to forge its own identity as the protector of the trade, a group identity reflected in the large numbers of Telecom/Telstra managers and supervisors who retained their union membership even when they 'left the tools'.

The importance of this vocational training system, from a union perspective, was not just the technical excellence of the training, but the process of acculturation embedded in it, as the 'artisan' handed on the skills (and identity) of the craft to the trade apprentice or technical trainee:

> Originally most of us were trained in a five year tech and training scheme which was when they had their training schools spread around Melbourne and the first year was full time and then the other years were part time ... You'd spend your time working with techs, *you were their trainee and they'd show (you) their on-the-job skills* ... (male technician, *emphasis added*)

This system of structured training and skill recognition did not encompass the union's other key constituency. The Australian vocational training system has, in keeping with the patriarchal goals of wage earner security, privileged male trades and consciously excluded women from access to the apprenticeship system (O'Donnell and Hall, 1988). Thus, an apprenticeship system never existed for telephone operators, and ATPOA could not define its industrial identity in quite the same way as the ATEA.

Nevertheless, the organization and location of operator work provided fertile ground on which to build labour organization among telephone operators. In particular, the concentration of large numbers of (mostly) women in relatively large workplaces gave rise to a workplace culture of considerable vigour and vitality. Former members of ATPOA look back on their workplaces as sites of extensive social activity, which extended well beyond the workplace.

The concentration of ATEA members in suburban and regional exchanges and depots generated a similar dynamic. In this sense, union organization was only the formal representation of collectivism in the workplace, much of which developed organically:

> Well, I believe that in those days Telstra used to make morale as one of their considerations ... staff were encouraged to run functions and ... I was involved in that; you had more people, and the families of all of the people at work were brought in for social functions, sporting, cultural and recreational activities and everybody joined and used to pay a shilling a week or 10 cents a week to join and they gave concession buying schemes and sporting carnivals and theatre nights and all those sorts of things. That kind of social, cultural atmosphere was encouraged and people did get a lot out of it in the job. (male technician)

The stability of employment within the PMG/Telecom undoubtedly contributed to this collectivism – workers speak of the comfort of knowing, barring acts of gross misconduct, that theirs was a 'job for life'.

> It was different, you had a job for life. You don't anymore. Basically if you were employed at Telstra you basically had to go and shoot your manager to get sacked. Now it is different. (female operator)

Two final points on union organization within telecommunications need to be made. First, the occupational origins of Australian unionism, and the legal boundaries imposed on unions to prevent them recruiting outside the registered coverage, greatly constrain the flexibility of the T & S Group in adjusting to changes in the industry. The T & S Group is part of a so-called 'super union', the CEPU. The growth of this type of union has been encouraged by the peak national union confederation, the Australian Council of Trade Unions, over the previous ten years. While nominally industry based, many of these super unions are conglomerates of occupational unions, and such is the case with the CEPU. Thus the major postal union has become the Postal and Telecommunications Branch of the CEPU, and by an accident of occupational unionism, continues to have a minority of its members in the telecommunications industry. Also within the CEPU, the Electrical Division has rights to cover some telecommunications work in the private sector. This overlapping coverage has, to follow the term used by Peetz (1998) and Pocock (1998), given rise to tensions over 'market share', leading to allegations of membership poaching, even within the CEPU. And finally, although the CEPU is the majority union, the Community and Public Sector Union (CPSU) retains a significant base of members within Telstra, obviously arising from the ancestry of Telstra as a government department. The CPSU has its own Telecommunications Section for this part of its membership, which covers workers in administrative and retail positions, but again with some overlap with the CEPU.

Second, union strength in the industry has historically been facilitated by the benign attitude of government departments to union organization. Thus, the union was represented on disciplinary and appeals boards within Telstra, which provided an obvious motivation for workers to join the union. The tradition of union recognition within Telstra, and especially its predecessors, can be seen in the willingness of managers to remain union members, and in the provision of such facilities as payroll deduction for union dues.

A union in crisis

Like many other union branches, by the mid-1990s, the Victorian T & S Group was facing a major crisis. As Table 5.1 indicates, the collapse in the organization's membership has been precipitous. In the seven years to June 1999, the union's membership fell 37 per cent, which suggests not just declining industrial relevance, but an acute financial crisis that threatens its organizational viability. The extent of membership loss revealed in Table 5.1 has prompted a fundamental rethinking of the organization's operations.

At least partly, the union's difficulties arise from technological change, involving the replacement of electromechanical switching equipment by fully electronic and digital technologies. This has generated job losses throughout the telecommunications network, particularly among technicians. The new electronic switching technology involves much less maintenance work and what remains is mostly associated with the simple replacement of computer boards. Where once the diagnosis and repair of equipment involved basing large numbers of permanent staff in most suburban and country exchanges, the computerization of exchanges allows for the diagnostic work to be per-

Table 5.1 *Membership of the T & S Group, CEPU, Victorian Branch, 1992–8 (financial members only)*

	Technicians	Operators	Total
1992	7099	1300	8399
1993	6737	1224	7779
1994	5964	1309	7273
1995	5833	1473	7309
1996	5964	1657	7621
1997	5366	1452	6818
1998	4884	1114	5998
1999	4506	864	5310

Source: Victorian Branch, T & S Group, CEPU

formed at central locations, leaving many local exchange technicians with the simple task of replacing nominated boards.

> They've gone from having, I worked at W, for 35 years and we would have had about 6 to 8 on the staff looking after three exchanges spread around the local area. None of those are there now. All of us are gone and those exchanges are now only visited on an 'as needs' basis as the work comes out either from the service delivery centres that are new connections or for maintenance or from our own centre for equipment type faults or maintenance. There is no resident staff in any of the exchanges now. (male technician)

The union has, however, survived technological change in the past, and its sternest challenge actually arises from the radical reconfiguration of the industry. This has been driven by the determination of Australian governments (both Labor and conservative) to create a telecommunications 'market' out of the previously public sector, monopoly carrier. This market-based reform model has involved:

- the corporatization and part-privatization of the public sector authority, Telstra; and
- the entry of new, private sector telecommunications carriers into the industry, involving complicated access arrangements to the Telstra phone and data network.

For the union, this reform model presents challenges on a number of fronts. Within Telstra, the union has seen a transformation in management culture in which the pursuit of a business ethos has been paramount. Part of this cultural transformation involves converting open management encouragement to union membership into an aggressive anti-union environment (see Barton and Teicher, 1999). This aggression is complemented by the contracting out of work previously undertaken within the organization, and a radical scaling back of Telstra's training infrastructures, where the craft identity of union members had traditionally been formed.

In keeping with this entrepreneurial project, job losses within Telstra have been considerable. Between 1988 and 1998, staff numbers fell from 86,832 to 57,234 (Barton and Teicher, 1999). Despite the job shedding associated with technological change, the union contends that the extent of job loss has been driven by management's determination to lower the ratio between the number of the organization's staff and the number of its telephone lines. This ratio is a common international benchmark, used by financial markets to calculate the likely profitability of a telecommunications carrier. The union believes given the geographical peculiarity of Australia, that benchmarks are inappropriate but are nevertheless being applied by management to impress potential investors in the lead up to full privatization (see the CEPU campaign video, *Keep Telstra Public*, 1996).

The revolution in management culture within Telstra is evident not only in the overall reduction in the organization's workforce but in the use of non-standard employment practices. These include the widespread use of casuals among the ranks of telephone operators, a process accelerated by the prohibition of restrictions on the use of non-standard employment by the Workplace Relations Act, and the contracting out of work previously performed in-house by permanent employees. The latest example of this organizational disaggregation is NDC Ltd, formed from Telstra's Network Design and Construction division. This corporatization will see 7000 Telstra staff shifted out of the parent organization into a wholly owned subsidiary, which will competitively bid for Telstra's own construction work and that of other telecommunications providers (see *The Age*, 22 January 1999).

For the union, the final effect of the management revolution within Telstra has been the determination of the corporation to dismantle its in-house training system:

> After your five years you came out fairly well trained if not … experienced. We got the experience on the job and then they used to have what was called the senior techs exam and you could study for that or you could do courses … to qualify you to sit for those exams. Once you did that, it was considered to be the last exam and from then on you used your efficiency

or your whatever to gain information. That worked fairly well, it was a very good grounding for everybody, the training scheme was very good, Telstra thought it was costly of course and eventually abandoned it ... (male technician)

What remains of in-house training within Telstra involves a fundamentally different pedagogy to that of the old apprenticeship and technical-training schools. Skill acquisition is now largely mediated by technology, principally computer-mediated learning, without the processes of acculturation associated with earlier practice.

At least in theory, the union's difficulties in Telstra should be compensated for by recruitment opportunities in the new market entrants. However, here the union confronts new private sector entrants who actively oppose union organization, and deploy the full panoply of human resource management techniques to bind employees to the corporation.

The first new entrant Optus, now a subsidiary of the multinational Cable and Wireless, uses its in-house training to build its corporate culture and prevent the company from becoming infected with the traditions of the craft (and craft unionism). As a result Optus fills its requirements for technical workers not by recognizing relevant vocational qualifications, but by training its own workers, recruited regardless of their occupational background:

They actually didn't say to you, 'here is the job, you are going to apply for that job', they just said 'we are looking for people to work at Optus we'll tell you what you are going to do'. So, you went in there and you didn't really know what you were applying for. My job, I had no idea. I didn't know what I was going to apply for ...

They kicked a lot of people with the trades out, completely. They didn't want to employ them at all, because they try to teach us from the beginning. (male technician)

From crisis management to strategy

The dramatic reduction in the T & S Group's membership initially prompted two specific initiatives on the part of the union. First, faced with the dismantling of the public sector agency to which the union's fortunes were tied, the T & S Group engaged experienced union officials from outside the organization and dedicated these new resources to private sector recruitment through activities like occupational health and safety.

The second initiative of the T & S Group to deal with the membership crisis was financial. The union's officials and administrative staff accepted a 10 per cent wage cut to alleviate the pressure on the union's finances.

Nevertheless, it would be idle to suggest that the difficulties facing the T & S Group could be resolved simply through cost cutting, no matter how noble. As the full extent of the membership decline became apparent in 1994, the union developed a recruitment strategy, and reviewed it in early 1997. This strategy combined a defensive element to retain membership in Telstra, and a more developmental element to build organization in the new private sector of the industry, where possible by 'migrating' with the members leaving Telstra. While the 1994 plan emphasized resource allocation questions to implement this strategy, the 1997 review raised questions of structural design within the union to position it in the private sector.

The union's challenge is to successfully appeal to two quite different groups of workers.

Modernizing craft-organizing practice

Changes in the telecommunications industry have combined to loosen the control of union members over the work of the craft. This loosening of the job control traditionally exercised by the union has prompted a fundamental re-evaluation of the union's organizing practice. In particular, the union has had to rethink how it intervenes in a labour market increasingly characterized by casual and contract forms of employment, and a vocational training system where the traditions of the apprenticeship have been replaced by a training market.

To meet this challenge, the union has used corporate forms as access points to the 'new' telecommunications workforce, and in doing so sought to modernize and reconfigure its influence over its traditional area of coverage. These initiatives included the following. First, a labour placement agency was established. This initiative is a latter-day 'union hall hire', an organizing practice in Australia that historically has been evident on the waterfront and in mining industries. The agency places T & S Group members with employers looking for IT and telecommunications skills, and offers them – through a partnership agreement with a private training provider – discounted training in high-growth segments of the market, especially the installations of local and wide area networks. The obvious goal for the union in this venture is that members will take their union cards with them, and plant the seeds for further organizing in private industry. Second, a vocational training agency was established. The transformation of the Australian vocational training system, in which both public training colleges and private training organizations bid for government funding to deliver vocational training opens up opportunities for unions to re-engage in the politics of craft and occupational identity.

This modernization of the craft-organizing practice is important for three reasons. First, it re-establishes the presence of the union in the site where the identity of the 'skilled' telecommunications worker is formed (the training system). This allows the union to contest the corporate use of training as a venue of cultural formation. Second, the objective circumstances for a revival of craft unionism are favourable. As the industry retreats from investment in training, the prospect of skill shortage is strong. Third, the technical work-force in telecommunications is increasingly located not in centralized workplaces but in civil society. To reach the workforce, external labour market infrastructure like job placement has a role to play.

On the first of these points, the difference between the structured training programmes of the traditional public sector employers, which proved such fertile ground for labour organization, and current industry practice has already been briefly discussed. Thus, the purpose of human resource strategy within Optus appears to be to tie the loyalty of the employee to the enter-prise, a debt of gratitude that individuals owe for their newly acquired human capital:

> they basically said 'well we taught you that', 'you knew nothing when you came here, we taught you all that' and one of the bosses actually said 'you know, I could get a burger flipper to do that, I'd teach him that eventually, it'd only take me 20 minutes' and that is where the background thing comes in. There are a lot of different backgrounds out there, some elec-tronic, some plumbing, some all different things and when it really comes down to it, they say 'well we taught you all this stuff'. (male technician)

Objectively, conditions for revival of craft tradition are good as the industry attempts to minimize its training investment. Thus Table 5.2 shows how the performance of the communications industry deteriorated between 1989 and 1996. For a revitalization of a craft-organizing practice, skill shortages are a favourable environment; the question may be whether the union can hold on long enough to take advantage of them.

Finally, the labour market services offered by the union provide an incentive for workers to come to the union, rather than the union having to establish contact with workers in a workplace climate that is hostile yet diffuse:

Table 5.2 *Training performance of the communications industry, 1989–96*

	Percentage of gross wages and salaries invested in training	Training hours per employee
1989	3.7	9.1
1996	3.2	6.3

Source: Australian Bureau of Statistics, *Employee Training Expenditure*, Catalogue No. 6353.0.

> If there is going to be a meeting, it is pretty hard, we are all over Melbourne from one end to the other, it is nearly impossible, unless there is something that is really pissing somebody off, or the whole lot of us, it is really hard to get everyone together. It is nearly impossible. (male technician)

The geographical dispersion of workers away from the centralized depots that once characterized the public sector telecommunications industry is accompanied by the colonization of civil society for the postmodern enterprise. Thus, workers maintain stock inventories in their own homes:

> A lot of us guys keep equipment in our garages because it is just a joke trying to get equipment. They don't give the installers enough time to go to the stores to get more gear, you've got to have it all in your van or car boot, it's too much to carry. (male technician)

The limits of a craft model? Organizing in call centres

The intervention of the union in labour market services therefore has a sound strategic rationale because the vocational training and job placement agencies of the union provide access points to a workforce fragmented by management strategy and technology. However, in the organization of the call-centre industry, the union faces a somewhat different challenge. There, the organizing task is less about maintaining the status of the trade or calling and more about asserting the dignity of labour in an industry that both draws on the emotional labour of workers (Taylor, 1998), while simultaneously relying on the ease of rostering – and replacing – the commodity of labour.

In appealing to this mostly female workforce, the union meets the limitations of craft organization. Women members, despite their loyalty to the union, report that the organization is 'still a tech's union', and that the specific interests of operators are difficult to raise in the structures of union decision making.

> The thing is that the guys around the table feel we are irrelevant to them. We have to actually force to have a break to go away and have a sit and talk in another room, because all of it is their issues and as far as they are concerned, operators are just 'down there' somewhere and you tell me, we are supposed to be a union, supposed to be one equal, but we are not equal, they don't see our problems as important enough. (female operator)

Although internal gender politics remain contested, the union continues to devote resources to private sector call-centre recruiting, and with some success. One such case involves the organization of a mostly female work force of 30 in a small private, telephone call centre. This is an example of effective unionization that shows the *interrelationship* between 'servicing' and 'organizing'.

In this case, the union was approached by a small number of workers in early 1998. The response of the union involved not 'recruitment' in the sense of 'selling' a membership, but the provision of information, advice and emotional support to the workers. One described her motive for contacting the union in these terms: 'Initially to understand more about the workplace agreement (offered by the employer) and find out how it could be stopped' (female operator). Providing these resources helps to build a relationship of trust between the union and the workers, a relationship forged during covert meetings held at all kinds of venues and at all hours of the day (and night): 'It has been terrific, (the union industrial officer) has been available weekends, nights, you know the amount of work!' (female operator). This process may begin with only one person, who builds an underground network of activists, quietly steering waverers in the workplace toward the union, often while concealing their own membership from management for long periods of time: 'There was incrimination [*sic*] as soon as the supervisors found out that a union had been contacted, it sort of had to go underground' (female operator). Throughout this period, the activists working for the union remained vulnerable to victimization, not necessarily through a threat to their employment, but through more indirect threats to desirable rosters and other working-time arrangements.

In the literature this organizing phase is known as a 'pre-union formation'. It involves breaking down the fear held by individuals in the face of management discretion to terminate their employment, or in other ways harm their interests, and the building of a sense of strength, newly found in the power of unity and collective identity. It is only after this point has been reached that the process of actual bargaining can begin – only when the gap in power resources between management and workforce has been narrowed sufficiently to limit the prospects of individual victimization. The success of the union in this case culminated in the negotiation and certification of an enterprise agreement; for the workers concerned, the benefit of this agreement was not so much the wages outcome, but the greater transparency and regularity attached to the rostering of working hours.

Social movement unionism

From what has been said about the T & S Group's efforts to restore craft organizing, it might be easy to mistake the union as a convert to 'business' unionism. In point of fact, the union has a strong tradition of community activism.

Although 'social movement unionism' (Hyman, 1994) is not a part of the lexicon of Australian unionism or labour studies scholarship, many unions – particularly those on the 'left' – exhibit characteristics that elsewhere are associated with this style of unionism. The current leadership of the T & S Group came to office in the mid-1970s on a left-wing reform ticket, following a long struggle within the ATEA between the socialist left and the Catholic right factions of Australian unionism (see Reinecke and Schultz, 1983, Chapter 9).

The social activism of this leadership is evident in the branch's participation and support for a variety of community organizations. These include an anti-privatization community group, solidarity organizations with overseas union activists and a community radio station.

The relationship between these activities and the union's political and industrial strategies varies. The anti-privatization campaigns have lifted the profile of the union as an industry union, and promoted several organizing initiatives among non-union workers whose attention was captured by this political activity. The community radio station sponsored by the union, and others among the Victorian union movement, also provides a communication channel for activists during strategic industrial disputes (for example, the famous 1998 Australian maritime dispute).

However, the union is also modernizing this community activism to provide it with points of intervention in the corporate times in which it lives. Following the tactics of mining unions campaigning against the multinational Rio Tinto company, the T & S Group established the lobby group 'Shareholders of Telstra' (SHOT), and duly attended the corporation's inaugural general meeting of shareholders. At that meeting, SHOT raised a number of issues, including human resources policy and executive remuneration, to the embarrassment of management and howls of protest from the mainstream media about the 'proper' role of trade unions.

Other Australian unions, like Textiles Clothing and Footwear Union with its community-based campaign to organize clothing outworkers, have moved toward social movement unionism. As these strategies develop, theories of Australian unions as creatures of a tribunal-based industrial relations system will have to be modified, in the course of which international conceptions of social movement unionism may have more local application.

Conclusions

In recent years, the union movement has conceived of its response to crisis in terms of a shift from a 'servicing' model to an 'organizing' model. Some researchers have followed, and used this dichotomy to evaluate union performance (McDonald *et al.*, 1997). Yet it is not clear how this framework might be applied to the T & S Group. The difficulties facing the T & S Group arise not from a failure of organization but from unprecedented changes in the objective conditions facing the union. These involve a neo-liberal revolution in public sector management and an acceleration in technological change associated with the convergence of telecommunications and information technologies.

This conjunction of events has provoked a crisis in the union, symbolized by a precipitous decline in membership and rooted in the erosion of collective identities on which the T & S Group built its organization. The union has chosen not to embrace the workplace organizing model favoured by the ACTU, but sought to refashion instead the way it relates to the occupational identities it has traditionally appealed to. Whether this project of modernization succeeds only the events of the immediate future will determine, but through the course of 1999 the union at least stabilized its membership base. The divergence of the T & S Group from official conceptions of union renewal suggests some care needs to be taken in analysing 'national' models of union strategy.

References

Australian Bureau of Statistics *Employer Training Expenditure*, Canberra: Australian Bureau of Statistics, Cat No 6353.0.

Barton, R. and J. Teicher (1999) 'The Consequences of Deregulation and Privatisation for Industrial Relations in Telstra', in Teicher, J. (ed.) *Public Sector Industrial Relations: Australian and International Perspectives*, National Key Centre in Industrial Relations, Monograph No 12, Melbourne: Monash University, pp. 161–93.

Bronfenbrenner, K., Friedman, S., Hurd, R., Oswald, R. and Scheer, R. (eds) (1998) *Organizing to Win: New Research on Union Strategies*, Ithaca: ILR Press.

Castles, F. (1985) *The Working Class and Welfare*, Sydney: Allen & Unwin.

Castles, F. (1988) *Australian Public Policy and Economic Vulnerability: A Comparative and Historical Perspective*, Sydney: Allen & Unwin.

Houghton, J. and Paltridge S. (1991) *Telecommunication Equipment Manufacturing in Australia: Opportunities and Policy Options*, Centre for International Research on Communication and Information Technologies, Policy Research Paper No. 15, Melbourne: CIRCIT.

Hyman, R. (1994) 'Changing Trade Union Identities and Strategies', in Hyman, R. and Ferner A. (eds.), *New Frontiers in European Industrial Relations*, Oxford: Basil Blackwell, pp. 108–39.

McDonald, D., Strachan, G. and Houston, L. (1997) 'Unionism in the Hunter Valley: An Exploratory Regional Study', *Labour and Industry*, 8 (2): 49–66.

O'Donnell, C., and Hall, P. (1988) *Getting Equal*, Sydney: Allen & Unwin.

Peetz, D. (1998) *Unions in a Contrary World: The Future of the Australian Trade Union Movement*, Cambridge: Cambridge University Press.

Pocock, B. (1998) 'Institutional Sclerosis: Prospects for Trade Union Transformation', in *Labour and Industry*, 9 (1): 17–36.

Reinecke, I. and Schultz, J. (1983) *The Phone Book: The Future of Australia's Communications on the Line*, Melbourne: Penguin.

Taylor, S. (1998) 'Emotional Labour and the New Workplace', in Thompson, P. and Warhurst, C. (eds) *Workplaces of the Future*, London: Macmillan Business, pp. 84–103.

6 FROM ORGANIZATIONAL BREADTH TO DEPTH? NEW ZEALAND'S TRADE UNIONS UNDER THE EMPLOYMENT CONTRACTS ACT

Pat Walsh and Aaron Crawford

Introduction

During the 1990s, New Zealand trade unions experienced a sustained period of significant membership decline. Trade union density fell from 45 per cent in 1989 to 17 per cent in 1999 (Crawford *et al.*, 2000). This chapter seeks to explain the reasons for this dramatic fall in membership and to identify and discuss the responses that New Zealand's unions made to it. It is argued that the strategic response by New Zealand unions to this dramatic membership collapse derived from the new organizational configuration brought about by the events of the 1990s. The historical configuration of New Zealand's union movement was as a 'creature of the state'. Industrial relations legislation established a system of state-sponsored conciliation and arbitration that imposed on unions a prescriptive set of rules and regulations. These, on the one hand, set limits to their organizational structure and operation, but on the other hand guaranteed their existence, their membership and their financial security. The abolition of this system in the 1990s deprived unions of the protections it offered even as it freed them from the constraints it imposed. However, most unions suffered more from the former than they benefited from the latter, in part because legislative reform coincided with other developments unfavourable to union organization. The adoption of a comprehensive set of neo-liberal economic policies, particularly the removal of almost all forms of border protection, and significant changes in the labour market made independent contributions to the fall in union membership.

The configuration of the union movement changed sharply from one in which numerous unions, nestling gratefully under the protections offered by the state, represented a high proportion of workers across the entire economy to one where fewer unions represented fewer workers in fewer sectors of the economy. This changed organizational configuration was reflected in new strategic responses by unions. Common to many of them was a deter-mination to consolidate the relevance of the union at the workplace to both employer and employees. Faced with widespread membership defection and with managerial strategies designed to establish a direct relationship with employees, unions sought to demonstrate their capacity to represent employee interests effectively while making a significant contribution to organizational efficiency. To achieve the former, unions placed a new emphasis on effective forms of workplace organization and more participatory forms of operation; to achieve the latter, unions showed their commitment to collaborative labour/management relationships and to innovative forms of work design aimed at achieving high-performance workplaces. All unions agreed with the need to organize effectively at the workplace but many disagreed with the need to cooperate with management. For them, the most effective way to represent their members was as an opponent of management rather than its partner. The tension between the union supporters of these two approaches remains unresolved.

The institutional context

For almost 100 years, a system of union registration was the key to union organization in New Zealand. Unions applied to the Registrar of Unions, a state official, for registration as the union to represent a particular category of workers. These categories were usually occupational although a small number of industry unions were formed. Once the Registrar had approved the registration of a union, no other union could be registered to represent that particular group of workers and only a registered union could partici-pate in the collective bargaining procedures that were also prescribed by the state. Thus, a registered union enjoyed monopoly bargaining rights for all workers covered by its membership rule. From 1936, they also enjoyed the benefit of compulsory membership. In return for this institutional security, unions accepted a high degree of official regulation of their activities.

The basis of private sector wage fixing was the system of minimum rate awards, negotiated in state-provided conciliation councils with recourse, if needed, to compulsory arbitration of unsettled interest disputes in the Arbitration Court. Awards, like the unions, which negotiated them, were typically occupational. Awards had blanket coverage, which meant they applied to all employers of the occupations covered by the award, and to all relevant employees, regardless of whether they were party to, or even aware of, the negotiations. Public sector unionism operated in a substantially different legal context. However, from 1948, they did enjoy negotiating and arbitration rights and although membership of most public sector unions was voluntary, the great majority of potential recruits did in fact join the relevant union (Walsh, 1993).

Although the Labour Relations Act 1987 began the reform of the law relating to trade unions, the character of the system did not change fundamentally at that stage. The National government, elected to office in 1990, responded to employer dissatisfaction with the system (NZBR, 1987) and introduced the Employment Contracts Act 1991. The Act abolished the institutions associated with the award system and ended the historically privileged position of unions (Anderson, 1991; Hince and Vranken, 1993; Walsh and Ryan, 1993; Dannin, 1997). Awards and agreements were replaced with employment contracts. Employment contracts could be individual, where they bound a single employer and a single employee, or collective where they bound two or more employees. The Act gave no explicit preference to either type, leaving both the form and content as matters for negotiation.

The Employment Contracts Act abolished the special legal status of trade unions and indeed the Act omitted any reference to trade unionism altogether. The automatic link between union membership and industrial representation was ended, and unions were required to establish their authority separately to negotiate on behalf of each individual member. While workers were free to authorize a 'bargaining agent' to negotiate on their behalf, and the employer was required to 'recognise' the appointed agent's authority, there was no obligation to begin or to conclude negotiations for an employment contract.

The new shape of the union movement

The 1990s saw a dramatic contraction of the organized sector of the New Zealand economy. The changed configuration of the union movement can be characterized as a shift from organizational breadth to organizational depth. This is shown by union membership and density data and by data on collective bargaining. Aggregate union membership fell from 603,000 at the enactment of the Employment Contracts Act to 302,000 by 1999, a fall of 50 per cent in less than a decade (Crawford *et al.*, 2000). As noted above, union density fell from 45 per cent to 17 per cent of the workforce. The proportion of the workforce covered by collective bargaining fell by more than 40 per cent (Crawford and Harbridge, 1998).

The new configuration of union depth is shown by the concentration of union membership in a small number of unions in specific sectors of the economy and in a lower proportion of workplaces. Membership collapse occurred unevenly across the economy. As a result, union membership is now heavily concentrated in a few sectors. Almost three-quarters (74 per cent) of the unionized workforce is employed in only two sectors – public and community services (51 per cent) and manufacturing (23 per cent). Another 18 per cent of union members are employed in transport and communication and in financial and business services. These four sectors account for 92 per cent of union members. Membership of unions has fallen so sharply amongst workers in agriculture, mining, construction and energy and in the retail, wholesale and hospitality industries that these sectors account for only 8 per cent of union members. This pattern of sectoral concentration of union members is paralleled by their concentration within a smaller number of unions. Between 1984 and 1990, while the average size of unions doubled, the proportion of union members belonging to one of the ten largest trade unions remained stable at around 45 per cent. Since the passage of the Employment Contracts Act, however, there has been a marked trend towards greater concentration of union membership. Although the average size of unions has declined, the share of total union members belonging to the ten largest unions has jumped from 45 per cent in 1990 to 78 per cent in December 1999 (Crawford et al., 2000).

Union membership is now heavily concentrated in a small proportion of workplaces. Data from one workplace survey undertaken at the midpoint of the Employment Contracts Act decade, show that in 1995 only 19 per cent of workplaces were unionized (Walsh and Brosnan, 1999). However, at those workplaces, 57 per cent of workers were union members. Both the breadth and depth of unionization was greater in the public than in the private sector. In the public sector, 92 per cent of workplaces were unionized and at those workplaces, 74 per cent of workers belonged to a union. In the private sector, the comparable figures were 13 per cent and 47 per cent. Unsurprisingly, unions were stronger at larger workplaces with 74 per cent of workplaces with more than 50 employees (which is large by the standards of the New Zealand economy) being unionized and 51 per cent of workers being union members. Interestingly, although only 11 per cent of workplaces with fewer than nine employees were unionized, 64 per cent of workers at those workplaces were union members.

The picture of the union movement at the end of the Employment

Contracts Act decade is one of depth rather than breadth. Fewer unions represent fewer workers who are concentrated in a narrower range of economic sectors and a smaller proportion of workplaces than in the past. However, where unions have a presence, it is a relatively strong one. The central question, then, is what explains the huge fall in union membership and the new shape of the union movement?

Legislative change is one major reason for the decline (Freeman and Pelletier, 1990). In New Zealand, the direct impact of the institutional changes in the Employment Contracts Act was immediate and substantial. During the first nineteen months of the Act's operation, aggregate union membership fell by around 30 per cent. The reasons for this dramatic effect are severalfold. First, and perhaps most significantly, the Employment Contract Act ended compulsory unionism, enabling those who were members only because of legal compulsion to resign or, in the case of newly employed workers, not to join. A second reason for the membership decline was the decline in collective bargaining associated with the Act. Following the removal of the blanket coverage of awards, unions found negotiating enterprise agreements for the thousands of small workplaces previously covered by awards quite beyond their limited and quickly declining resources. For workers in these workplaces, the absence of a collective contract reduced the incentive to be a union member.

Third, and crucially, specific provisions of the Act and their interpretation by the courts placed significant obstacles in the way of unions seeking to pursue collective negotiations on behalf of their members (Dannin, 1997; Harbridge and Honeybone, 1996). Case law under the Employment Contracts Act established that even where unions had secured authorization to represent their members, employers could flout this in a number of ways. As Hughes (2000) has observed, the courts held that employers were permitted to express to their employees 'robust' criticism of unions, either in general or with reference to the particular union representing their employees and that employers could bypass the union and communicate directly with union members over issues in negotiations. These forms of communication included employer comment on the position adopted by the unions, information packs about the employer's proposal (which might include requests for feedback) and warnings of the consequences of non-settlement on the employer's terms. Other approaches sanctioned by the courts included the presentation of draft contracts to employees with, on occasions, financial incentives to sign, and, often related to this, a 'take or leave it' negotiating stance, a refusal to negotiate or even to meet, and captive audience speeches by employers to workers. The combined effect of legislative and judicial sanctioning of these approaches made for a bleak industrial landscape for unions and imposed severe impediments in the way of effective collective organization.

Shifts in the labour market were a second contributor to union decline and to the changed shape of the union movement in New Zealand. The sharp rises in unemployment experienced in most Western economies during the 1980s have been suggested as an important reason for union decline (Bain and Price, 1983; Tyler, 1986). Certainly, increases in unemployment are likely to be responsible for some proportion of the decline in the number of union members witnessed between 1985 and 1989 (a period in which, despite the fall in aggregate membership, union density actually increased). The experience during the 1990s, however, has been different. Unemployment in New Zealand has fallen from a high of 11.1 per cent in the March 1992 quarter to 6.3 per cent in 1999. However union membership and density have continued to fall during this period. This suggests there has been a decoupling of the linkages between union growth and the business cycle. This may be partly explicable by data on employment trends. Proponents of structural explanations of union decline move the focus of analysis to the composition of employment, particularly the shift from manufacturing to service sectors, the increasing prevalence of contingent forms of employment, and changes in firm size (Troy, 1990; Peetz, 1998). In New Zealand, only two industry groups – business and financial services and community, social and personal services – have seen any growth in the number of full-time employees over the course of the last decade. Significantly, the decline in union density in those sectors is below the average for the economy as a whole. Without exception, full-time employment in traditional union strongholds has fallen sharply and part-time employment has increased across all sectors of the economy. Moreover, official data clearly show that across all industries, the bulk of employment growth since 1987 has been in small firms (those employing less than ten full-time equivalent workers) which are notoriously difficult for unions to organize effectively. In large workplaces where unions have traditionally fared better, employment fell precipitately between 1987 and 1994 and this decline has not been offset by subsequent increases (Crawford et al., 1999). The aggregate data hide important inter-industry differences. For instance, in both periods, manufacturing employment has fallen for units of every size grouping except those employing five or fewer full-time equivalent workers.

A deliberate strategy of union amalgamations also contributed to the new shape of the union movement. Union amalgamations were made necessary by the organizational difficulties many unions faced under the Employment

Contracts Act. The number of unions had in fact been declining prior to the Employment Contracts Act because of a requirement in the Labour Relations Act 1987 that unions have a minimum of 1000 members in order to retain their registration. The rationale for this requirement was that larger organizations would provide a better resource base for organizing and servicing members and benefit from economies of scale (Department of Labour, 1985a and 1985b). The Act set off a flurry of amalgamations amongst smaller unions, more than halving the number of registered unions between 1985 and 1989. Although the New Zealand Council of Trade Unions (CTU) has promoted a coordinated approach to union amalgamations (NZCTU, 1994, 1998), amalgamations during the 1990s were governed more by the dictates of survival rather than by any logic of rational representation. The amalgamation process under the Act has been controlled by individual unions and there has been an observable shift towards the establishment of 'conglomerate' unions that span several sectors or industries. This trend, which is evident internationally (Visser, 1998), has resulted in the sharp increase in membership concentration.

Union responses

The dramatic contraction in the organized sector of the economy carried with it a significant risk of industrial and political marginalization for New Zealand's unions. A fall in membership and collective bargaining coverage at that speed and on that scale weakens considerably any union claim to be a major player with employers and the state in industrial and political decision making. This was compounded by other developments, which posed independent challenges to the decision-making role of unions. Strategic human resource management practices have sought to individualize the employment relationship and have encouraged employers to establish direct relationships with their employees unmediated by unions. As a result, many employers become increasingly unwilling to involve unions in their relationships with their employees and, with a weakened union movement, feel under less pressure to do so. More generally, product market deregulation greatly reduces the sectoral interests employers previously shared and leads them away from an industry or sectoral focus and towards the 'centrality of the firm' (Regini, 1992). Related to this, the 1980s and 1990s also saw the decline of employer support for neo-corporatist approaches to economic and industrial policy formation in favour of policies driven at enterprise level. Similarly, governments see fewer reasons to consult with a contracting union movement. Ideologically driven shifts in the state's perception of its role (Sharp, 1994; Boston; *et al.*, 1996) further challenged the political relevance of unions. New Zealand's pursuit of radical neo-liberal policies initiated by the Labour government elected in 1984 put an end to the 'historic compromise' that had guided Labour policies (Jesson, 1989). Neo-liberal economic policies led to the dismantling of national tripartite bodies in which unions had negotiated compromises with the state.

Marginalization weakens the ability of unions to provide an effective voice for workers on industrial and political matters which further reduces the appeal of membership. Any hope for the renewal of trade unionism relies on a successful response to both threats of marginalization. The union response to the decade of decline and the threat of marginalization reflected the changes that had occurred in the shape of the union movement. Unions, now organized more narrowly but in greater depth, sought to demonstrate their relevance to both employees and employers in the organizations where unions retained significant membership. Their response was in two parts. One recognized that an effective union response to massive membership defection depended upon a strong workplace presence. Historically, this had not been vital. Legislation required all workers covered by an award to be a member of the negotiating union and protected unions against membership challenges by rival unions. Harbridge and Honeybone (1995: 244) conclude:

> Historically, New Zealand unions had a poorly developed approach to recruitment strategy, mounted few public union organising drives, relied extensively on the law of compulsory unionism as their primary recruitment technique, and undertook little (if any) training in recruitment matters for union officials.

In both the private and the public sector, unions dealt with employer associations or other organizations at a national or sectoral level and negotiated awards and agreements that were also enforced centrally. Unions mapped on to this structure and allocated their resources accordingly. There were notable exceptions to this in some of the traditional industrial unions representing manual workers, such as in shipping, on the waterfront, in the meat-freezing industry and in road transport and the pulp and paper industry. Most unions, however, saw little need for a strong workplace presence and, in any event, had few resources for the development of this. One study in the second half of the 1980s concluded that most employers were untroubled in their day-to-day management of the workplace by the intrusion of either elected or full-time union officials (McAndrew and Hursthouse,

1991). By the 1990s, unions recognized that the industrial relations focus had shifted. The issues for which workers needed union representation were now very much at a workplace or company level. Multi-employer awards and agreements, the mainstay of the traditional system, had all but disappeared, although there were important exceptions, notably in the dairy, plastics and metals industries, and in the hospitality and commercial cleaning sectors. However, whereas prior to the Employment Contracts Act more than half the workforce was covered by a multi-employer agreement, and in the public sector this applied to virtually all employees, by 1999, multi-employer collective bargaining was very restricted. Economic deregulation meant widespread organizational restructuring and associated downsizing in both the private and public sectors. Increasingly workers needed effective union representation at their workplace rather than centrally. Unions recognized that they needed to reorganize themselves to meet the needs of their members.

In response to this, New Zealand's unions embraced much of the organizing model that had gained widespread currency in the USA as a strategy to address declining membership in the USA (Bronfenbrenner, 1998). The value of a simple dichotomy between organizing and servicing models has been called into question (Hurd, 1998; Boxall and Haynes, 1997), but New Zealand's unions adapted innovative strategies and tactics from their American counterparts. The organizing model implies a fundamental shift in the roles of, and the relationship between, officials and rank-and-file membership in union affairs. A key aspect of this shift is the establishment of a strong union presence at the workplace.

The organic nature of the organizing approach is attractive to unions because it accords with the image of trade unions as democratic, membership-driven organizations. It is difficult to establish whether, in the New Zealand context, the reality has matched the rhetoric. Union officials remain important actors and retain a key role in determining the direction of union policy and continue to service membership needs through their expertise in bargaining and grievance handling. Nonetheless with the shift to decentralized bargaining a deliberate strengthening and broadening of the role of union delegates (elected shop stewards) is apparent (Yarrell, 1994; Oxenbridge, 1995). It has been argued that New Zealand unions were stronger at the workplace under the 'highly unfavourable' Employment Contracts Act, than their Australian counterparts under the arbitration system (Brosnan and Walsh, 1997). This apparent paradox is explained by reference to the demise of centralized bargaining under the Employment Contracts Act, effectively 'compelling unions in New Zealand to focus their organising efforts at the workplace' (Brosnan and Walsh, 1997: 88). In contrast, Australian unions were still able to focus on state and federal arbitral bodies and on bargaining at those levels, at least in the first half of the 1990s.

The second plank of the union response to decline was to recognize that union success depended on their capacity to show to employers that unions could contribute to improved organizational performance. This was a departure from the historical union position, which rejected any notion of union responsibility for organizational efficiency. This implicitly, if unwittingly, supported managerial prerogative by accepting management's right to organize the workplace in such a way as to ensure its efficient operation. In this view, the union's job was limited to the extraction of the best possible deal for its members. By the 1990s, unions recognized the need for change. If they continued in this position, they ran a serious risk of being seen as irrelevant by both workers and employers. Their response was the adoption of what in the New Zealand context was called strategic unionism. This entered New Zealand discourse via the Australian Council of Trade Union's publication *Australia Reconstructed*. Drawing on the perceived successes of European labour movements, this new approach involved a broadening of the scope of union activities beyond the narrow concern with wages and conditions of work and set a new agenda for labour's dealings with employers and with the state (TUEA, n.d.). The micro-level aspects of the strategic unionism model embraced by the CTU and some of the larger unions found expression in the 'workplace reform' movement (Street, 1994). Workplace reform is a general term for a broad range of organizational change strategies typically motivated by the need or desire to improve productivity through the introduction of more flexible work practices. Frequently this is set against the background of the alleged paradigmatic shift away from Taylorist or Fordist production systems. Agreement on the appropriateness of this new agenda was and remains by no means unanimous. Critics of this approach see it as largely adopting a compromised and conciliatory stance towards capital (Gay and MacLean, 1997). Some unions have strongly opposed workplace reform as collaborationist. As one official from the Manufacturing and Construction Workers Union states:

> Buying into the 'competitive world, lower costs equals job security argument' is replacing the traditional solidarity between workers with workers solidarity with their employer ... (Clarke, 1992: 8)

Some unions have refused to buy into workplace reform programmes, and have continued to maintain a traditional stance in their dealings with employers (Dannin, 1997). In contrast, others have taken a 'new realist' approach, arguing that employers will seek to change the organization of work regardless of union opposition. Consequently, it was argued, unions are left with the choice of becoming involved in the process or risk being bypassed altogether (Tolich, 1992; Haworth, 1993). As with the development of a strong workplace presence, the Engineers Union was instrumental in the development of the workplace reform agenda in New Zealand (Perry *et al.*, 1995) and incorporated aspects of this agenda into its proposals for award restructuring (New Zealand Engineers Union, 1987). The bulk of its membership was employed in the manufacturing sector, which was severely affected by the post-1984 reforms, and where, as a consequence, employer interest in reforming work practices was keenest.

In a similar vein, other unions have sought to establish and secure an ongoing role in the workplace through a shift in the relationship with management. The Public Service Association (PSA) recently determined to pursue a partnership strategy under the banner 'Partnership for Quality'. The strategy aims to allow the union to influence decision making at the workplace through a 'constructive engagement' with management (PSA, 1997). The coalition Labour government, elected in 1999, has endorsed this approach and signed a partnership agreement with the PSA. By doing so, it has made clear its expectation that public sector employers will adopt this approach and accept the union as a major participant in workplace decision making. The Dairy Workers Union and the Dairy Employers Association attempted to follow a path of workplace reform through award restructuring. A formal agreement – the 'Memorandum of Understanding' – was brokered with the intervention of the CTU and against a background of bitter industrial disputation. The Memorandum committed the parties to a cooperative and industry-based approach to workplace reform, including commitment to job security, the development of consultation, training and pay system reform (Perry *et al.*, 1995). The industry-level focus of workplace reform initiatives in the dairy industry made it an important model for the type of approach advocated by the CTU.

It is perhaps too early to offer comprehensive assessments of the success of these initiatives. Certainly one key issue that has arisen is that of ownership (PSA, 1999; Law, 1998). Law's (1998) survey showed many Dairy Workers Union members were sceptical of the cooperative approach advanced at industry level due to the perception that the centrally negotiated initiatives did little to change the day-to-day realities on the shop-floor. Moreover the multi-employer collective contract was broken up into separate company agreements in 1997, potentially destabilizing the industry focus of the reforms. The Engineers Union has recognized the potential and actual opposition from groups of its members who see various workplace reform initiatives as threatening their craft status (Boxall and Haynes, 1997). Similarly, not all employers are amenable to the union's involvement. In balancing these competing pressures, the Engineers Union has adopted an approach of what it terms 'strategic engagement', where the union's strategy takes account of members' concerns and is contingent upon the employer's stance.

The future

In 1999, a Labour/Alliance coalition government was elected with an election manifesto commitment to repeal the Employment Contracts Act. The Employment Relations Act 2000 constitutes a clear attempt by the new government to provide New Zealand's trade unions with the opportunity to restore their role in the economy and society. It does this in several ways. The Act takes a positive public policy stance towards collective organization; it recognizes the inherent inequality in the employment relationship and the need to address that through collective organization; it establishes a good-faith obligation that will rule out many practices hostile to collective organization that had become common under the Employment Contracts Act and it includes union access and bargaining provisions very favourable to unions.

The objects clause of the Employment Relations Act sets out its primary policy objective as 'to build productive employment relations through the promotion of mutual trust and confidence in all aspects of the employment environment and of the employment by acknowledging and addressing the inherent inequality of bargaining power in employment relationships' and 'by promoting collective bargaining'. The Act states explicitly that one of its objects is to promote observance of the principles underlying International Labour Organization (ILO) Conventions 87 on Freedom of Association and 98 on the Right to Organise and Bargain Collectively. This support for collective organization contrasts sharply with the Employment Contracts Act whose provisions were found by the ILO to be in breach of Convention 98 (Haworth and Hughes, 1995). A public policy stance, such as this, which takes a positive attitude towards trade unions and that manifestly values the contribution they make to the society and economy is more likely to encourage collectivism than the policy stance underpinning the Employment Contracts Act which took a negative attitude toward them.

The Employment Relations Act introduces a broad concept of good faith employment relations. This includes but is wider than good faith bargaining. The Act sets out a general obligation to conduct employment relationships in good faith and defines these relationships very broadly to include not only employer/employee relations but relations between a union and an employer, a union and its members, and between unions. The good faith requirement applies to but is not limited to the negotiation and interpretation of a collective agreement and to any proposal by an employer that *might* (emphasis added) impact on the employer's employees. It is important to note, however, that the good faith obligation does not require agreement on a collective agreement or on any matter for inclusion in a collective agreement. The scope of the good faith provisions is remarkable, and provides a strong basis for union activity. They rule out practices that have become increasingly common in the last decade and that pose major obstacles for unions in their efforts to establish collective organization. The range of issues covered by the good faith obligation is very wide. Indeed, the open-ended reference to employer proposals 'that might impact on the employer's employees' shows that it is the government's intention that no aspect of employment relations should fall outside the good faith obligation. The good faith provisions include information disclosure obligations, which are also defined broadly and have the potential to transform the bargaining process in ways favourable to unions.

Under the Employment Contracts Act, unions had to secure the agreement of the employer to gain access to the workplace for recruitment purposes. The Employment Relations Act, in contrast, grants virtually unrestricted rights to unions for recruiting purposes and very wide access rights to discuss employment matters or union business with their members. The bargaining provisions in the Act are also favourable to unions. Unions enjoy the exclusive right to negotiate a collective agreement; they are automatically a party to the collective agreements they negotiate; members who fall under the agreement's coverage clause are automatically covered by the agreement; and membership fees are automatically deducted. None of this was the case under the Employment Contracts Act. The Employment Relations Act also seeks to facilitate multi-employer bargaining. It restores the right to strike in support of the negotiations for a multi-employer agreement (provided other conditions relating to the legality of strikes are met) and it establishes specific procedures to be followed in the negotiation of multi-employer agreements. The Act also prohibits the employment of replacements for striking workers.

The Employment Contracts Act's strong individualizing thrust was another obstacle for unions in their efforts to maintain collective bargaining coverage.

The Employment Relations Act, however, imposes hurdles for employers to overcome in their efforts to negotiate individual contracts. In workplaces where there is a collective agreement, the Act encourages non-union members to join the union and be covered by the collective agreement. In these circumstances, employers are not free, as they were previously, to negotiate an individual contract with non-union members without any reference to the collective contract. Two provisions bear upon this. First, when an employer receives notification from a union that it intends to begin negotiations for a collective agreement, the employer is obliged to advise non-union members of the existence and scope of the bargaining. Second, and potentially very importantly, when an employer negotiates an individual agreement with an employee who is not a union member but whose work falls under the coverage clause in the collective agreement, there is a 30-day interregnum in which the terms and conditions of the collective agreement are deemed to apply to the non-member. The employer is obliged to give that employee a notice that informs the employee that a collective agreement covers the work done by the employee and that the employee may join the union that is a party to the collective agreement.

Conclusion

Historically, trade unions operated across the breadth and on the surface of the New Zealand economy. Compulsory arbitration and compulsory membership freed them from the organizing tasks facing the union movements of most countries while other institutional aspects of the industrial relations system limited the capacity of those unions with more ambitious vision. Most unions focused their limited resources on the negotiation of occupational awards with central employers' associations, which applied to all workers falling under their coverage clauses. Some unions had a strong workplace presence but these were the exception. In the decade following the Employment Contracts Act, however, the shape of the union movement changed comprehensively. Breadth yielded to depth. The number of union members has halved and more than 90 per cent of those are employed in only four sectors of the economy and are concentrated in the large workplaces of those sectors. The strategic direction of the union movement reflects this sea change in configuration but does so unevenly. Although not all unions have formally embraced the organizing model they have all sought to establish a more effective presence at the workplace and to involve members more fully in the operation of their union. Secondly, unions have focused on showing employers that their contribution can be instrumental in enhancing organizational capability and performance. This has led many unions into collaborative labour/management relationships. This remains controversial within the union movement with some unions continuing to pursue a more traditional oppositional stance to employers. However, the recent merger decision by the two rival central union federations, which had taken up opposing positions on this, may indicate a lessening of the divide on this issue.

The Employment Relations Act 2000 seeks to provide a legislative basis for trade union renewal by levelling the industrial relations playing field to a considerable degree. The Act does not restore the right to make union membership compulsory nor does it restore the blanket coverage bargaining provisions of the traditional award system. There is no move towards interest arbitration and no compulsion to conclude negotiations for a collective agreement. However, in other important respects the Act gives New Zealand's unions the opportunity to repair some of the damage done to their movement during the last decade. The Employment Relations Act starts from the premiss that employment relationships involve inherent inequality and that collective organization by trade unions is the most effective way to redress this inequality. From the outset, therefore, unions are seen as legitimate, significant and positive institutions, which can contribute to the achievement of important public policy objectives. The provisions of the Act aim to give unions a chance to contribute to achieving those objectives. The requirement to conduct employment relationships in good faith and the wide scope of the good faith obligation is a key provision. Not only will it rule out a range of practices inimical to collective organization but it will introduce a number of obligations that will benefit unions and collectivism. The provisions regarding the structure and operation of unions give them a strong organizational base for the recruitment and subsequently the effective representation of members. The provisions regarding bargaining support the negotiation of collective agreements, including multi-employer agreements, and considerably reduce the capacity of employers to impose individual agreements upon unwilling employees. The Act establishes an environment in which unions are able to operate more effectively than under the Employment Contracts Act. Whether and to what degree unions recover the ground lost in the last decade now depends upon the energy and commitment of unions and the support they can engender from members.

References

Anderson, Gordon (1991) 'The Employment Contracts Act 1991: An Employers' Charter?' in *New Zealand Journal of Industrial Relations*, 16 (2): 127–42.

Bain, George and Price, Robert (1983) 'Union Growth: Dimension, Determinants, and Density', in Bain, George (ed.) *Industrial Relations in Britain*, Oxford: Basil Blackwell, pp. 3–33.

Boston, J., Martin, J., Pallot, J. and Walsh, P. (1996) *Public Management: The New Zealand Model*, Auckland: Oxford University Press.

Boxall, Peter and Haynes, Peter (1997) 'Strategy and Trade Union Effectiveness in a Neo-liberal Environment', *British Journal of Industrial Relations*, 35 (4): 567–91.

Bronfenbrenner, Kate (1998) 'Reversing the Tide of Organizing Decline: Lessons from the US Experience', *New Zealand Journal of Industrial Relations*, 23 (2): 21–34.

Brosnan, Peter and Walsh, Pat (1997) 'Why Are New Zealand Unions Stronger at the Workplace under the Employment Contracts Act Than Australian Unions under the Accord?' in Bramble, Tom, Harley, Bill, Hall, Richard and Whitehouse, Gillian (eds) *Current Research in Industrial Relations*, Proceedings of the 11th AIRAANZ Conference, Brisbane, Queensland, 30 January–1 February 1997, pp. 78–88.

Clarke, Graeme (1992) 'Reform Secures Employer Control', *Labour Notes*, 7 (Sept): 8–9.

Crawford, A. and Harbridge, R. (1998) 'External Legitimacy in New Zealand: An Update', *Journal of Labor Research*, XIX (4): 711–21.

Crawford, Aaron, Harbridge, Raymond and Walsh, Pat (1999) 'Unions and Union Membership in New Zealand: Annual Review for 1998', *New Zealand Journal of Industrial Relations*, 24 (3): 383–96.

Crawford, Aaron, Harbridge, Raymond and Walsh, Pat (2000) 'Unions and Union Membership in New Zealand: Annual Review for 1999', *New Zealand Journal of Industrial Relations*, 25 (3): 291–302.

Dannin, Ellen (1997) *Working Free: The Origins and Impact of New Zealand's Employment Contracts Act*, Auckland: Auckland University Press.

Department of Labour (1985a) *Annual Report of the Department of Labour for the Year Ended 30 June 1985*, (G.1), Wellington: Department of Labour.

Department of Labour (1985b) *Industrial Relations: A Framework for Review* (Volume 1), Wellington: Department of Labour.

Freeman, Richard and Pelletier, Jeffrey (1990) 'The Impact of Industrial Relations Legislation on British Union Density', *British Journal of Industrial Relations*, 28 (2): 141–64.

Gay, Maxine and Maclean, Malcolm (1997) 'Six Years Hard Labour: Workers and Unions under the Employment Contracts Act', *California Western International Law Journal*, 28 (1): 45–64.

Harbridge, Raymond and Honeybone, Anthony (1995) 'Trade Unions under the Employment Contracts Act: Will Slimming Be Fatal?' in Boxall, Peter (ed.) *The Challenge of Human Resource Management: Directions and Debates in New Zealand*, Auckland: Longman Paul, pp. 231–49.

Harbridge, Raymond and Honeybone, Anthony (1996) 'External Legitimacy of Unions: Trends in New Zealand', *Journal of Labor Research*, 27 (3): 425–44.

Haworth, N. (1993) 'Unions in Crisis: Deregulation and Reform of the New Zealand Union Movement,' in Frenke, S. (ed.) *Organized Labour in the Asia-Pacific Region: A Comparative Study of Trade Unions in Nine Countries*, Ithaca, New York: ILR Press.

Haworth, N. and Hughes, S. (1995) 'Under Scrutiny: The ECA, the ILO and the NZCTU Complaint 1993–95', *New Zealand Journal of Industrial Relations*, 20 (2): 143–62.

Hince, Kevin and Vranken, Martin (1991) 'A Controversial Reform of New Zealand Labour Law: The Employment Contracts Act 1991', *International Labour Review*, 130 (4): 475–93.

Hughes, John (2000), 'Good Faith and Collective Bargaining under the Employment Relations Bill', *Employment Law Bulletin*, 4, April, pp. 53–60.

Hurd, Richard (1998) 'Contesting the Dinosaur Image: The Labor Movement's Search for a Future', *Labor Studies Journal*, 22 (4): 5–30.

Jesson, Bruce (1989) *Fragments of Labour: The Story Behind the Labour Government*, Auckland, Penguin Books.

Law, Michael (1998) 'Mopping up after Spilt Milk: A Survey of Union Members in the Dairy Industry', in Harbridge, R., Gadd, C. and Crawford, A. (eds) *Current Research in Industrial Relations: Proceedings of the 12th AIRAANZ Conference*, Wellington, 3–5 February 1998, pp. 212–20.

McAndrew, Ian and Hursthouse, Paul (1991) 'Reforming Labour Relations: What Southern Employers Say', *New Zealand Journal of Industrial Relations*, 16 (1): 1–11.

New Zealand Engineers Union (1987) *Strategies for Change: Representing Workers in a New Environment*, Wellington: New Zealand Engineers Union.

NZBR (1987) *Freedom at Work: Why New Zealand Needs a Flexible, Deregulated Labour Market*, Wellington: New Zealand Business Roundtable.

NZCTU (1994) *Unions Organising for the Future: Report of the NZCTU Search Conference*, Wellington: New Zealand Council of Trade Unions.

NZCTU (1998) *The Review of the New Zealand Council of Trade Unions: 1998 Report of the CTU Review Committee*, Wellington: New Zealand Council of Trade Unions.

Oxenbridge, Sarah (1995) 'Organising the Secondary Labour Force: The New Zealand Experience', in Sonder, Larry (ed.) *Current Research in Industrial Relations: Proceedings of the 9th AIRAANZ Conference*, Melbourne, February 1995, pp. 347–56.

Peetz, David (1998) *Unions in a Contrary World: The Future of the Australia Trade Union Movement*, Cambridge: Cambridge University Press.

Perry, Martin, Davidson, Carl and Hill, Roberta (1995) *Reform at Work: Workplace Change and the New Industrial Order*, Auckland: Longman Paul.

PSA (1997) *Partnership and the PSA's Strategic Direction: Policy on Partnership with Employers*, Wellington: Public Service Association.

PSA (1999) 'Ownership the Key', *PSA Journal*, 86 (3): 5.

Regini, Marino (1992) 'Introduction: The Past and Future of Social Studies of Labour Movements', in Regini, Marino (ed.) *The Future of Labour Movements*, London: Sage Publications, pp. 1–16.

Sharp, Andrew (ed.) (1994) *Leap into the Dark: The Changing Role of the State in New Zealand since 1984*, Auckland: Auckland University Press.

Street, Maryan (1994) 'Business and Labour', in Deeks, John and Enderwick, Peter (eds) *Business and New Zealand Society*, Auckland: Longman Paul, pp. 193–205.

Tolich, Paul (1992) 'Workplace Reform: The Key to a Quality Future', *Labour Notes*, 6: 6–8.

Troy, Leo (1990) 'Is the U.S. Unique in the Decline of Private Sector Unionism?' *Journal of Labor Research*, 11 (2): 111–43.

TUEA (n.d.) *The Compact and Current Union Issues*, Wellington: Trade Union Education Authority.

Tyler, Gus (1986) 'Labor at the Crossroads', in Lipset, Seymour (ed.) *Unions in Transition: Entering the Second Century*, San Francisco, ICS Press, pp. 373–92.

Visser, Jelle (1998) 'European Trade Unions in the Mid-1990s', in Towers, Brian and Terry, Mike (eds) *European Annual Review 1997*, Oxford, Blackwell Publishers, pp. 113–30.

Walsh, Pat (1993) 'Has the Evil Been Remedied? The Development of Public Sector Unionism in New Zealand', in Walsh, Pat (ed.) *Pioneering New Zealand Labour History: Essays in Honour of Bert Roth*, Palmerston North: Dunmore Press, pp. 102–26.

Walsh, Pat and Brosnan, Peter (1999) 'Redesigning Industrial Relations: The Employment Contracts Act and Its Consequences', in Boston, J., Dalziel, P. and St John, S. (eds) *Redesigning the Welfare State in New Zealand*, Auckland, Oxford University Press, pp. 117–33.

Walsh, Pat and Ryan, Rose (1993) 'The Making of The Employment Contracts Act', in Harbridge, Raymond (ed.) *Employment Contracts: New Zealand Experiences*, Wellington: Victoria University Press, pp. 13–30.

Wilson, Suze (1994) 'Organised Labour in the Employment Contracts Act Environment', in Morrison, Phil (ed.) *Labour Employment and Work in New Zealand: Proceedings of the Sixth Conference 24–25th November*, Victoria University of Wellington, pp. 281–92.

Yarrall, Phillipp (1994) *Recruitment Strategies for the Canterbury Hotel & Hospital Workers Union*, unpublished Diploma of Industrial Relations Research Paper.

7 A STORY OF CRISIS AND CHANGE: THE SERVICE AND FOOD WORKERS UNION OF AOTEAROA

Sarah Oxenbridge

Introduction

The Service and Food Workers Union (SFWU) represents workers across a wide range of low-wage service and food manufacturing sectors in New Zealand (NZ). In the course of studying this union in 1994, a picture emerged of an organization severely shaken by near financial collapse. This was the result of massive membership losses stemming from the enactment of the Employment Contracts Act (ECA) in 1991. This Act overturned labour relations legislation and practice which, for more than a century, was based on negotiation of national industry-wide occupational awards, compulsory union membership, and compulsory arbitration of disputes. In 1991 New Zealand shifted from being one of the most heavily regulated labour markets in the Organization for Economic Co-operations and Development (OECD) to become one of the least regulated. Trade unions no longer had a prescribed role or function under the new law, which made no mention of unions and which implicitly encouraged individual employment contracts (see Crawford and Walsh, Chapter 6). By 1998, around 75 to 80 per cent of workers were employed on individual contracts, and union density had dwindled to 19 per cent (Chapter 6 and Oxenbridge, 1999a). Several unions, including the Clerical Workers and the Communication and Energy Workers Unions, were plunged into insolvency due to massive membership losses and financial difficulties. Those unions operating in the low-wage service sector, such as the Clerical Workers Union, the National Distribution (retail sector) Union, and to a major extent, the Service Workers Union (SWU),[1] relied most heavily on compulsory unionism to generate members.

The shift to voluntary union membership, membership loss, financial crisis, and diminished resources – particularly reduced staff levels – all acted as spurs for reform in the SWU. They forced officials to engage in major revisions of their organizing strategy, which led to the adoption of rank-and-file organizing methods.

This case study offers insights into how and why unions choose certain survival strategies, particularly those necessitating reform of organizing practices, when faced with threats to survival. Why, for instance, did the SWU choose change over maintaining the *status quo*, which was arguably the easier option? The story of the SWU demonstrates how leadership values, leadership change, and a tradition of building activism can all contribute to an organizational propensity for innovation and change.

One of the most interesting facets of the SWU's experience is the degree of conflict between those officials seeking change and those resisting change. Key officials endeavoured to introduce new organizing practices, yet most staff simply chose not to adopt the new approaches. This shows that trade unions, by their very nature, tend to attract staff with strongly held views, which may translate into resistance to change. Change engineers who are planning reforms in trade unions might bear this in mind. The SWU's experience indicated that change cannot be decreed, or forced through an organization, no matter how urgent or necessary for survival it is perceived by officials to be. Change may take successive attempts, and is best viewed as an incremental process.

This case also demonstrates that organizational and cultural change in unions may only ultimately transpire as a result of three constituent elements working together. These are leadership change; structural change through internal union restructuring; and generational change, through turnover and recruitment of new union staff. In the SWU, this three-pronged mix of elements, along with the exchange of ideas between national labour movements, acted to bring about eventual change.

This chapter traces the process of reform in the SFWU, focusing on each successive phase of the process along with the barriers to, and levers for change. It is based on interviews with 31 full-time officials, mainly divisional leaders, secretaries, and organizers. In NZ unions, organizers are responsible for organizing, recruitment, contract negotiation and enforcement, and handling grievance and disciplinary cases. Most interviews were conducted in 1994 and 1995, and follow-up interviews were conducted in later years. The SWU's case demonstrates how a range of external and internal (union) imperatives for change may work in cohesion to bring about change. But more importantly, it proves that even where unions face seemingly insurmountable barriers to organizing, they are sufficiently adaptable to build membership activism and indeed survive, a feat deemed remarkable by many SWU officials.

A profile of the SFWU

The Service Workers Union of Aotearoa was registered in May 1991 as a result of an amalgamation between eight regional unions. It merged with the United Food and Beverage Workers Union (UFBWU) in 1997 to become the SFWU. The union's six main industry divisions organize security officers and cleaners and caretakers working in the commercial and education sectors; workers in restaurants, accommodation and licensed hotels, catering companies, and casinos; and health and care workers in nursing and residential care homes, public hospital domestic staff (orderlies, catering, cleaning, security, and laundry workers) and homecare workers. The clerical division covers administrative and clerical workers in schools, betting agencies, and airlines. Members in the community services division are employed in community organizations and voluntary agencies. The merger with the UFBWU brought with it membership in food and beverage processing and manufacturing, and laundry and chemical workers.

The SFWU is dominated by female members, and has significant proportions of Pacific Island and indigenous Maori members. In 1999, female members made up around 67 per cent of SWU members. A 1993 survey of women members found that 80 per cent were European, 12 per cent Maori, and 5 per cent Pacific Island, which approximated the mix of ethnic groups in NZ society (Harbridge and Street, 1995). More recent 1999 figures indicate that the proportion of Maori members has increased as a result of the UFBWU merger, and that 62 per cent of members work more than twenty hours per week (full time). The remaining 38 per cent are classified as part-time workers.

Little accurate statistical data on the proportion of young, Maori and Pacific Island members was available, although concentrations of Pacific Island and young members are highest in the hospitality sector, with significant numbers of Pacific Island members also in hospitals and the commercial cleaning sector. Since 1994, increasing numbers of Asian workers from Vietnam, Myanmar, Thailand, India, Indonesia, the Philippines and China have joined the union. New migrant workers are prominent in the commercial cleaning and hospitality sectors, particularly in Auckland.

The SFWU is structured into northern and central (North Island) regions and a southern (South Island) region. The union's two largest regional offices are located in Auckland and Wellington. Each region appoints a regional secretary who oversees staff in a number of smaller district offices. In 1994 the SWU employed 71 staff. By late 1999 this had dropped to 63 employees. Between 1991 and 1994, officials in each of the six industry divisions were responsible for industrial strategy, whereas policy, financial and resource allocation decisions were made by regional and national secretaries and national and regional executive committees made up of elected lay representatives. After 1994, the six industry divisions were abolished, although they remained in the union rules and for purposes of representation on executive committees.

The impact of the Employment Contracts Act

At the time of the passage of the Employment Contracts Act (ECA) and the SWU amalgamation in May 1991, the combined membership of the SWU's constituent amalgamating unions is recorded as 69,000 actual members and 50,000 full-time equivalent (FTE) members. However, a key interviewee noted that there was widespread doubt among officials as to the accuracy of these figures. Actual membership was believed to be significantly lower because at the time of amalgamation computerized membership figures were out of date and included thousands of resigned and non-financial workers.

Eighteen months later, at December 1992, membership had halved to 25,000 FTEs. By March 1997, it dropped to 19,000 actual members, despite membership increases resulting from several amalgamations between 1994 and 1997. Overall, between 1991 and 1997 membership declined by 72 per cent, even when including increases resulting from amalgamations. By 1999, membership stood at around 21,000 actual members, including approximately 5000 ex-UFBWU members. Membership losses continued due to the 1997–8 Asian crisis and economic downturn and widespread redundancies, particularly in the food manufacturing and traditionally highly unionized public hospital sectors. However, new sectors, such as the casino industry and subcontracted healthcare, cleaning, catering, and community care, all expanded from the mid-1990s. The SWU officials were quick to seize opportunities and extend their coverage by organizing these sectors.

Imprecise membership data and overoptimistic financial projections based on expected membership levels resulted in a serious financial deficit in the year ending January 1993. Consequently, officials embarked on radical restructuring measures during 1993, when around one-third of the union's employees were made redundant. Programmes of restructuring and rationalization of union functions, in preparation for and in response to the ECA, were constant in the SWU from the late 1980s onwards. Leaders applied strategies of cost-cutting and amalgamation, and reformed financial planning, administrative and information systems, staff management, and recruitment monitoring functions.

Organizing under the ECA: problems and approaches

Multiple impediments hindered officials' attempts to recruit workers and develop strong workplace representation under the ECA. They included high levels of labour turnover, young and casual workers, employer anti-unionism, and small worksites. In 1999, for example, the SFWU's 21,000 members were spread across 3700 worksites, an average of six per site. And turnover was such that while officials recruited around 3500 new members each year, they were required to recruit 4500 in order to grow. In light of these factors, it is not surprising that officials achieved greater success when certain structural factors were present. These included workforces concentrated in large groups, or concentrated nationally through multi-site contracts, and establishments employing older, full-time workers.

These structural elements shaped the mix of organizing and servicing approaches used. Where employers were neutral towards union involvement, the site was of medium to large size, and union officials felt there was some possibility of negotiating a contract, they attempted to organize collectives around contracts. Conversely, workers in small sites with hostile employers were recruited individually around servicing-based 'insurance' appeals. In general, most SWU officials used insurance appeals, consistent with 'servicing' models of unionism (see Fletcher and Hurd, 1998). They recruited around union staff resolving work-related problems for individuals, negotiating and enforcing contracts, representing workers in grievance and dispute cases, and discounted membership services. Most officials employed the same approaches used under the award system, when their role mainly involved enforcing awards and handling grievances.

What is of interest about the SWU is that this servicing orientation operated in tandem with activist organizing approaches. A number of SWU officials described themselves as community or grassroots organizers. They spoke of how, at the workplace level, they educated workers about the need for collective problem solving and action, and endeavoured to build workers' confidence and self-sufficiency. Their organizing focus also reached beyond the workplace, encompassing local communities and national and international social justice campaigns, and they built links between union members and organizations involved in these campaigns.

Most community organizers were former officials of the NZ Clerical

Workers' Union or the Northern or Wellington Hotel & Hospital Unions (H&HU) which had histories of campaigning or activist unionism (Oxenbridge, 1999b). There was a particularly strong tradition of community organizing in the SWU's Wellington office, where some community organizers were former H&HU officials, and others had been employed after 1991 by the SWU Wellington regional secretary, who was himself a community organizer. The Wellington office demonstrated how the degree to which SWU regional offices were dominated by community, or servicing-oriented staff, was a function of historical legacy and regional secretaries' organizing orientations.

From the late 1980s onwards, the SWU and its predecessor unions were reconfigured as a result of pressure from these community organizers and lay activists for greater participation of women, Pacific Island, and Maori workers in democratic structures. Senior lay and paid officials established standing committees for these groups, and allocated places for committee representatives on regional and national executive committees. They also employed greater numbers of Pacific Island, Maori, and women organizers. By 1994, staff structures were largely representative of membership profiles, and national secretaries were elected in 1993 and 1996 who were of Pacific Island descent and female (respectively). Despite these changes, staff and leaders lamented the decline in membership activism under the ECA, and spoke of the need to boost membership participation in union decision-making structures.

Membership decline, again combined with pressure from standing committees, also spurred leaders to target the organization of women, Pacific Island, Maori, and young workers to a greater degree under the ECA. Consistent with literature describing participative, activist organizing strategies used by American unions (Banks, 1991; Crain, 1994), officials organized these workers by: organizing around specific issues of relevance to them; using participative 'female' styles of organizing; tailoring promotional material to non-English-speaking workers; and building visibility by networking with students, community groups, churches, and workers' centres.

On the whole, however, officials were prevented from spending a sufficient amount of time organizing new members. Consistent with Kelly and Heery's (1994) research, they were overwhelmed by servicing demands. Leaders constantly stressed the need for greater organizer presence and visibility on worksites, yet this conflicted with a massive increase in time-consuming grievance and disciplinary cases, which kept organizers off worksites. The difficulties organizers faced as they attempted to encourage stewards to recruit members contributed to a growing belief that responsibility for recruitment should be broadened to all members, rather than just individual stewards.

The need for greater levels of recruitment and membership activism, combined with a tradition of community organizing and a shift towards more participative union practices, led officials to seek out new modes of organizing more attuned to the ECA environment. As a consequence, staff sought to institute worker-to-worker and contract campaign organizing techniques. The following sections describe their efforts to bring about organizing reform.

Initial steps towards reform: 1984–92

The first shifts towards organization-wide organizing reform occurred between 1984 and 1990. In the early 1980s a change of leadership occurred in the Northern H&HU, the SWU's largest pre-constituent union. The new secretary and other officials instituted changes that, officials stated, transformed the union from a 'patsy union with a history of being in the pocket of the boss', to an 'activist' or 'organizing' union. Senior officials were certain that the National Party would win the 1990 general election and introduce voluntary unionism soon after. Consequently, in the late 1980s, senior officials visited unions in America, Britain, Europe, and Australia to study different industrial relations systems and union organizing strategies. These officials were, in the words of a former secretary, 'able to bring back a perspective of what life might be like under a change of law' in a deregulated labour market. Along with enhancing the participation of women and minority workers in democratic structures, officials set about strengthening steward structures, devoting more resources to organizing campaigns, and employing organizers skilled in community organizing methods.

In 1989, educators in the Service Workers Federation and the Northern H&HU brought out officials from the American United Food and Commercial Workers Union to explain worker-to-worker organizing techniques to staff. Staff also participated in case study exercises based on American organizing education programmes that illustrated contract campaign processes. The objective of this initiative, as described by the 1993–6 national secretary, was 'to shock staff into understanding what was going to come' and persuade them that new methods of functioning were required. Nevertheless, few officials adopted these techniques. In hindsight, SWU leaders believed that this was because staff were still operating within a system of compulsory unionism, and thus could not envisage how or why they should use worker-to-worker techniques. Despite this, neither the former secretary nor his successor, who held the post from 1993 to 1996, felt that these attempts at change had failed. Rather, they explained that the techniques were adopted gradually by some officials, whereas others simply chose not to use them. Interestingly, it appears that these leaders – who had reformed steward and democratic structures during the 1980s – did not openly support educators' endeavours to promote organizing reform between 1989 and 1992.

In the period following these early training seminars, education officers incorporated worker-to-worker techniques into steward education pro- grammes and several officials with community organizing backgrounds studied the methods and started using them. These officials stressed that they and other H&HU community organizers had used similar rank-and-file methods well in advance of the 1989 seminar. One interviewee stated:

> For those who'd come from a community organizing background, what (the educator) had to say was just articulating ideas that were already around. What was talked about then, and agreed, was that we have to organize in this way. But others thought 'Who's this bloody [educator] telling us what to do, bringing back things from America?' They shouldn't have been couched as something that came back from America. That was a mistake. It was already present in New Zealand.

Renewed efforts at change: 1993–6

Most SWU officials reacted to the ECA by adhering to an arbitrationist, ser- vicing orientation. In the turbulent period following the ECA's introduction, officials focused on negotiating collective employment contracts as quickly as possible to secure access to worksites, even though in many instances only a minority of workers on these sites were members. They based recruitment around contract negotiations and dispute handling, and engaged in con- cessionary bargaining, which the northern health division leader described as 'the concept of organizing as being deals done with the boss'. She com- mented further that the SWU responded to the ECA by 'imitating the old award system'. This resulted in minority membership representation, weak organization, lowered wages and conditions, and negative perceptions of the union among workers, who associated it with wage cuts.

Officials became disenchanted with this state of affairs, and interviews conducted in 1994 revealed a strong determination to cease using concessionary strategies and focus instead on building activism through rank-and-file organizing. This led certain individuals once again to look at alternative organizing approaches. During 1993 and 1994 the New Zealand Council of Trade Unions (CTU), Communication and Energy Workers Union (CEWU) and the Finance Sector Union (FinSec) funded speaking tours of American unionists from the Communication Workers of America (CWA) and the Service Employees International Union (SEIU) who advocated the use of organizing model techniques. The SWU's northern health division leader attended one such seminar in 1993. Soon after, she and northern health organizers began trialling organizing model techniques, with much success. She used organizing methods employed by the CWA and SEIU, such as 'mapping' worksites to assess levels of union support, employee surveys, establishing workplace organizing committees (WOCs) and communication networks, holding meetings in workers' homes, and worker-to-worker organizing campaigns.

By 1993 the SWU had a new national secretary who was supportive of efforts to implement organizing model methods. He stated that his support stemmed from the fact that these methods had proven successful in the northern health sector, which had experienced membership growth during 1993–4; because grassroots organizing was aligned with his philosophy of 'genuine effective unionism'; and because staff levels had been reduced, meaning that greater organizing responsibility would have to be devolved to members. He stressed that they had adopted the organizing model as a matter of sheer survival, given the financial catastrophe experienced in 1993.

Following her efforts in the northern health division, the divisional leader tried to promote the use of organizing model methods throughout the entire union. In mid-1994 she and the national secretary urged the union's executive committees to appoint her to the newly created position of national organizing and education coordinator. Once appointed, she endeavoured to educate staff and members about the organizing model concept at conferences in 1994. Her brief involved training all organizers in membership education techniques and assisting them in planning organizing campaigns. However, interviews with staff conducted directly prior to and following the conferences uncovered significant resistance to the model. Staff prevented her from planning and directing their organizing campaigns, which meant that she was only able to oversee organizing activities in her former division (northern health).

Barriers to change

Staff opposition to organizing reform stemmed from a number of factors. Officials felt that organizing model methods could not be used on small sites; that the union had insufficient resources to conduct often lengthy organizing model campaigns; and that members were not sufficiently skilled to undertake many of the complex responsibilities required of them under the model. One such official commented:

> You cannot get delegates (stewards) elected and say 'Now it's your job', when it's not. We're the paid officials, not the delegates. We're there to help and support and train them, and always be there for them. . . . Because it is a dangerous position . . . You've also got to build up a rapport with the delegate's employer, so that you can come and go, and you take in and bring out the animosity with you, and it doesn't stay there for the workers to deal with.

Some asserted strongly that, even if the model was implemented successfully, organizers would have to continue to service members' needs to a high degree. This was because members felt vulnerable and feared for their jobs if they became involved in union activities and because they lacked the confidence required to engage in organizing campaigns. Some felt that part-time workers were reluctant to fight for improved conditions as they were not committed to their jobs, and claimed:

> Because of the types of members we represent we will always need to be a servicing body. Organize where possible – great, I believe in membership-driven organization – but if we want to keep some sites unionized, it's a matter of servicing.

Community organizers and those who supported organizing reform initiatives predicted that organizers would resist change on the basis of the prevailing servicing orientation embedded in the SWU's culture. These predictions were confirmed by interviews with servicing-oriented officials, most of whom resisted being trained in organizing model techniques by stating that they were 'already using organizing model methods'. According to the model's proponent, a servicing orientation prevailed because organizers gained immense satisfaction from helping people. Most were highly committed to the union and their job, and agreed with the concept of worker empowerment, yet they found it difficult to devolve responsibility to workers on a daily basis. The model's advocate, along with certain community organizers, considered that adoption of the model required a culture shift within the organization. They commented (respectively):

> I firmly believe that you can't impose that sort of change of attitude, from servicing to organizing. It's that whole thing of changing the culture of an organization. If you ask a lot of people why they're in this job, they'll say they're in it to help people, not empower people. We've got a lot of organizers who get the rewards from achieving the results themselves, rather than helping the members to achieve results.

and

> I think there's got to be a lot of grassroots change in organizers' attitudes. Partly it's about who we employ. We should be employing people with community links who naturally gel with an organizing model, rather than telling old hacks who have been around for years that that's the way they have to organize, because that's a real problem already ... We need to have an organizing philosophy and an organizing strategy. If you've got the philosophy you'll find the model quickly enough, and people do it all over the world. It's a matter of what particular models are appropriate in different divisions and regions, and are appropriate for different organizers who have different skills and different levels of adaptability.

In essence, at the time of interviews in 1994 SWU officials comprised three groups: servicing-oriented officials who were either overtly resistant to adopting organizing model techniques, or were confused about their practical application; organizing model supporters who used rank-and-file organizing techniques; and community organizers who also used activist approaches, but who expressed concerns about the process by which the organizing reform was being engineered.

Four key factors influenced the extent of staff opposition to, or support for, organizing model techniques. First, amongst servicing-oriented organizers, resistance stemmed from adherence to the notion of the 'professional' organizer who serviced members (Heery and Kelly, 1994), and a belief that 'organizers' work' should not be devolved to members. Some held misconceptions about the model, believing that *all* organizers' duties would be devolved to members, leaving organizing staff without jobs. More generally, many organizers were self-conscious and defensive about the recruitment methods they used. This was a function of constant leadership scrutiny of officials' recruitment numbers as financial conditions worsened. Consequently, organizers took exception to others within the organization telling them that their recruitment methods were wrong and that they should use new methods.

Regional and divisional leaders' organizing orientations constituted a second factor determining uptake of the new methods. These leaders acted as gatekeepers in terms of the dissemination of organizing model techniques among their staff. In the Wellington office, for example, key officials were community organizers, and the central region secretary actively promoted rank-and-file techniques. In contrast, southern region leaders chose not to use organizing model training programmes and resources made available to them. Similarly, the level of autonomy granted to *divisional* leaders enabled servicing models to remain entrenched, with senior leaders unable to influence either divisional cultures or the proportion of divisional resources allocated to organizing.

A third important factor influencing support for organizing model techniques centred around criticisms voiced by community organizers. These officials were not opposed to the organizing model concept or philosophy, as most had used grassroots and worker-to-worker organizing strategies since the 1980s. They were, however, unhappy with the somewhat rushed process officials had used to implement reforms. Some felt that the model had been imposed on staff, who had been prevented from debating issues surrounding its implementation. In response to these criticisms, the model's proponent highlighted the tensions that existed at the time between the need to build consensus, and the need to implement urgent strategic responses to financial crisis and membership decline.

As noted earlier, community organizers were unhappy that worker-to-worker organizing methods had been depicted as 'new', and American, when H&HU and SWU organizers had used them for many years previously. When interviewed, an ex-SEIU official who toured NZ and trained SWU staff in organizing model techniques during the mid-1990s concurred that many officials had displayed resistance to 'American' organizing methods. Consequently, both she and the SWU's organizing model proponent stated that, when training officials in later years, they were careful to stress that the organizing model was neither new, nor American. Rather, they positioned it as a traditional 'back to basics' campaigning approach. They also took care to explain that the servicing/organizing dichotomy was simply a theoretical construct for analysing organizer practice, rather than a means of demonstrating that servicing was inherently 'wrong'. The challenge, they suggested, was for unions to get the balance right between organizing and servicing.

The SWU's experience reveals the difficulty proponents face in translating their zeal for organizing reform into adoption by organizational actors. Consistent with the experience of Conrow (1991) and Grabelsky and Hurd (1994), SWU staff endeavoured to block change because a culture that devalued organizing endured, and was continually reasserted among servicing-oriented staff. In concert with these American studies, SWU staff were threatened by the new strategy; they feared increased workloads and burn-out; they argued that devolving organizing responsibilities to members would result in weakened control; and many were committed to a 'professional' definition of their role. We turn now to look at how such resistance was mediated through structural change.

Structural reform

When interviewed in 1995, one year after her appointment as organizing co-ordinator, the model's proponent was pleased that many organizers who were formerly resistant to the model had begun to accept the need to employ these techniques. They did not, however, use them in practice. As before, they claimed that they were prevented from establishing workplace organiz-ing structures because of urgent individual casework and negotiation demands. Alongside this, the high level of autonomy granted to divisional and regional leaders continued to prevent union-wide strategic change.

The coordinator became frustrated at not having sufficient authority to initiate change, as she could only become involved in organizing campaigns if invited by divisional leaders. Consequently, in March 1995 she established a pilot interdivisional organizing team in the Auckland office to test the via-bility of reallocating the servicing workloads of some organizers to other officials, thus enabling organizers to concentrate solely on organizing tar-geted sites. Two months later, falling northern region membership led to voluntary redundancies. The reduced size of the divisional teams prompted senior officials to question whether organizing on a divisional basis was sus-tainable. This, combined with the success of the pilot organizing team and the organizing coordinator's need to bring about further changes, led the Auckland office to embark on a process of restructuring, and reorienting organizing.

Suggestions for change were canvassed among staff, who, guided by the organizing coordinator, determined that they should be permanently restructured into two teams of organizers and advocates, similar to structures in some American local unions. This would enable organizing team members to concentrate solely on building workplace organization and educating members. Advocacy team members would perform contract negotiation, enforcement, and grievance work. Staff were appointed to teams based on their preferences, although leaders retained the power to make final decisions on the placement of staff. Two northern assistant secretaries' positions were established to direct the work of the teams, and the organizing co-ordinator filled the position of assistant secretary (organizing and education). Her new role provided her with the mandate she needed to implement change, as she was now able to direct organizers' work on campaigns and appoint staff.

Thus, resistance to organizing reform among servicing-oriented officials resulted in structural change in the northern region office. Ostensibly, restructuring served to ameliorate resistance, as servicing-oriented staff assumed roles as advocates. For example, all northern region cleaning division staff, who had argued that organizing model methods were not relevant to their sector, chose to be advocates. Looking to the longer term, however, it might be that structural reform represents only a partial or short-term solution to the problematic issue of a lack of organization-wide commitment to rank-and-file organizing (see also Fletcher and Hurd, 1998).

Both Conrow (1991) and Fletcher and Hurd (1996: 6, 1998: 48–9) sound warnings about the negative effects of separating representation functions. According to Fletcher and Hurd (1996), the split between field represent-atives and organizers may result in a lack of cohesion, member dissonance, and ideological division. They warn that this structural option should be avoided by unions unless these obstacles can be overcome. Judging from the experience of the SWU and the American unions studied by Conrow as well as by Fletcher and Hurd, it seems that the benefits derived from specializa-tion must be balanced with officials' workload, job variety, and coordination needs. Unions must build enough overlap and flexibility into team structures to enable effective coordination, and to allow staff to move in and out of teams as needs dictate. By 1999, after four years of fine-tuning, the national secretary stated that organizing teams were able to decide which organizers specialized in particular functions, as well as performing some advocacy (servicing) tasks, such as dealing with employers who tried to fire activists or contract them out. However, her goal for future years was to separate the two functions further, to allow organizers and activists to spend more time on external organizing using home visits.

In essence, servicing demands are a key impediment to organizing. Organizing and servicing functions are interlinked, and neglect of servicing responsibilities may affect the union's ability to recruit workers. Separating these activities through specialization constitutes one means of dedicating commensurate time to each. However, longitudinal research is needed to assess whether the benefits flowing from this structural choice outweigh the costs.

In summary, a combination of factors drove change in the SWU (see Oxenbridge, 1997). These included first, and most crucially, precipitating events in the shape of the ECA and voluntary unionism, membership decline, financial crisis, and staff reductions. Other intra-union stimuli included leadership change and leadership support of experimentation with new strategies. While leaders initially failed to support officials advocating worker-to-worker approaches between 1989 and 1992, leadership composition had changed by the time a second attempt occurred in 1994, and the new national secretary was supportive of organizing reform.

Data also demonstrated how a tradition of building membership participation (such as those initiatives implemented during the 1980s) and the presence of union educators may influence both exposure to new organizing methods, and willingness to devolve responsibility to members using organizing model methods. The proponents for reform of organizing methods in the SWU were either educators, or became educators. They played an important role in exposing union officials to organizing model and other foreign strategies and promoting their adoption.

Application of the organizing model

As noted earlier, officials adopted rank-and-file intensive organizing methods originally designed by SEIU and CWA officials. In her role as organizing co-ordinator, the model's advocate also revised steward and membership education programmes to reflect the new thrust. She developed short education modules for WOC members that could be used in workplaces during lunch breaks and after work hours. Members of WOCs organized workmates around petitions on working conditions that were presented to management, and used other low-risk, non-confrontational 'solidarity' actions, such as all workers wearing union badges and stickers, or stopping work for short periods, simultaneously. In a similar fashion to American unions, most campaigns were conducted around issues of fairness, workplace justice and dignity.

Within eighteen months of first trialling organizing model techniques, officials turned their attention to new organizing targets, such as casino workers. During casino campaigns, they drew on the support and expertise of

Australian and American unions organizing casinos. By 1996, organizing committees were established in a significant number of companies, and increasing numbers of northern region organizers were running membership education programmes. To maintain momentum on worksites between contract campaigns, officials involved active WOC members in external organizing campaigns on neighbouring sites. However, because the ECA caused employment relations activity to become focused at the single enterprise level, SWU staff encountered difficulties persuading activists to look beyond their workplace. As a consequence, 'members as organizers' education programmes were established in the northern and central regions to promote external organizing by volunteer organizers on a systematic basis. From 1996 onwards, the number of volunteer organizers working out of the Auckland and Wellington union offices increased steadily. The organizing coordinator outlined the programmes' objectives:

> The members as organizers programme is about first of all getting people to organize their own workplaces properly, but also to help us with the place down the road ... It's understanding that it's building unionism – that it's not just about their workplace, and that if the workplace down the road isn't organized, theirs isn't going to stay organized, or they're not going to stay with the benefits. I haven't come across any difficulty with our members understanding that concept.

In the years following 1994, some organizers who had resisted adopting organizing model methods, or were critical of the process by which they were instituted, resigned voluntarily. Others were devolving organizing to workplace activists, yet not without difficulty. The organizing coordinator stated:

> What [one organizer] says is that she has to continuously practise organising, and that the temptation to fix problems is always there. So if a member says they've got a problem, she says to them 'Go and find out who else has got the problem.' And she never leaves a stewards' or WOC meeting without leaving them with something to do. And it's those sorts of techniques that other organizers haven't learnt to do.

The impact on members

This study focuses primarily on reactions to the organizing model among union staff. Obviously, it is equally important to consider the effect of reform on members. What, for example, are the long-term outcomes of top-down reform initiatives, as opposed to membership-initiated pressures for change? It seems that the staff-directed mode of reform evident in the SWU occurred partly as a consequence of a compliant membership, in that members were willingly guided by officials who initiated and coordinated organizing campaigns. It may be surmised that in many unions, top-down organizing reform is more likely to occur than bottom-up change. This is because union staff are more likely to be exposed to new or foreign organizing strategies than members, and because staff are more aware of financial pressures necessitating radical change. This also appears to have been the case in British and Australian unions that have adopted US-style organizing approaches (see Cooper and Walton, 1996; Heery *et al.*, 1999).

How did members react to efforts to transform organizing practices? The only information available comes from the model's advocate, who had found widespread enthusiasm for organizing model methods among members. Support, she asserted, was also evident in the significant number of enrolments for volunteer organizer training courses, and increased levels of workplace organization and activism. She added, however, that there had been some opposition to activist organizing methods among long-standing stewards.

Over the 1994–7 period, she reshaped membership education programmes to stimulate critical analysis of the political and social context in NZ. These programmes reinforced the notion that the SWU was not merely asking members to cooperate in existing union institutions, but was encouraging them to create and build their own movement. This, she stated, would lead to genuine transformational organizing, enabling workers to gain confidence and challenge the *status quo*. However, officials may face future difficulties balancing the needs of newly empowered workplace leaders – who may seek control of leadership structures, decision-making functions, and resource allocation processes – with an arbitrationist legacy of institutional control by paid officials and union managers. It might be expected that there is a fine line between paid officials supporting a certain level of membership activism, and feeling unease at the prospect of a loss of control at the hands of members. Once again, longitudinal research may shed light on the long-term effects of rank-and-file empowerment on union governance structures.

The exchange of ideas

A degree of convergence was evident in terms of the rank-and-file organizing strategies used by the SWU and American service sector unions. This was the result of first, cross-pollination of ideas between unions – for example, transference of the organizing model – and second, indigenous development of like strategies, in the case of SWU community organizers' approaches. Evidence supported Heery's (1996) claim that mimesis (the modelling of union organization on other organizational forms) has increasingly accounted for the spread of new union strategies across national borders. The SWU's experience indicated that mimesis is promoted by the presence of union educators or research-oriented staff and inhibited by resistance from other staff.

From 1993 onwards, the SWU's organizing model advocate worked closely with educators from the Australian Council of Trade Union's (ACTU) Organising Works programme (see Cooper and Walton, 1996). Together with the programme's director, she produced organizing model training resources that have been widely used by unions across NZ, Australia, and Britain. From 1995 onwards, she and others developed systems for gathering information about organizing targets (particularly multinational casino and contract catering and cleaning companies) through linkages with overseas unions and international confederations. This information has enabled officials to plan strategies for organizing new market entrants prior to their establishment in NZ. The SFWU has also started using the Internet to build international union support around campaigns to organize NZ hotels belonging to anti-union multinational chains.

The model's proponent has visited and formed links with the Trades Union Congress (TUC), the American Federation of Labour-Congress of Industrial Organisations (AFL-CIO), and the ACTU, along with visiting 'organizing unions' in Britain, America and Australia, to exchange ideas and strategies. Representatives of these unions and federations have also visited SFWU officials in NZ to learn of their experiences. Further exchange of ideas has occurred through transfers of staff. During 1999–2000 the SFWU employed a graduate of the TUC's Organizing Academy, while a community organizer from the Wellington office worked for SEIU local and international offices over the same period. All of these initiatives to build international linkages are grounded in a tradition of contact with overseas unions which began in the SFWU in the 1980s.

Conclusions

The process by which the SWU reformed organizing illustrates how organizational actors sought to replace the ascendant servicing orientation with an activist or organizing culture (see also Grabelsky and Hurd, 1994). The SWU change engineers found that cultural change takes time. In some instances it may occur only as a result of generational change, when staff leave the organization and are replaced by officials whose value systems are aligned with the new culture promoted by change agents. Increasingly, the SWU has appointed organizers with activist organizing backgrounds. Leadership and structural change have also facilitated organizing reform. A new southern region secretary has been appointed, for example, and divisional structures have been dissolved. Each of these changes lessens the likelihood of resistance to new ideas.

Some SWU officials claimed that American organizing model strategies could not be effectively implemented in NZ. These claims may be rebuffed with reference to the successful outcomes of organizing model campaigns in both the SWU and other organizing unions such as FinSec. In the SWU, organizing reform has resulted in the creation of new teams of volunteer (member) organizers, the recruitment of young stewards and activists, increased membership and activist numbers in the Auckland and Wellington health and community services divisions, and membership growth in the Wellington cleaning sector. When asked to provide evidence of the success of the changes she had implemented, the general secretary stated that membership activity and the union's profile had increased significantly due to the massive expansion of membership training programmes. The reforms had been highly successful, she believed, in terms of both the extent to which strong, enduring workplace structures had been built, and the numbers of members and activists who had been exposed to organizing and education programmes. Additionally, in 1998 greenfield external organising campaigns began in earnest in existing membership sectors – such as nursing homes and health trusts – and in new sectors, including Internet workers and professional musicians.

She believed that a key indicator of success was the fact that in 1999 the SFWU only lost 368 members. She directly attributed this marked reduction in membership losses to organizing campaigns in the northern and central regions. A loss of 368 members may not seem like evidence of success. However, to union leaders it represented a significant turnaround from the massive yearly membership losses of the last eight years and offered hope that – despite increasing levels of turnover, contracting out of members' jobs, and redundancies – the SWU has turned the corner and might now begin to increase membership.

It is difficult to measure the success of reforms after only four years, as building membership is a long-term process, particularly in a country where unions disappeared from public view for most of the 1990s. While the outcomes of the reforms are not immediately apparent, they will lay the basis for future membership growth. Whether union reform leads to long-term survival remains to be seen. It might be said that true change has occurred only recently, as it has taken six years for the model's advocate to garner full support for the reforms from all sectors of the union. By 1999, she had the unequivocal support of the union leadership (regional secretaries, the president, and the national executive), all of whom have taken on a greater role in driving change.

The case of the SWU shows that change in trade unions can be an iterative, sometimes intricate process, as evidenced by the successive attempts made by the model's advocate to break free of the servicing treadmill and dedicate specific resources and staff to greenfield organizing. This was necessary, she believed, to ensure long-term membership growth. While the focus of the years 1994–8 was on building workplace organization, by 1999 it had shifted to external organization of entire industries and educating members about the need to organize non-union competitors to protect their own wages and conditions. In the year 2000 the Auckland office planned to establish an external organizing unit with new staff dedicated to organizing in new, priority areas, including three young organizers recruited from the TUC's organizing Academy and the NZ Students' Association. External organizing teams will be established in all three regions, and the membership organizing programme will be expanded. Around 20 per cent of national union income has been allocated to external organizing.

Since 1995 other NZ unions such as FinSec, the Nurses organization, the Engineers' Union, and the (now defunct) CEWU have promoted organizing model strategies in their unions. Yet, as in America, relatively few unions use these methods extensively, due to many of the same barriers to adoption (Fletcher and Hurd 1998: 42–3). Traditional union policies of recruitment around servicing, and union amalgamations, are more common responses to membership loss than is organizing reform. Pressures for mergers and absorptions increased after 1991 as unions faced financial hardship. Some unions boosted the range of services offered to members, although it quickly became apparent that workers did not join for these services, but for union protection. In the late 1990s several unions adopted a policy of seeking partnership with employers. This strategy was in turn rejected by some of these unions, who found that mutually beneficial partnerships are rare in a labour relations environment where power rests with employers.

In 1999, the NZCTU had a change of leadership. The newly elected president and secretary are committed to building organizing and campaigning among affiliates, who, they argue, should devote 20 per cent of their time and resources to organizing (Campbell, 2000). The new secretary (FinSec's former national secretary), and the new vice-president (the SFWU's national secretary), are both long-standing supporters of activist organizing. They will play an important role in transmitting organizing strategies throughout the union movement, drawing on their own experiences of implementing reforms. Their election signals a decisive shift in the Council's direction which differs markedly from that supported by previous leaders (see Oxenbridge, 1999b).

If other NZ unions *are* to shift to organizing, what can they, and unions more generally, learn from the SWU's experience? It is hoped that this study will alert unions to the potential pitfalls inherent in the reform process, thus allowing them to avoid them. Unions, for example, may wish to develop their own organizing model training programmes, tailored to local and industry circumstances, to avoid resistance to what might be seen as an American approach that bears little relevance to officials' specific circumstances.

Additionally, in the same way that union officials are increasingly becoming involved in organizational change processes in companies, as representatives of workers, union managers and leaders must also consider carefully the employment relations implications of organizational change within their organizations. Union human resources need to be actively managed throughout the change process, just as they do in any other organization. Issues related to matching staff competences to tasks, restructuring workloads, changing job descriptions and role definitions, and specialization of functions all came to the fore in the SWU during the process of change. Union managers must also use voluntary redundancies, attrition, and staff turnover strategically to enable them to promote and appoint new staff who 'fit' with the culture they are promoting. They must be aware of the need to build a critical mass of like-minded, organizing-focused staff, in order to build momentum and provide mutual support for one another.

In summary, two key themes emerge from the story of crisis and change in the SWU. The first is the importance of structural reform as a means of forcing change to accord priority to organizing. The second is the need for union leaders to understand and manage employment relations dynamics during the change process. Whether these factors come to the fore in other unions as they attempt change is for future research to determine.

Acknowledgements

The authors would like to thank Darien Fenton, National Secretary of the SFWU, for her help over the course of this research. This chapter draws and expands upon earlier analyses of the SFWU's efforts at reform published as Oxenbridge (1997) and Oxenbridge (1998).

Note

1. The SFWU is referred to as the SWU (Service Workers Union) throughout most of this chapter because the focus is on events occurring prior to the SWU's amalgamation with the United Food & Beverage Workers Union in 1997, when it became the SFWU.

References

Banks, A. (1991) 'The Power and Promise of Community Unionism', *Labour Research Review*, 18 (2): 17–31.

Campbell, G. (2000) 'Windows of Opportunity', *Listener*, 15 January 2000: 22–4.

Conrow, T. (1991) 'Contract Servicing from an Organizing Model', *Labor Research Review*, 17: 45–59.

Cooper, R. and Walton, C. (1996) 'Organizing and Recruitment in Australia: The Response of Unions to the Membership Crisis', paper presented to the AFL-CIO/ Cornell Union-University Research Conference on Union Organizing, Washington DC, 31 March–2 April 1996.

Crain, M. (1994) 'Gender and Union Organizing', *Industrial and Labor Relations Review*, 47 (2): 227–48.

Fletcher, B. and Hurd, R. (1996) 'Beyond the Organizing Model – The Transformation Process in Local Unions', preliminary draft of paper presented to the AFL-CIO/Cornell Union-University Research Conference on Union Organizing, 31 March–2 April 1996, Washington DC.

Fletcher, B. and Hurd, R. (1998) 'Beyond the Organizing Model: The Transformation Process in Local Unions', in Bronfenbrenner, K., Friedman, S., Hurd, R., Oswald, R. and Seeber, R. (eds) *Organizing to Win: New Research on Union Strategies*, Ithaca, NY: Cornell University Press.

Grabelsky, J. and Hurd, R. (1994) 'Reinventing an Organizing Union: Strategies for Change', *Proceedings of the Industrial Relations Research Association 46th Annual Meeting*, 3–5 January 1994, Boston, 95–104.

Harbridge, R. and Street, M. (1995) 'Labour Market Adjustment and Women in the Service Industry: A Survey', *New Zealand Journal of Industrial Relations*, 20 (1): 23–34.

Heery, E. (1996) 'The New New Unionism', in Beardwell, I. (ed.) *Contemporary Industrial Relations: A Critical Analysis*, Oxford: Oxford University Press.

Heery, E. and Kelly, J. (1994) 'Professional, Participative and Managerial Unionism: An Interpretation of Change in Trade Unions', *Work, Employment and Society*, 8 (1): 1–22.

Heery, E., Simms, M., Delbridge, R., Salmon, J., Simpson, D. and Stewart, P. (1999) 'Union Organising in Britain: A Survey of Policy and Practice', paper presented to the British Universities Industrial Relations Association Conference, 1–3 July 1999, Leicester.

Kelly, J. and Heery, E. (1994) *Working for the Union: British Trade Union Officers*, Cambridge: Cambridge University Press.

Oxenbridge, S. (1997) 'Organizing Strategies and Organizing Reform in New Zealand Service Sector Unions', *Labor Studies Journal*, 22 (3): 3–27.

Oxenbridge, S. (1998) 'Union Organising in New Zealand', *Union Research Bulletin*, 2, April 1998, pp. 12–15.

Oxenbridge, S. (1999a) 'The Individualisation of Employment Relations in New Zealand: Trends and Outcomes', in Deery, S. and Mitchell, R. (eds) *Individualisation and Union Exclusion in Employment Relations: An International Study*, Sydney: Federation Press.

Oxenbridge, S. (1999b) *Trade Union Organising among Low-Wage Service Workers: Lessons from America and New Zealand*, University of Cambridge ESRC Centre for Business Research Working Paper No. 160, March 2000.

8 THE DILEMMAS OF SOCIAL PARTNERSHIP AND UNION ORGANIZATION: QUESTIONS FOR BRITISH TRADE UNIONS

Peter Fairbrother and Paul Stewart

Introduction

An important debate is beginning to crystallize about the development and future direction of British trade unionism, in which the role of the Trades Union Congress (TUC) assumes particular significance. After two decades of union membership decline and marginalization, and a series of individual union initiatives to address these problems, in 1996 the TUC initiated a programme of change and development known as the New Unionism organizing campaign. Following discussions within the TUC and a consideration of developments elsewhere, the TUC focused on a choice between social partnership unionism (based on European experiences) and an organizing model (based on American-Australian experiences). The working out of this choice is of critical concern for the future of UK trade unionism.

In the debates about UK trade unionism, the terms 'organizing' and 'social partnership' have been used in contradictory and confusing ways. Taking 'organizing' first, the term has proved elastic. On the one hand, and most usually, it has referred to union strategies towards membership recruitment and retention whereas, on the other hand, it has been used to designate a model for the construction of more active and participative unionism, with an emphasis on representation and accountability. The latter emphasis has not been notable in public debates on the subject. Second, the notion of social partnership unionism is equally flexible in meaning. One meaning refers to a social democratic, European form of participation, with its focus on tripartite-type arrangements, whereas another restricts it to the promotion of employer-trade union agreements without involvement of government agency. On the latter point there is a second order of argument, with trade unions accepting such agreements as a means of securing representation and recognition, while a more radical goal would be to attempt to secure employer acceptance of union participation in key elements of company strategies. At this stage it is not clear how these various aspects of trade unionism fit together, although increasingly the emphasis by the TUC and many affiliate-unions has been on an accommodative form of unionism, rather than a trade unionism concerned with renewal and resistance (Fairbrother, 2000a). In this chapter we shall address the key dilemmas and contradictions this circumstance has thrown up, notably in the context of the ongoing tensions between social partnership and organizing.

The argument presented in the chapter is that the tensions indicated by these themes present the TUC and affiliated unions with a series of choices that signify the form and character of emerging trade unionism. There are six stages to the argument. First, a brief review of the problems faced by unions is presented. We consider the TUC and its affiliates follow this in the second section through a review and assessment of the recent history of British trade unionism, identifying the circumstances of the re-examination of trade unionism. Third, the details of what has been termed 'New Unionism' are presented, pointing to the way in which the TUC has drawn on models of organizing and partnership unionism elsewhere, in somewhat inchoate ways. Fourth, the notion of 'organizing' and the way it has been promoted by the TUC is considered. Fifth, the limitations of the partnership strategy and its relation to organizing are examined. Finally, the form and character of the trade unionism that is in the process of emerging are assessed.

British trade unionism in crisis

The current uncertainties facing British trade unions come after three decades of extensive economic restructuring and political realignment. During this period, membership levels fell, the workplace base of many unions was eroded and marginalized, and unions faced an ongoing recomposition of the workforce. From a peak of over 13.2 million union members in 1979, membership fell to 7.85 million by 1998 (Certification Officer, 2000: 20). Trade union density declined from a high of 55.8 per cent in 1979 to 29.5 per cent in 1999 (Waddington, 2000: 585). After seventeen consecutive years of decline, the longest on record, union membership increased in absolute terms by 105,000 in 1999, although union density declined marginally (Waddington, 2000; see also Certification Officer, 2000: 20). However, it is unclear whether this will be maintained in view of the extensive redundancies that have taken place in British manufacturing between 1999 and 2002.

Among the TUC unions the picture is no more encouraging. In the period 1974 to 1979, the TUC unions increased their membership by 1.5 million workers, but dropped from 8.4 million members in 1989 to 6.6 million in 1998 (TUC, 1998). A key feature of this decline was the increase in non-recognition and the decline of collective bargaining. Only a third of workers are union members and a minority of the workforce is covered by collective bargaining (McIlroy, 2000: 15). The enormity of these problems has been acknowledged by the TUC, which has highlighted the growing problem of non-union membership, even where workers are covered by recognition agreements (TUC, 1998: 57).

One feature of this decline was the recomposition of the economy, with a collapse of employment in heavy industry, where union density was traditionally high, and the growth of private services, where the figures remain correspondingly low. However, it is equally important to note that these figures mask the continuing relative strength of unionism in the public sector and its converse weakness in the private sector (Waddington, 1992a; Fairbrother, 1996, 2000b). Nonetheless, it is necessary to keep in mind that within the public sector and the privatized utilities there has been a marked unevenness in membership patterns. Specifically, the Association of Teachers and Lecturers (ATL) and the Communication Workers Union (CWU), both recorded aggregate membership increases of 15,000 (total membership 168,000) and 14,000 (total membership 287,000) respectively, and UNISON a decline of 28,000 (total membership 1,272 million members) (Certification Officer, 2000: 21). This unevenness suggests a progressive weakening of public sector unionism, related to the reforms to decentralize bargaining, the introduction of internal (quasi-market) competition, which continue to test the abilities of unions to respond effectively (Carter and Poynter, 1999; Waddington, 2000). In contrast, it would appear that the decline in the private sector is ongoing, at least for the time being, where there has been a continued decrease in union density, despite a relative upturn in the economy (TUC, 1998; Fairbrother, 2000b).

These difficulties are compounded by recent developments in the electoral sphere of politics and the relationships between unions and government. The historical acceptance of the separation of the representation of working-class interests into politics (Labour Party) and narrow economic interests (unions, including the TUC), meant the TUC leadership had neither the ideology nor legitimacy, let alone the capacity, to challenge the incoming Conservative government of 1979. Faced with hostility and increasingly restrictive legislation, the TUC leadership looked to the prospect of a re-elected Labour government (Fairbrother, 2000b; McIlroy, 2000).

With Labour's electoral victory in 1997, there was a difficult period of re-evaluation of the relationship between the government and trade unions. On the one hand, the trade unions had the appearance of success with the implementation of minimum wage legislation and the Fairness at Work legislation. To a limited extent there was recognition by the government of long-standing union aspirations, although in both cases the final outcome was less than they had campaigned for during the period of Conservative rule. On the other hand, it became very clear in the first few weeks of the Labour government that the unions no longer had the type of privileged position that they aspired to in the neo-corporatist 1970s (McIlroy, 1995). This distancing of the Labour Party from the trade union movement further encouraged the TUC leadership to pursue strategies focused on both membership recruitment and union-employer partnership, as part of an integrated solution to union problems. One hope was that at the very least a Labour government would now provide a positive legal framework in which unions could flourish (Fairbrother, 2000b).

The place of membership recruitment and retention

At the outset it is important to emphasize that the most prominent feature of the focus for reform to date has been on the conditions for increasing union membership and retention. This concern has a relatively long history and has taken place in the context of a major decline in membership over the last two decades and particularly during the 1980s (Waddington, 1992a). According to the Workplace Employment Relations Survey (Cully et al., 1999), by 1998 nearly half of all workplaces had no union members or presence and of all workplaces of between ten and 24 workers, only one in five had any trade union members. Shop stewards were still numerically important with just less than a quarter of a million across all sectors, but there were no stewards in over 25 per cent of all workplaces covered by collective agreements. More-over, with continuing decline consequent upon occupational change there has been a hollowing out of employment in sectors of traditional union strength, with white-collar workers now accounting for around 40 per cent of all unionized employees.

Added to this occupational and sectoral shift the UK labour market has witnessed a significant increase in non-standard employment (Dex and McCulloch, 1997; Heery, 1998a). The consequent implications of this development for recruitment and retention are slowly being addressed by key unions, notably in higher education, by the National Association of Teachers in Further and Higher Education (NATFHE), and in retail and distribution, by the Union of Shop, Distributive and Allied Workers (USDAW).

Yet the problem posed by a combination of the rise of non-standard employment and membership loss provides compelling evidence of the difficult position for trade unions more generally. Most significantly in retail where USDAW (involving the supermarket chain Tesco) and the Transport and General Workers Union (TGWU) (with the supermarket chain, Sainsbury) have secured a variety of forms of collective agreements, these unions face substantial membership turnover, which for USDAW alone stands at around 20,000 per annum. In a different area of employment, the large public sector union UNISON, which had a membership goal of 1,500,000 for the year 2000 (on a membership base of 1,266,000 in 1999) on its own estimate was losing around 160,000 members a year.

Union dilemmas

Despite the bleak prospect of lower union density and representation, it is important to remember that unions have maintained a significant presence amongst the major private sector employers. More significantly, unions have started to utilize the changed climate following the election of the Labour government in 1997 to seek union recognition in previously unrecognized areas or where collective bargaining is absent. Such agreements have been sought in the chemical sector, with companies such as British Petroleum, Exxon, and Tioxide. They are also being sought in the so-called new economy, in the call-centre sector, for example Cable and Wireless and Cellnet, part owned by British Telecom. In the case of retailers, such as Marks and Spencer plc, recognition has long been the goal of USDAW and with the new legislation, the Employment Relations Act 1999 (which came into force in June 2000) a legal vehicle has been provided to help secure this objective. This company has long pursued a paternalist-unitarist agenda but with recent sector restructuring, including the turmoil of the company's collapse of market share, there may be an opportunity for USDAW to secure recognition (see Turnbull and Wass 1998 for an assessment of the contradictions on retail management's pursuit of employment 'care' in an era of competitive restructuring).

Of particular concern for many unions has been low unionization rates amongst young people. First, the decline in the recruitment levels of young workers by the end of the 1990s was drastic, with 'only one in five of those aged between 20 and 29 ... a union member' by the end of the 1990s

(Income Data Services, 1999: 3). In contrast, the proportion of union members who are women is increasing, reflecting changing patterns of employment as well as increased openness on the part of male focused and dominated unions. By the 1990s more than 35 per cent of TUC union membership were women, with the female membership of the largest union, UNISON, at 65 per cent. More than half the members in another twelve were women. However, there is still a gap between male and female union density (38 per cent and 31 per cent respectively).

Membership rates apart, what is more telling is the relatively low level of female representation within unions. Despite years of advocating positive encouragement of female members, and the imposition of *de facto* quotas in some unions, such as UNISON, the representation of women, particularly at the senior levels, remains distressingly low. Of the ten unions with the largest female membership in 1991, only Manufacturing Science and Finance (MSF) had the same percentage of women members on the national executive and as full-time officers as the percentage of female members in the union; the remainder were lower in both categories (McIlroy, 1995: 178).

Of equal importance is the position of black workers in trade unions. Black workers have a higher union density than white workers, with those of an Afro-Caribbean background having the highest density of any social group (mid-40 per cent). This pattern of union membership is against a background where many unions had adopted exclusionary policies in some cases formally and certainly informally until at least the 1970s. Historically, black workers were employed in low-paid and unskilled jobs, often grouped in particular industries, such as foundry work and notably the public sector. Building on an emergent black consciousness and anti-racist campaigns during this period, union policy began to shift, and in the 1980s the TUC abandoned its colour-blind ('we are all workers') policy and sought to advocate more progressive policies (McIlroy, 1995: 36). In 1994, the TUC designated three seats on the General Council for black and ethnic minority trade unionists (McIlroy, 1995: 179). However, it remains the case that very few black members hold formal officer positions in unions, at local levels and nationally, although there are exceptions to this pattern, particularly in the public sector.

Thus the pattern of union membership is changing in decisive ways, albeit slowly. The problem is that unions have found it difficult to address these issues in a clear-cut and effective manner. With the beginnings of a distancing between the Labour Party and trade unions, individual unions began to look to their own forms of organization and practice (Fairbrother, 2000b). In particular, they sought to reverse falling membership levels, both within particular trade unions as well as across the unionized workforce as a whole (Undy *et al.*, 1996). Major unions, such as the TGWU and the General, Municipal and Boilermakers (GMB) embarked on focused recruitment campaigns. Organizational rationalization was also seen as an appropriate response and there have been a series of mergers involving major unions within the Civil Service, the public sector more generally and manufacturing, aimed at relaying the foundation of unionism in these sectors on a firmer basis (Waddington, 1992b). However, the reality of many of these mergers fell far short of the promises (Carter, 1991). But they do illustrate the scale of the problems faced and the outer limit of the package of measures adopted to deal with the problems of the 1980s and 1990s.

The legacy of the 1980s: from new realism to new unionism

The current dilemmas of the TUC and affiliated unions have their origins in the early 1980s. Then the TUC faced a series of problems, when it was first systematically excluded from the tripartite bodies of the 1970s and when trade unions faced severe membership decline. The TUC commissioned a series of reviews in which the dominant argument was that unions were unlikely to regain the prominence they had in the 1970s, as individual unions, nor would the TUC be able to reassume the role of influential representative of the trade union movement as a whole. In these circumstances it was argued that the most promising future lay in the elaboration of service model unionism. The evolution of the policy towards service model unionism was at first slow to develop. The initial analysis was to develop a programme of criticism, campaigning and support for a return to the co-operative relations between union leaderships and past Conservative governments (McIlroy, 1995: 209). By 1983 it had become apparent that this approach was failing and that a more proactive approach was necessary, which became known as 'New Realism' (TUC, 1984). The new emphasis was one of acknowledging that the unions individually and the TUC centrally were pressure groups, whose leaderships would deal pragmatically with any government in office. Such a stance was predicated on the view that unions represent and organize in the industrial arena, and that there is a self-limiting ordinance against union activity on political matters (TUC, 1984: 10, para. 28). Although the government turned down the argument for cooperation and conciliation, the sentiments expressed in the document formed part of the leitmotiv for policy development.

Concurrently, there were the beginnings of attempts amongst some affiliated unions to encourage a more activist strategy in relation to membership organization and representation. On the one hand, the formerly accommodative public sector unions, such as local government workers, civil servants and nurses, continued to develop their organizational and activist base (Fairbrother, 1989). Of more immediate note, the National Union of Mineworkers (NUM) during the early 1980s challenged the more cooperative relations advocated by the TUC and the majority of affiliated unions (McIlroy, 1995: 214–15). The 1984–5 NUM strike was part of an attempt to promote a more critical and active approach in dealing with industrial and political relations. However, defeat discredited national strikes as a way of challenging the Conservative governments of the day. Even so, public sector unions continued to reorganize and promote workplace-based forms of action (Fairbrother, 1989). Nonetheless, this uneven and contested action did not result in a shift in the focus of the TUC.

Against a backdrop of further deteriorating employment trends and membership decline, and considerable infighting amongst unions about the appropriate strategies to be pursued, the TUC leadership established a Special Review Committee in 1987 (McIlroy, 1995: 215–19). The thrust of the reports was to encourage and develop recruitment strategies, as well as addressing the problems of union membership retention (TUC, 1988a, 1988b, 1989). During the first part of the 1990s, the TUC began to consider the question of organization, in particular focusing on representation and recognition, emphasizing formal recognition of union representatives, supported by law, including European law and directives (TUC, 1991; 1995: 5).

These reports were very much part of the preparation for a relaunch of the TUC as a modernized and improved trade union centre. The aim was to reposition the TUC in relation to its affiliates, so that they could be served by more effective and focused campaigns. The emphasis on service model unionism was coupled with more effective lobbying and pressure group approaches to employers, governments and the Labour Party. This shift partly coincided with the changes taking place in the Labour Party and the advent of New Labour.

The emergence of 'new unionism'

The New Unionism Task Group was established in 1996 to research and make recommendations for recasting the TUC and its affiliates under the label of New Unionism (TUC, 1996a, 1996b, 1996c, 1996d). It drew conscious parallels with the New Unionism of the late nineteenth century that witnessed extensive development in trade union membership and organization amongst unskilled workers. This focus was seen as an example of how British unions in the past had been able to replenish their numbers by reaching out to workers formerly excluded from the core membership areas, the relatively secure and well-organized workers. As in the late nineteenth century, the argument is that unions should now address the concerns of excluded, marginalized, and unorganized workers, mostly in forms of non-standard employment. The focus should be on membership recruitment and retention, extending and developing the representational base within unions, and advocating social partnership agreements and arrangements (TUC, 1997a, 1999). Reference was made to part-time workers, women (many of whom are employed part-time) and young workers (Heery, 1998a).

There were three aspects to the relaunch of the TUC. First, the representative structure of the TUC was reorganized and the policy committee arrangements overhauled. A small Executive Committee was established, issue-based Task Groups set up, and other committees, such as the Women's and Race Committee, refocused. As part of this reform the TUC introduced a more flexible department structure, emphasizing project work and promoting managerial forms of organization and operation. Second, the TUC presented itself as the spokesperson of the employees and workers broadly defined, in unions or as non-union members. Accompanying this broad definition of the TUC constituency there has been a more explicit recognition of its social diversity and variation, particularly with reference to the young and women. Third, there has been a distinctive emphasis on what the TUC defined as union organizing, especially with reference to recruitment and retention (Heery, 1998b: 351–66).

The historical context for this programme is crucial. It was an attempt to break from the organizational and policy inertia of the 1980s and 1990s. McIlroy (1995) has characterized the earlier period as one of political minimalism that accommodated Conservative anti-union legislation, 'sweetheart' agreements and massive defeats of unions, including both the print workers and mineworkers. Part consequence, part enabling, of the wider neo-liberal project on labour market reform, the TUC was increasingly marginalized by confident Conservative governments during this period. The restraints placed by legislation (outlawing secondary action and restricting the *de jure* power of picketing) upon pre-existing forms of labour movement activity presented significant obstacles to the establishment of any kind of broad-based organizing strategy and solidarity campaigning. Nonetheless, the TUC still counselled that things would be different with the return of a Labour government.

The focus of the Task Group was on strengthening existing areas of membership as well as extending the representational basis into currently unorganized or lowly organized areas of employment. Particular reference was made to the need to organize part-time workers, women and young workers. In developing the New Unionism programme, there was conscious reference to and modelling on exemplary trade union movements, elsewhere in the world. Specifically, reference was made to the USA, Australia and the Netherlands, each of which had gone through a process of refocusing and rebuilding their trade union movements (TUC 1996b, 1996c, 1996d). The view was that 'many of the training and organizing techniques used are transferable and adaptable to the UK' (TUC, 1997b: 41).

In elaborating this reform programme, the TUC faced two choices. On the one hand, it looked east to Europe, and particularly the Netherlands, at models of social partnership, on campaigns to recruit part-time workers and women workers (Heery, 1998a: 357, 1998b: 344). Such a focus could also be expressed in social partnerships with employers and governments to secure a raft of employment rights, depending on a 'revived social democracy' (Heery, 1998b: 355). On the other hand, the TUC looked west and south, to Australia and the USA, at the organizing activity, especially on recruitment and retention, taking place in those countries. Deciding between the two strategies lies at the heart of the relaunch, although as noted by Heery this is not a choice that will be made in a vacuum; it will be in the context of profound political and economic constraints and competing views about trade unionism (Kelly, 1997).

A partial view of organizing

While the tensions between social partnership and organizing define the New Unionism project, a second order concern has been to promote a view of organizing acceptable to the affiliate unions. The problem has been that the advocacy of a more participative and relevant mode of representation touches on the internal affairs of affiliate unions, not the province of the TUC. In this respect the question for the TUC has been to try to put flesh on the rhetoric of restructuring for reorganizing and recruitment in ways that elicit the support of affiliate unions.

Central to the New Unionism agenda has been the development of the Organizing Academy. (For details, see Heery *et al.*, 1999.) The General Council of the TUC set out its agenda in terms of an orientation towards organizing rather than servicing:

- promote organizing as the top priority and build an organizing culture;
- boost investment of resources – people and money – into organizing and strengthen lay organization;
- help unions strengthen their existing bases and break into new jobs and industries and win recognition rights;
- sharpen unions' appeal to new workers, including women and youth and those on non-standard contracts employed in poor working conditions (TUC, 1997b: 39).

While the Organizing Academy is but one element of the New Unionism agenda the fate of the latter can nevertheless be seen to be closely associated with the strategies, prognoses and outcomes of the Academy. The TUC's New Unionism Task Group had high hopes for the Academy. The view was that the Organizing Academy would provide the vehicle to train and equip organizers with the skills and strategies to trigger a broader shift towards an 'organizing culture'. By recruiting 'new' workers – especially women and young people – there would be an injection of fresh ideas and impetus into the trade union movement (TUCs, 1997b: 44).

The Academy began in January 1998 with a cohort of 36 trainees out of 4000 applicants (in the second year, 1999, a second group of 33 entered the Academy). The initial group of participating unions sponsored between one and six trainees. These 16 sponsoring unions included some of the largest, the Amalgamated Engineering and Electrical Union (AEEU) and UNISON, as well as some of the most beleaguered, the Iron and Steel Trades Confederation (ISTC), National Union of Knitwear, Footwear and Apparel Trades (KFAT) and Society of Telecom Executives (STE – subsequently Connect: The Union for Professionals in Communications).

The objectives behind the Organizing Academy are:

- the creation of lead organizers across the labour movement sponsored by the TUC and participating unions;
- arrangements for the recruitment, coaching, mentoring and placement with unions of mainly young dedicated organizers – to become a permanent institutional resource for union organizing;
- to draw together all involved with the 'centre and participating unions in shaping, overseeing, managing and delivering the programme' (TUC, 1997b: 44);
- create an institutional (union organizing) response to employer hostility;
- refocus union officers and officials to become organizer-recruiters (TUC, 1997b: 38–45).

Although the evidence of the Academy's success in transforming trade union cultures is limited, research suggests that there are difficulties deriving from tensions inherent within the New Unionism project (Simms, 1999). Simms (2000: 11–12) estimates that trainees have successfully recruited 5500 recruitees directly (plus 11,000 via campaigns involving trainees) in Year One and 12,000 (plus 18,000 via campaigns involving trainees) the following year. Although the TUC has set an annual target of half a million new members, these figures represent an important achievement against the background of nearly two decades of membership decline. On recognition agreements the evidence is more mixed. Trainees were involved in 37 successful initiatives but the labour movement as a whole only achieved 75 for 1999 (Heery *et al.*, 2000: 19–20).

In view of this limited success, it could be argued that the development of the New Unionism agenda requires spreading the organizing ethos to workplace organization and subsequent branch recruitment initiatives and campaigns (Heery *et al.*, 2000: 19–20). Yet while the broader question of diffusion of new organizing techniques may not be so difficult to identify in terms of reinforcing mechanisms drawing in those above the level of the trainee, the success of involving workplace activists is somewhat more difficult to ascertain. Certainly, there is considerable unevenness in the success of organizing at the workplace level, despite the Academy now having obtained sufficient support to continue into the immediate future (Heery *et al.*, 2000: 19–20).

There is, however, evidence of a scepticism among some unions about the Academy. According to the New Unionism Research Project at Cardiff Business School, although a majority of sponsoring unions supports the establishment of the Academy, the results should be interpreted with some caution. A survey of national officers indicated that, while the Academy was important in promoting recruitment, a majority thought the Academy had not been important in promoting organizing in their union (New Unionism Research Project, 1998, No. 3: 11). Moreover, in respect of trainees' experiences of the training objectives, Simms (2000) comparative survey of 26 Year Two Academy entrants and the first cohort identifies a critical constituency of trainees where Academy sponsoring unions, 'emphasize employer-supported recruitment and play down an organizing agenda' (p. 15). Furthermore, 'there is a division between the training and aspiration of a portion of trainees and their everyday experience as recruiters within their sponsoring unions' (p. 15).

Thus, despite the concerns of some within the TUC that the success of trade unionism in Britain depends upon the strategic commitments of those few large and leading unions to the 'organizing culture', including the Academy, evidence of a sea change is mixed (Heery *et al.*, 1999). Less optimistically, a number of affiliates have withdrawn their sponsorship of the Academy and it remains to be seen whether this represents a permanent or temporary divorce from the TUC's prescriptive approach to organizing. These unions include the AEEU, CWU, Institution of Professionals, Managers and Specialists (IPMS), Management and Professional Officers Union (MPO), MSF (includes Communication Managers Union), whose withdrawal reflects both disappointment at outcomes (benefits of participation in terms of costs and a view that there has been an insufficient increase in membership) as well as disagreements over the nature of the Academy and the role of the trainee organizers more generally.

The limitations of partnership

The other side of the TUC strategy for reform has been the promotion of social partnership as a means of securing union recognition and the capacity to organize. This strategy has as its central leitmotiv the aim of working with 'good' employers while cajoling the 'bad' into recognition agreements. Central to this objective has been the Employment Relations Act 1999, which provides a legal framework for securing union recognition (formal acknowledgement of the right of unions to recruit members and negotiate on their behalf). This legislation plus the statutory minimum wage represent a partial achievement of union aspirations relating to worker and trade union rights, but they are less than had been hoped for prior to the election of the Labour government. As a result, there is a tendency to view government as the legal midwife rather than the central figure in the social partnership agenda.

In 2001, the TUC added another dimension to its reform programme with the establishment of the Partnership Institute. Based on research in 1997, which resulted in the 'TUC Partnership Principles' (www.tuc.org.uk), the aim of the Institute is to provide research information on partnership arrangements, training programmes for trade unionists on partnership agreements, and to promote what is seen by the TUC as best practice on these questions. The background to the Institute was recognition within the TUC that there was a powerful push for such agreements among a number of trade unions. While not central to the relaunch of the TUC it nonetheless points to some of the central tensions within the TUC about the way forward. The Institute has a director and 26 'consultants' and began life working with five organizations covering health, electronics, food and finance (see TUC, 2001).

In one recent assessment of the accomplishments of unions in the recent period, it was noted: 'Unions have made some inroads in areas that until recently have been virtually impenetrable' (*Labour Research*, September 1999: 11). The means of achieving this success has been via recognition agreements as part of a social partnership programme (TUC, 1999). Recognition agreements have been maintained at Rover (now Rover-MG and BMW), Ford, British Aerospace and British Telecom – the traditional sectors – and secured in retail, notably the supermarket chains Tesco, Somerfield and Morrison. One key feature of these efforts has been to locate them as part of the emergent social partnership ethos promoted by the TUC. These agreements are claimed to be indicative of a more positive approach by many employers, the 'good employer', towards trade unions. As leading business partners themselves highlight, this allows for what one described as the development of 'long-standing, constructive relationships with its trade unions' (cited in *Labour Research*, September 1999: 11).

A second aspect to the social partnership strategy, articulated within the recently established Partnership Institute, has been to secure a basis for union cooperation and involvement in managerial strategies of change (TUC, 1999, 2001). The civil service unions, for example, in securing a partnership agreement as part of the modernizing strategy, provide a clear example of this approach by the New Labour government. This Agreement, between the Cabinet Office, Public and Commercial Services Union (PCS), IPMS, and the Association of First Division Civil Servants (FDA), and the Council of Civil Service Unions (CSSU) is seen as the means to achieve 'continuous improvement' in the civil service, on work organization, increased use of information technology, and the delivery and provision of public services (PCS, n.d.).

The emphasis amongst affiliate unions has been on organizing as recruitment and the negotiation of social partnership agreements, but as a means of embedding unions within the emergent economy, there are relatively few examples of unions wholeheartedly embracing the organizing agenda. A notable exemplar is the MSF which launched its own 'Organising Works' campaign in 1997. Carter (2000; see also Chapter 9) in a review of this programme distinguishes the variable experience of MSF's 'Organising Works', with reference to two National Health Service branches. He highlights the problematical implementation of new organizing initiatives and the crucial importance of local leadership and organization in the articulation of the national policy portfolio. The study links the tension between servicing, organizing and recruitment to the uneven practice of officers in facilitating membership involvement in national policy initiatives and illustrates the manner in which the perception of policy can be critical to its success. Where local officers interpret organizing initiatives as dependent on membership involvement one may glean some measure of success (Carter, 2000: 131).

Concurrently, another union, the ISTC has begun experimenting with what has been termed 'community unionism' (ISTC, 1999). Against the backdrop of declining steel work employment and the continued degradation of steel communities, the ISTC has begun to explore the boundaries of unionism, focusing on the provision of services for ex-steel workers and recruitment in non-unionized areas of a wide range of workers, including substantial numbers of young male and female workers, in such areas as computer manufacture and assembly, plastics manufacture, food supply, employment agencies and call centres (ISTC, 1999: 18–21). While this is a notable achievement, the dilemma for the union is not just to present itself as a community union, but also to ensure systems of representation for these new and different members.

The diversity in experience and approach to organizing and social partnership by unions raises questions about the wider New Unionism agenda within which the Organizing Academy is located. Recently Danford *et al.* (2002) have studied the variants in 'partnership and organizing strategies' (p. 4) taken up by National Health Service and local government workplace unions in the south-west of England. The distinctive operationalization of strategies by officers in the GMB and MSF has a direct bearing on the outcome of 'mobilizing around critical incidents' (p. 21) and it introduces the broader theme of social partnership within which New Unionism can be anchored. Many of the tensions and operational difficulties associated with the trajectory of the Academy may in part be linked to how union officers at national, local and workplace level perceive the role of organizing and recruitment in relation to union development and workplace employment relations. An echo of these dilemmas can be found in Carter's recent diagnosis of the organization and operation of MSF (2000). More broadly, these analyses suggest an uneasy tension within the TUC's promotion of a social partnership agenda and its commitment to an organizing strategy.

Thus there are persistent stresses and contradictions (between organizing and partnership) in the broader New Unionism agenda. In relation to institutional reform within the TUC, the idea is that the Academy would be a key public flagship of the New Unionism with a portfolio of interlinked activities generated by the soon-to-be-active trainee organizers who would proselytize the wider project while promoting a new 'organizing culture'. Complementing this organizational arrangement, the Partnership Institute provides an alternative focus involving affiliated trade unions. Ironically, this initiative signifies the institutionalization of the tension between organizing on the one hand and partnership on the other hand. However, if the leading theme of the New Unionism has been to turn around decades of decline the immediate results have been somewhat mixed at best and at worst unpropitious.

Heery (1999) argues that the Academy is premised on bridging the gap between grassroots activity and nationally led partnership agreements. In theory, as Heery has pointed out, these can conflict but as he suggests, this need not necessarily be resolved in a pessimistic scenario. Rather than privileging a radical dynamic, clearly present in one reading of what he terms 'movement unionism', the careful 'sequencing' of 'partnership' and 'movement' can allow for employer and union reciprocity. Thus, 'Partnership is built from below and thus can institutionalize the collective power of workers, rather than being offered as an alternative to that power' (1999: 20). In making explicit the strategy of 'organizing-for-partnership' in this way, the potential bifurcation, inherent in attempts either to inject a radical agenda to organizing or a partnership for partnership's sake approach, is resolved in favour of a more radical version of social partnership unionism. However, the danger remains that 'movement' will be subordinate to 'partnership' since it is 'partnership; that is the object of union activity in this scenario, rather than organizing *per se*.

Assessment

It is against this complex of developments that the prospects for trade unionism in the UK are being worked out. There are three features to consider. First, a number of unions have begun to reorganize and re-examine themselves in the light of membership decline and uncertainties about recruitment. Such developments have taken place against the backdrop of long-term membership decline and with the emergence of significant areas of non-union membership mostly, though not only, in the private sector. Second, in addressing these dilemmas, some union leaderships have begun to advocate the advantages of social partnership. More generally it can be argued that there has been an advocacy from the TUC of a managerial unionism together with centralized forms of union organization and activity as a condition for participation in the social partnership experiments (Heery and Kelly, 1994; Heery, 1996; Ackers, 1995 and Smith, 1995). Third, in contrast, the question of union organization has come to the fore as the basis for any union revival.

The dilemma for the TUC is that the claims for organizing and partnership derive from different social and political contexts, which are seen as models for revival and renewal. The location of organizing in the USA has a specifically combative history quite at odds with the way it is envisaged by the TUC. Indeed, much of what goes by the way of organizing against recalcitrant employers in the USA does not dovetail with the carefully orchestrated approach of the TUC (Carter *et al.*, 2000). This caution is most notable where large campaigns have been developed around union and community opposition to corporate strategies involving plant closures. Certainly, organizing for union growth and renewal in the US (and Canadian) contexts is quite different from the idea of union organizing for renewal in the British context.

Whilst it could fairly be argued that the TUC saw social partnership as part of a wish list to propose to the New Labour government, the reality of Labour in power has highlighted the limited scope for the possibility of a social democratic imperative in the current period. Part of the problem for the TUC is that there is considerable evidence that the Labour government has little intention of accepting anything other than a limited agenda of industrial citizenship. Moreover, it could be argued that this Labour government position undermines the particular vision of social partnership at the heart of New Unionism.

Thus, there is a tension between the emphasis on organization and the focus on social partnership. In general, the focus on social partnership presupposes effective organization, otherwise partnership relations are unequal and the union becomes a supplicant rather than an active partner. The solution for many is the promotion of a managerialist unionism, centralized and professional, as necessary to secure the benefits of partnership while maintaining the integrity of the union. In this perspective, the future for unions is clear; it emphasizes the importance of centralized, effective union organization, achieving a fruitful and productive balance between active workplace unionism and forward-thinking centralized leaderships (arguably Heery and Kelly, 1994; McIlroy, 1997; Terry, 1996). In contrast, a participative form of unionism is more likely to emphasize autonomy and independence rather than cooperation and accommodation (Fairbrother, 2000b). In either case the question at stake is the form of unionism that is promoted by the TUC and within unions.

The way in which unions will resolve this tension is unclear, with some arguing for the combination of 'movement' (that is organizing) unionism and partnership (Heery, 1999) and others emphasizing the salience of an organizing strategy in its own right (Fairbrother 2000a, 2000b; McIlroy, 2000). The critical issue confronting advocates of a relation between organizing and social partnership is that the arguments presuppose a set of state relations that are not evident in the UK. In the case of corporatist models evident in social democratic Europe the assumption is that a proactive government creates the conditions for an institutionalized accommodation between workers and management, in the form of works councils and related arrangements (Martinez Lucio and Stuart, 2000). Such state regulation is non-existent in the UK and thus one of the conditions for social partnership is absent. More than this, the argument for 'movement' unionism presupposes that effective unionism provides the foundation for social partnership. However, the weakness in this account is that it overlooks the character of relations between collective worker organization and employers, based on the alienated relation between labour and capital. In such circumstances, an organizing unionism should be seen as necessarily operating *in* and *against* the employment relationship.

These outcomes leave the New Unionism project with its heady optimism from the days of a prospective Labour Party victory, drawing on US 'best practice' and European social democratic collectivism, somewhat becalmed. Whether this inertia suggests that centralism is the antidote to the new tepid political environment remains to be seen. Certainly, the form of unionism that has long prevailed in this country is at a crossroads (Williams, 1997; Fairbrother, 2000b). It may be that the shop steward form of engineering and manufacturing unionism, restricted to immediate workplace concerns, is no longer a model of effective and participative unionism. However, there remains the possibility that this form of union representation can be both innovative and combative around the politics of production, extending to the revival of industry-specific union coordinating groups and the like (see Danford and Upchurch, 1999 on the durability of shop-floor power in the engineering industry). For sure, unions elsewhere, particularly in the public sector and the privatized utilities, have begun to reorganize in complementary ways, placing on the agenda, yet again, the position of unions in the polity. These previously centralized and often acquiescent unions have, as much as those in manufacturing, continued to face a dramatic restructuring of social relations of production and service provision. In such circumstances, union groups have begun to reorganize. Thus, in the public and private sectors, trade unions face very particular challenges that place the union form of organization at the forefront of contemporary class struggle.

Acknowledgement

We wish to thank Bob Carter for advice on the argument and Steve Craig (NATFHE) for providing us with some critical source material in the preparation of this chapter.

References

Ackers, P. (1995) 'Change in Trade Unions since 1995: A Response to Heery and Kelly', *Work, Employment and Society*, 9 (1): 147–54.

Carter, B. (1991) 'Politics and Process in the Making of MSF', *Capital and Class*, 45: 35–71.

Carter, B. (2000) 'Adoption of the Organizing Model in British Trade Unions: Some Evidence from MSF', *Work, Employment and Society*, 14 (1): 117–36

Carter, B. and Poynter, G. (1999) 'Unions in a Changing Climate: MSF and UNISON Experiences in the New Public Sector', *Industrial Relations Journal*, 30 (5): 499–513.

Carter, R., Fairbrother, P., Sherman, R. and Voss, K. (2002) 'Made in the USA: The TUC, the Organizing Model and the Limits of Transferability', *Work and Occupations*, in press.

Certification Officer (2000) *Annual Report of the Certification Officer 1999–2000*, London: Certification Office for Trade Unions and Employers' Associations.

Cully, M., Woodland, S., O'Reilly, A. and Dix, J. (1999) *Britain at Work: As Depicted by the 1998 Workplace Employee Relations Survey*, London: Routledge.

Danford, A., Richardson, M. and Upchurch, M. (2002) '"New Unionism", Organizing and Partnership: A Comparative Analysis of Union Renewal Strategies in the Public Sector', *Capital and Class*, 76: 1–27.

Danford, A. and Upchurch, M. (1999) 'Trade Union Mobilisation at the Workplace Level: Three Sectoral Case Studies in the South West of England', *Working Paper*, Employment Studies Research Unit, University of the West of England.

Dex, S. and McCulluch, A. (1997) *Flexible Employment: The Future of Britain's Jobs*, Basingstoke: Macmillan.

Fairbrother, P. (1989) 'State Workers: Class Position and Collective Action', in Duncan, G. (ed.) *Democracy and the Capitalist State*, Cambridge: Cambridge University Press, pp. 187–213.

Fairbrother, P. (1996) 'Workplace Trade Unionism in the State Sector', in Ackers, P., Smith, P. and Smith, C. (eds) *The New Workplace and Trade Unionism*, London: Routledge, pp. 110–49.

Fairbrother, P. (2000a) *Trade Unions at the Crossroads*, London: Mansell.

Fairbrother, P. (2000b) 'British Trade Unions Facing the Future', *Capital and Class*, 71: 47–78.

Heery, E. (1996) 'The New New Unionism', in Bearwell, I. (ed.) *Contemporary Industrial Relations: A Critical Analysis*, Oxford: Oxford University Press, pp. 175–202.

Heery, E. (1998a) 'Campaigning for Part-time Workers', *Work, Employment and Society*, 12 (2): 351–66.

Heery, E. (1998b) 'The Relaunch of the Trades Union Congress', *British Journal of Industrial Relations*, 36 (3): 339–60.

Heery, E. (1999) 'Social Movement or Social Partner? Strategies for the Revitalisation of British Trade Unionism', European Community Studies Association Annual Conference, 2–6 June, Pittsburgh.

Heery, E., Delbridge, R., Salmon, J., Simms, M., Simpson, D. and Stewart, P. (1999) *The Organizing Academy Summary Report*, Cardiff: New Unionism Research Project, Cardiff Business School, Cardiff University.

Heery, E. and Kelly, J. (1994) 'Professional, Participative and Managerial Unionism: An Interpretation of Change in Trade Unions', *Work, Employment and Society*, 8 (1): 1–22.

Heery, E., Simms, M., Delbridge, R., Salmon, J. and Simpson, D. (2000) *The Organizing Academy: An Assessment*, Cardiff: New Unionism Research Project, Cardiff Business School, Cardiff University.

Income Data Services (1999) 'New Unionism', *IDS Focus*, 91 (Autumn): 3–14.

Iron and Steel Trades Confederation [ISTC] (1999) *ISTC Today: The Free Magazine for ISTC Members and Their Families*, Issue 1.

Kelly, J. (1997) 'Challenges to Unions in Britain and Europe', *Work, Employment and Society*, 11 (2): 373–6.

Labour Research (1999) 'Big Business: Unions Make Inroads', *Labour Research*, September 1999, pp. 11–13.

Martinez-Lucio, M. and Stuart, M. (2000) *Swimming against the Tide: Social Partnership, Mutual Gains and the Renewal of 'Tired' HRM*, Leeds: Centre for Industrial Relations and Human Resource Management. Discussion Paper Series, IH00/03 University of Leeds.

McIlroy, J. (1995) *Trade Unions in Britain Today*, second edition, Manchester: Manchester University Press.

McIlroy, J. (1997) 'Still under Siege: British Trade Unions at the Turn of the Century', *Historical Studies in Industrial Relations*, 3 (March): 93–122.

McIlroy, J. (2000) 'New Labour, New Unions, New Left', *Capital and Class*, 71: 11–45.

New Unionism Project (1998) No. 3, Trade Union Research Unit, Cardiff University.

PCS (n.d.) *Partnership Working in the Civil Service: An Agreement between PCS, IPMS, FDA, the CCSU and the Cabinet Office*, London: Centurion Press.

Simms, M. (1999) *New Unionism Research Bulletin*, No. 6, New Unionism Research Project, Cardiff Business School, Cardiff University.

Simms, M. (2000) *New Unionism Research Bulletin*, No. 7, New Unionism Research Project, Cardiff Business School, Cardiff University.

Smith, P. (1995) 'Change in British Trade Unions since 1995: A Response to Heery and Kelly', *Work, Employment and Society*, 9 (1): 137–46.

Terry, M. (1996) 'Negotiating the Government of Unison: Union Democracy in Theory and Practice', *British Journal of Industrial Relations*, 20 (1): 1–19.

Trades Union Congress (1984) *TUC Strategy*, London: Trades Union Congress.

Trades Union Congress (1988a) *Meeting the Challenge: First Report of the Special Review Body*, London: Trades Union Congress.

Trades Union Congress (1988b) *Services for Union Members: Special Review Body Report on Services*, London: Trades Union Congress.

Trades Union Congress (1989) *Organizing for the 1990s: The SRBs Second Report*, London: Trades Union Congress.

Trades Union Congress (1991) *Towards 2000*, London: Trades Union Congress.

Trades Union Congress (1995) *Representation at Work: A TUC Consultative Document*, London: Trades Union Congress.

Trades Union Congress (1996a) *New Unionism: Organising for Growth. New Unionism: A Message from John Monks*, London: Trades Union Congress.

Trades Union Congress (1996b) *New Unionism: Organising for Growth. Organisers with Attitude: The USA Experience*, London: Trades Union Congress.

Trades Union Congress (1996c) *New Unionism: Organising for Growth. The Wisdom of Oz: The Australian Experience*, London: Trades Union Congress.

Trades Union Congress (1996d) *New Unionism: Organising for Growth. Going Dutch: The Netherlands Experience*, London: Trades Union Congress.

Trades Union Congress (1997a) *Facing the Future*, London: Trades Union Congress.

Trades Union Congress (1997b) *General Council Report: Next Steps for the New Unionism*, London: Trades Union Congress.

Trades Union Congress (1998) *Congress 1998 – General Council Report*, London: Trades Union Congress.

Trades Union Congress (1999) *Partners for Progress: New Unionism in the Workplace*, London: Trades Union Congress.

Trades Union Congress (2001) *Winning at Work*, London: Trades Union Congress.

Turnbull, P. and Wass, V. (1998) 'Marksist Management: Sophisticated Human Resource Relations in a High Street Retail Store', *Industrial Relations Journal*, 29 (2): 98–111.

Undy, R., Fosh, P., Morris, H., Smith, P. and Martin, R. (1996) *Managing the Unions: The Impact of Legislation on Trade Unions Behaviour*, Oxford: Clarendon Press.

Waddington, J. (1992a) 'Trade Union Membership in Britain, 1980–1987: Unemployment and Restructuring', *British Journal of Industrial Relations*, 30 (2): 287–328.

Waddington, J. (1992b) 'Restructuring Representation: Trade Union Mergers 1980–1988', in D. Cox (ed.) *Facing the Future: Issues for Adult Education*, Nottingham: University of Nottingham, Department of Adult Education in association with The Society of Industrial Tutors.

Waddington, J. (2000) 'United Kingdom: Recovering from the Neo-Liberal Assault', in J. Waddington and R. Hoffmann (eds) *Trade Unions in Europe: Facing Challenges and Searching for Solutions*, Brussels: European Trade Union Institute, pp. 575–626.

Williams, S. (1997) 'The Nature of Some Recent Trade Union Modernization Policies in the UK', *British Journal of Industrial Relations*, 35 (4): 495–514.

9 RHETORIC AND REALITY: THE ADOPTION OF THE ORGANIZING MODEL IN MANUFACTURING, SCIENCE AND FINANCE

Bob Carter

Introduction

Manufacturing, Science and Finance (MSF) promotes itself as the union for skilled and professional staff in both the public and private sectors of the British economy. Founded in 1988 by the merger of the Association of Scientific, Technical and Managerial Staffs (ASTMS) and the Technical and Supervisory Staffs (TASS), it claimed on its foundation a membership over 600,000 spread throughout sectors as varied as manufacturing, insurance, health, tobacco and voluntary, and representing members with jobs ranging from managers, supervisors, technicians, laboratory staff to clerical workers. The merger was hailed at the time by both partners as an opportunity to increase the influence of trade unionism, promising that members would benefit from the greater power and influence of the combined organization (Carter, 1991). Within a short space of time, it was apparent that few if any of the benefits claimed could be realized, precipitating a crisis in the union and, eventually, the adoption of an organizing model in 1995. By 2000, the claimed membership of the union was 400,000, a financial crisis had resurfaced, and in part to address those problems the union merged with the larger Amalgamated Engineering and Electrical Union (AEEU in 2002). It is arguable that a major impetus for the merger will have been the failure to see benefits from its implementation of an organizing strategy. This chapter traces the background to the decision to adopt the strategy and questions the extent to which the union has confronted its past traditions and has been able to implement changes in practice to secure its future.

The two unions that formed MSF were organizationally and culturally very different. Technical and Supervisory Staffs had emerged from the drawing offices of major engineering companies and represented a relatively homogeneous membership (Mortimer, 1960; Foley, 1992). The leadership was closely associated with the Communist Party of Britain and was on the left of the trade union movement. While it had many well-organized offices, and a tradition in the 1960s of local industrial action to support improvements in terms and conditions (Roberts *et al.*, 1972), the internal life of the organization was stunted by the control of leading officials and an increasing emphasis on affecting the formal policies of the TUC and the Labour Party, rather than mobilizing its membership (Smith, 1987). Two factors influenced TASS's decision to merge with ASTMS. The first was its earlier failure to form an industrial union through a merger with the dominant manual worker union in the engineering industry, the Amalgamated Engineering Union (AEU). The second factor pushing TASS towards ASTMS was its uncertain future due both to changes in the labour process, which threatened the traditional functions of its membership (Cooley, 1980), and the overall decline of the engineering industry in Britain. During its period of association with the AEU, it had managed to join with a series of small craft unions but, despite these mergers, membership was only 50,000 above its 1979 figure, at 250,000. Moreover, cut off from the main crafts within engineering, to have a future it had to abandon the long-held idea of industrial unionism and seek a different principle of organization.

ASTMS differed from TASS in a number of respects. Although originally based upon supervisory workers and technicians, recruitment horizons had been progressively widened, reflecting a shift from organizing specific occupations and grades to all and any white-collar workers. With this shift, the ideology of the union increasingly emphasized the difference between the status and aspirations of white-collar employees and manual workers and promoted the parallel claim that the practice of the union was superior to the staid, old-fashioned and outdated practices of the manual unions. The union was rewarded for this shift by spectacular growth through direct recruitment and mergers that fed its sense of confidence. Between 1968 and 1979 the union increased its membership from 75,000 to 390,000 or by 520 per cent. The result was a union comprising heterogeneous categories of employees in varied sectors of the economy, with different traditions of self-organization and levels of trade union consciousness.

If TASS was clearly and easily identified as a left-wing union, characterization of ASTMS was much more difficult. The union was not averse to using left-wing rhetoric and had close ties at the highest levels with an organized left wing of the Labour Party, the Tribune group (Carter, 1983). At the time of the merger, many ASTMS officials were proud to claim that there were no substantial differences with TASS on broad policy issues. What undermined the credibility of this claim was the tenuous relationship that left-wing policies had to union practice and membership activity. This was also true of TASS, but it at least could point to a relatively recent period of membership mobilization and to a membership that on the whole was more homogeneous and was drawn from industries that had a tradition of organization.

A largely conservative membership of ASTMS had tolerated the apparent left-wing and militant stance of the union, which included support for the extension of public ownership, for two reasons. Firstly, there was no doubt that in relative terms many of the union's members felt badly treated by employers, certainly in relationship to the perceived improvements that manual unions had been able to secure in the 1960s and early 1970s. The ability of the union to articulate that sense of grievance in a loud and aggressive fashion was welcomed, especially as the union was happy to do it on their behalf, thus not causing individual relations at work to become soured or embarrassing. Secondly, it was recognized that most of the political positions that the union adopted had no immediate affect on membership activity or prospects. The policy that the union pushed particularly hard, the policy against government-determined incomes policies and for free collective bargaining, could be presented as left wing, but also resonated with membership antagonism to policies that effectively compressed differentials. There was little socialist ideology expressed here, with concern for differentials over other workers featuring more prominently than the inequality between capital and labour (Carter, 1986).

There were also definite limits to solidarity and collectivism between members within the union. Recruiting across different grades, some of which had responsibility for ensuring the reproduction of profits for employers, potentially promised to introduce class conflict within the union itself. The union attempted to minimize internal conflict by adopting a structure of semiautonomous occupational groups within the major companies in which it had a presence. This allowed policy to be determined close to members who were affected by decisions. More importantly, however, it ensured that no groups could be controlled by any policies derived from any others. Members who were supervisors, for instance, were in a group not therefore bound to respect picket lines when other members in the same plant were in dispute. Indeed, where managers, who were members, attempted to undermine disputes by threatening fellow members, the union took the position that as long as they were carrying out their contracted function (that is, managing) this was acceptable and the union would not discipline them (Carter, 1986).

Instances of internal conflict were, however, rare. The explanation for this relative absence rests with the low level of disputes in which members were engaged. The union recruited specifically on the basis that membership was an insurance policy rather than a commitment to wider values of collective strength and solidarity. This policy is amply illustrated by the following passage written by the then General Secretary and the Director of Research:

> If you feel unwell you visit a doctor; if you have a toothache you visit a dentist; if you are involved in litigation you visit a solicitor; if collective bargaining needs to be done, workers approach a trade union. We live in the age of the professional and in the case of trade unions this applies not only to the negotiators but also to their research, legal and educational staffs. (Jenkins and Sherman, 1977: 2)

The perspective had the result of recruiting individuals and reinforcing their individualism. Where the union fostered collective consciousness, it was as likely to be an occupational consciousness, as amongst hospital staff whose internal union organization bolstered their identity as technicians, radiographers and pharmacists, rather than employees and trade unionists.

The heterogeneous nature of the membership and rapid expansion led to an interesting period of internal government. The main membership challenge to the leadership came from the left, although for the most part they were as detached from membership ambitions, or lack of them, as the leadership. Despite occasional lurches towards exclusion of the left, and perhaps because of the relative security of the leadership built upon much expansion and success, internal control of the union was much more lax than in TASS. Annual Delegate Conferences frequently defeated the leadership motions and refused to accept reports. The general image that the union projected was therefore both arrogant and relatively undisciplined.

ASTMS needed to merge with TASS for its own specific reasons. Built rapidly during the 1960s and 1970s, ASTMS had a more torrid time during the 1980s. Without historic reserves, its overheads proved too large, as membership was lost. From a high point of 491,000 in 1979, it had a claimed membership of 390,000 at the point of merger. Although necessary for its survival, the merger with TASS made many in ASTMS fearful that the rather relaxed internal regime would fall prey to a rather more disciplined TASS machine.

The sources of the danger to ASTMS were twofold. The union was to go ahead without any prior agreement on the structure and future governance of the union. The two unions would maintain separate structures within the merged union, MSF, under joint general secretaries for a transitional period during which the structure of the union would be decided. The second concern of many in ASTMS was that, although smaller, TASS was much more centralized. With equal voting rights, and faced with a fractious ASTMS, this feature increased the likelihood that TASS members would win all the decisive votes. Initial impressions of the conduct of TASS leaders confirmed these fears in the eyes of ASTMS activists (Carter, 1991).

These fears caused an unprecedented galvanization of ASTMS activists to defend their traditional organization, including direct branch representation to annual conference and the right of branches and regions to retain a proportion of membership subscriptions. In this they were largely successful and the new union emerged having more of the structural characteristics and staffing profile of ASTMS than TASS. However, the internal battle was won at some considerable cost, as it left corrosive residues in the form of two factional organizations, MSF for Labour and Unity Left. The former was the mechanism for mobilizing ASTMS members over the internal questions of the union, but came increasingly to be an electoral machine. The latter represented the diminishing organization of full-time officials and lay activists that had dominated TASS. Neither side developed a programme to advance the fortunes of the union nor attempted to involve members in the union on wider issues.

There were policy changes following the victory of the ASTMS wing of the union, with an attempt to reintroduce features associated with ASTMS's earlier successes. The emphasis on servicing that had been a central feature of ASTMS was rearticulated. One outcome of this development was the attempt to get the union officially recognized as a high-quality provider of services to individual members through the award of an independent quality assurance kitemark. The General Secretary explained this orientation thus:

> We shall be highlighting individual representation as a priority for trade unionism. We have developed expertise in individual rights and representation. An increasing number of our members have individual contracts and profit or performance-related pay and they can turn to us for individual advice. (quoted in Bacon and Storey, 1996: 57)

This orientation found expression in a document, *MSF into the 21st Century,* placed before the 1994 Annual Delegate Conference (MSF, 1993). The document was replete with warnings of the need to change in response to the changed context within which unions were operating, but its advocacy of a servicing model of trade unionism was untenable. The union was neither attracting new members, nor adequately providing for existing ones. The conditions that had enabled ASTMS to grow no longer existed: white-collar employees now faced more aggressive employers without the support of generally confident shop-floor unions and in a climate of job insecurity. The very conditions that impeded growth also affected existing members, with many of them feeling the need to activate the insurance policy that was their union membership. Weakened union organization, and more individual issues, most of which could or should have been dealt with at workplace level, led to even more demands on full-time officers. When the conference rejected the document the limits of this orientation had already been reached.

The need for some confrontation with the problems besetting the union was soon made more obvious by a looming financial crisis. The union responded in 1995 by producing the *MSF Strategic Plan* (MSF, 1995a). Much of the plan addressed the financial problems of the union, which was registering a £8.4 million debt. Financial deficits stemmed from continued loss of members and inability to recruit sufficient new ones. The projected estimate was that the union would continue to lose 7.5 per cent of its membership per annum. The solutions adopted were the obvious short-term ones: the reduction in staff, both full-time officers and administrative, and the disposal of property. There was also a more concerted attempt to manage the union, with targets being set and officers being appraised for the first time. In this respect, the union reflected a movement towards managerialism, a trend that Heery and Kelly (1994) maintained was the dominant one within contemporary trade unionism.

Alongside the above changes, however, were further ones that attempted radically to change the practice of the union. Influenced by close family in Australia, one of the three Assistant General Secretaries advocated the adoption of the organizing model, and the policy of *Organising Works* was born. The context and manner of its adoption, however, were to cause it a difficult life. Reaction to the policy of *Organising Works* was coloured by its association with job losses. The internal strife of the union compounded adverse reaction by causing suspicion about the criteria of selection for redundancies. Finally, although the policy was predicated on the enthusiasm and commitment of officers and leading activists, they were involved little if at all in the formation of the policy. The policy as laid out formally promised to move away from union managerialism and instead encourage membership activity and involvement, but it encountered a legacy of membership inactivity and a leadership unable to encourage open debate. Whatever the formal policy of *Organising Works*, therefore, it has to be viewed within the context of the history of the union and its ongoing internal relations.

Organising Works

Organising Works was officially launched in October 1995. It was clearly and openly influenced by developments in the USA, Australia and New Zealand and the union circulated to full-time officers material from unions in those countries. An early account of the policy in one of the union's publications gave space to the views of Richard Bensinger, at the time, head of the AFL-CIO's Organizing Institute. The article described *Organising Works* as 'a back to basics approach that recognizes that the union is not there to do things for its members. While recruitment is essential, the emphasis is on empowering both existing and new members to take an active part in the union' (MSF, 1996: 6). The article also contrasted the union's approach to that of other parts of the British labour movement. It quoted the Assistant General Secretary charged with the policy:

> The TUC and other unions are talking about recruitment, while we are talking about organizing. The aim is maximum participation and involvement by ordinary members – to encourage ownership of the union by its members. Our role is to strengthen workplace organisation, and it's a change of culture for full-time officials and members alike. (MSF, 1996: 7)

More specifically, it was recognized by the union that the culture still supported the idea of the union as a servicing organization acting on behalf of its members.

An early assessment showed that MSF was some distance from being an organizing union:

> We can learn much from the techniques of selling and marketing and from recognising the need to give a good service to our members. However for some officers the debate has moved on to another plain. They see the union as a 'servicing' organization, the members as clients and the 'product' as industrial relations services. (MSF, 1995b)

But recognition of past failings has to be accompanied by a thought-out management of change process.

The necessary conditions for change, for building a consensus and support were, however, insufficiently developed, in MSF. There was neither consultation about the change in direction, nor after its adoption was there debate about how its spirit might be best implemented. The central message given publicly by the Assistant General Secretary was blunt enough:

Organising to recruit and retain members is the most important issue facing us today. It fundamentally affects the future – and survival – of MSF. No one should purport to say that s/he believes in MSF unless they see organising to recruit as their number one priority ... The choice is stark. Either we seize the chance of revitalising our union by recruiting, organising and mobilising members or we service an ever-declining membership. (Turnbull, 1997:19).

In private, criticism of the outlook of full-time officers was even harsher. Regional Officers were characterized by some national officials as being almost universally hostile to organizing. Explanations for this hostility pointed to Regional Officers' fear of losing status and power based on their specialized knowledge and expertise. It was also considered generational: given the lack of growth and turnover, most officials had done the job for a long time, in a particular way, in difficult circumstances, and were now being told this was wrong. New demands to organize threatened them especially as it was claimed that some were spending more time with employers than with members, were no longer attending branch meetings, and were remote from members. How widespread the validity of this judgement was is difficult to tell, but it did inform national views, which appeared to place the blame for union decline not on the changes in the environment in combination with union reactions to it, but solely on the practice of full-time officers. In the context of the union's bruising internal relations, it is hardly surprising that some staff found the approach of sections of the leadership threatening.

In interviews with Regional Officers, little overt hostility to *Organising Works* could be detected. There were differences about how it might be achieved, but a consensus emerged that workplace organization should be strengthened. There was some particular opposition to the way in which the union sharply counterpoised organizing to the traditional practice of servicing. Where the characterization of regional officers proved accurate was in its judgement that officers felt deeply that the work that they had done in very difficult circumstances was being belittled. What they thought was now being asked of them – that they should walk away from work that they were expected to do by both representatives and members – caused them a good deal of confusion and distress. Any sharp withdrawal from this work threatened their relations with key activists and they were reluctant to do this, certainly in the short term.

While sections of the union, and particularly regional officers, felt that 'one best way' of implementing organizing was being imposed, it seems that key national personnel neither fully shared the commitment to, nor understood, the perspectives advanced. The General Secretary, for instance, was not openly hostile to the initiative but there is little evidence of his genuine support for it. On the few occasions he addressed the subject directly, the perspectives he advanced are less than developed and collapse into a simple question of recruitment and numbers:

> Our influence with the government, your credibility with the boss, all depends on how representative we are, on how strong is the union organisation. I want the very best for every member, but so often, our ability to win fairness at work is undermined by weak organisation. That's why we've launched our 'organising works' initiative.
>
> After all, over 5 million say they would join a union – but have never been asked!
>
> Let's take away that excuse – invite your colleagues to join in – aim for 100 per cent membership.
>
> And let me know how you get on – or if I can help in any way. (MSF, 1997: 3)

Most of the union publications, for instance, continued to be dominated by pictures of the General Secretary at conferences, opening buildings and being joined by senior politicians. In this representation, the union continued to be synonymous with its top official, contrary to the central message of the organizing model. As a consequence, the union carried out insufficient organizational and educational work before and after the policy was launched. The pertinence of the traditions of the unions, and particularly of ASTMS, continued, with policy grafted on to practices that were contrary to the new perspectives, and with structures of the union left unchanged.

Interviews with National Officers revealed that this lack of clarity about the very model the union was promoting was replicated in a number of different ways. There was continuing support, for instance, from one national official for the idea of the union specifying a service contract with members, with different bands of members buying into different levels of service. In this model, people not wishing to take out a full subscription to the union could pay less to become an associate member, with access to perhaps legal advice, but with no rights to representation. Other officials conflated the concept of *Organising Works* with the existence of workplace organization. This meant that in some areas, like the insurance industry, officials considered their own lack of day-to-day involvement as evidence of having already achieved the goals of *Organising Works*. One official commented:

> Yes MSF already has a lot of the organizing model in place but perhaps hasn't recognized it. Servicing is done by delegates and, although they are not paid for it, it is a proper role for them. The question is how to add the recruitment side to it. (National Official, 1996)

There is no vision of membership involvement here and the servicing model is simply applied at a lower level of the organization.

It could be argued that one positive outcome of the *Organising Works* initiative has been that regional officers are more aware of the need to organize and recruit and are likely to give these activities a higher priority. At the same time, however, the lack of consensus over fundamental issues is also reflected in how these activities are perceived. Regional officers tend to see organizing and recruitment as an addition to the work they normally do, rather than a transformation of it. This can be illustrated by the following:

> You don't recruit cold in a sense of having people just willing to pay money and not create a demand ... I will spend Monday afternoon operating strictly under the *Organising Works* philosophy, which is that I'm recruiting members, but the consequence of that is that I will probably have two or three other meetings which will be service related. (MSF NHS lead officer, 1997)

The union nationally has therefore been able effectively to gain some ground through officers extending their work, rather than win the argument and seeing officers transfer their practice. Universal acceptance of *Organizing Works* was never likely, but the terms of the argument have not helped the centre's cause. Rather than emphasizing the underlying purpose of full-time officers' work, the debate about organizing versus servicing has suggested that particular tasks fall one side or the other of the divide. The latter can be illustrated by one officer's description of his considerable input into a union pamphlet on the government's Private Finance Initiative. Because it did not involve organizing directly, he believed that the work fell outside his brief to follow the policy of *Organising Works*:

> In terms of a strict *Organising Works* philosophy, the work I spend on it has no value whatsoever: it is not quantifiable, measurable. In terms of keeping and maintaining the structures and the members we've built up, it is invaluable because we will produce a guide that is better than most and our reps will go round and wave it at people and sell the organization and it

will enable them to cope with what is a massive subject ... (MSF NHS lead officer, 1997).

Viewed from outside the framework established within MSF, however, contributing to a document on Private Finance Initiative (PFI), is neither organizing nor servicing. If the document is restricted to full-time officers or simply aimed at influencing the government, then it reinforces passivity amongst the membership and falls within the servicing model. If, on the other hand, it is widely distributed to the membership, as is intended, and reinforces the conscious strategy to build confidence and activity, then it dovetails into an organizing model.

The argument can be extended. Too often, disciplinary and other case-work is automatically portrayed by the union as servicing. But if in the process of representing members the regional officer makes a conscious effort to educate and train an embryonic local leadership then it becomes an organizing activity. In defending the continuity of some of the existing work of regional officers, one officer coined the phrase, 'all servicing is an organizing opportunity'. In part because of the dogmatic presentation of organizing by the union nationally, some officers seized upon this statement as a defence of existing positions, to use the sentiment to maintain the need for both organizing and servicing. Used like this, the statement can be a cloak for the continuation of representation of members without the training and encouragement of local leadership and workplace organization.

The lack of clarity of policy and concepts added to a confusion and frustration that was compounded by some national officers' lack of recognition of the complexity of demands on regional officials, and the amount of time and resources needed to make the transition to another model of activity. Given the traditions of the union, the shift from officers' representation to self-sufficiency on most domestic matters will take a long time for most workplaces, even with resources available to aid the transition. One of the most successful examples of a move in this direction, the development of representatives' committees in the West of Scotland, had its roots in policies laid down locally from 1992 (Carter, 2000). The union, despite its emphasis on organizing as opposed to recruitment, did not seem to allow for that time, reinforcing many officers' belief that recruitment was being given priority even if it distorted organizing. Moreover, regional officers could point to the fact that from an early point in the implementation of *Organising Works*, they were given individual recruitment targets, by some national officers, a mechanism also at variance with the insistence that they move towards teamwork.

There was some variation in approaches by national officers, with some giving more thought to the practical problems that officers faced. The national officer for the NHS sector, for instance, produced guidelines that were aimed at strengthening workplace organization and at the same time acknowledged the demands that members could place directly upon officers. The new procedure made it clear that, other than in exceptional and defined circumstances, inquiries from individuals will be referred to local representatives and that: 'Officers will not be expected to explain why they have not responded to individual inquiries other than in the manner proposed' (MSF, 1996: 3). Regional officers greatly appreciated this development and it was adopted as union-wide policy. In practice, however, outside the NHS, officers did not encounter the support from national officials they thought they should be entitled to. When individuals complained to the national organization, officers were pressurized to respond to them directly, further undermining the confidence that they had in the integrity of the organization.

The heavy-handed nature of some of the demands made on them and the lack of sympathy with the complexities and difficulties faced by regional officers has alienated many of them. One national officer, opening up a meeting on recruitment with regional officers, is cited as stating that he was not interested whether officers had too many demands on them or work-related stress: all he wanted to know was how officers were going to increase recruitment over the next twelve months. If anything, this emphasis on recruitment has increased as the policy developed. National circulars have adopted the tactic of naming and shaming areas that have recruited poorly, describing one as a disaster area. According to one regional officer in 1999:

> In one of the regions that wasn't doing well they went in and created an 'A team' and a 'B team' and if you were in the 'B team' you were fucking useless. It was absolutely clear; they were told you are in the 'B team' because you are no good. How does that motivate people in a constructive way? I know it motivates people in a very negative way. The aim is to scare the shit out of people. To me the whole idea of teamworking is that you are open and honest with people – that's the last thing you can afford to be with people here. If you are honest, you are exposing weaknesses or being critical and before you know it has gone back and you are asked why are you saying this. It's the antithesis of the atmosphere that should be created to foster teamwork.

As already suggested, the turn to the organizing model appeared to place too much weight on the role of full-time officers at the expense of developing other layers of the union. Organizers have been appointed, but it is not clear that they have led to any major successes. Indeed, there is some doubt as to whether their appointment has been helpful given their relationship to regional officers. One assessment raises the question of responsibilities:

> I can honestly say that the organizer has made no impact on my work. When I try to involve the organizer things become confused with two people involved rather than one. Things become confused, with no clear demarcation in terms of who is doing what. Why people join unions is because of issues and they (organisers) don't deal with issues. I cannot see how you can have a situation where you can divorce issues from the organizing. The two go hand in hand. (regional officer, 1999).

Another assessment of the impact is more supportive of the idea in principle, but equally doubting of its effect in practice because it ignores the present level of commitment and motivation of the union representatives:

> The principle of organizing that the union pushes is that our job, and more particularly that of the organizers, is to get people into the union and then offer them training and support to organize themselves to solve their own problems. In theory, this sounds great but it rarely works because, even in companies where we are well organized, there is massive recruitment potential, but it is incredibly difficult to get the reps' organization and to motivate them and to get time out away from the job. That's where the very simplistic organizing philosophy starts to fall apart. Clearly if the reps won't do it, [achieve] the 1% target [hanging] above your head, you've got to do it. It is a very shallow approach to that principle. Constantly having to make compromises on a pure principle that looks all right on paper. (regional officer, 1999)

There are examples of representatives developing and taking on more responsibilities. The lead officer responsible for NHS organization in the West of Scotland commented that:

> It's developed so that this year, for the first time, I have noticed a decline in the individual casework and the reps are taking on more, automatically. Four or five years of encouraging members to go through their rep and building up the structures has meant that at last the problems are going through them and, depending on the ability of the rep and the strength of

our organization, are being settled at local level. (MSF NHS lead officer, 1997)

It should be noted, however, that the change stems from policies locally adopted that pre-date *Organising Works*. Elsewhere, not only have changes not taken place, but also awareness of the union's policy is still quite low. A survey of NHS representatives in 1996 indicated that 91 per cent knew little or nothing about *Organising Works* (MSF, 1997: 14). Interviews with local representatives indicate that it is still the case that many do not understand the policy to which the union is formally committed. Moreover this is neither a sectional nor local problem but a national one. In a study of MSF representatives across all sectors in the South West, 41 per cent had not heard of *Organising Works* and 60 per cent were not aware of the principles behind it (Danford and Upchurch, 1999).

Beyond the representatives, who are the activists, stand the membership who will have less awareness and less knowledge of the policy but are nevertheless crucial to its success. If they are unaware of it as a formal policy, it is also unlikely that they will glean the principles from the practice of the organization, certainly at a national level. Here the image of the union continues to project ambiguous messages. While it is true that the union carries the message of organizing sporadically in its publications and advertising, this is more than balanced by an approach that continues the servicing tradition. On its newly revamped website, the section describing the union carried the following:

How do we work?
A great deal of the work trade unions undertake is unseen and unsung. We help to oil the machinery of business by maintaining a reasonable balance between employer and employee and helping to sort out many problems – often before they become bigger issues. In other words, we help business to prosper. We want our members to work for successful companies and organizations: only by doing so can they have secure, well-rewarded and interesting jobs. (MSF, 1999a)

In presenting itself thus, the union has become the third party that the organizing model is ranged against. Nor is this a totally isolated aberration. A more emphatic embrace of the servicing model would be harder to find than material produced in the Irish section that read:

WHAT CAN I BUY FOR £1.98 A WEEK OR LESS?

You're usual drink – maybe, but without the mixer

A weekly magazine – just about

A daily newspaper – if you only read one twice a week

Your lunch – can you wash dishes?

Not a lot, you'll probably agree. If I was to tell you that it could give you access to representation and advice on salary, pensions, equality, job security, holidays, legal advice, health, safety & welfare issues including stress, health screening, bullying and much more ... would you be interested? (MSF, 1999b)

The material then proceeded to list all the services that the union provided.

In effect, organizing has been downgraded to a tactic advocated by the union for specific circumstances. In line with the British TUC (see Carter *et al.*, 2002), the union has responded to the Labour government's enthusiasm for the belief that unions and employers have common interests and that these interests should be formalized through partnership agreements. Where MSF can secure partnership agreements, it ignores the organizing model. The union made much, for instance, of 'an historic agreement, unprecedented in industrial relations ... signed between MSF and the Industrial Society' (MSF, 1997). What made it historic was that the agreement was conceived as a service level agreement (SLA). As the union stated:

In business an SLA would usually be signed by a company and its supplier, formalising arrangements between the two parties by setting out what standards of performance and delivery are required. But in this case MSF is the first union to sign up committing the union to provide a high level of service and maintain a fully-trained reps network. (MSF, 1997: 1)

The future of the union

Given the starting-points of membership passivity and factional leadership, the difficulties of obtaining lasting change in MSF cannot be under estimated. The leadership of MSF has failed to address either problem, or to provide coherence and direction. In the last election for General Secretary in 1996, for instance, leaflets supporting the outgoing postholder, who was successfully re-elected, made no mention of perspectives for the union. The necessary qualities of leadership it mentioned were almost exclusively individual ones, such as having vast experience, being an effective and successful front-line negotiator, representing MSF on the TUC General Council and Confederation of Shipbuilding and Engineering Unions (CSEU) Executive. In the lingering factionalism within the union, MSF for Labour, which supported him, acts as an electrol machine with no programme other than urging votes for its candidates and disparaging the opposition. Members are not empowered by this process but herded into camps.

The lack of direction had the further consequence of affecting personal relations at the heart of the leadership. A rift gradually developed between the General Secretary and an Assistant General Secretary and exploded spectacularly in 1999 with accusations by the latter of the General Secretary's financial impropriety (*Sunday Times*, 1999). The accusations ended with the accuser suspended and eventually leaving the union with compensation believed to amount to as much as £500,000.

The willingness to pay this sum indicated that the union leadership had doubts about the utility of public disclosure of the issues in a tribunal case. In this their judgement was almost certainly sound, as was subsequently indicated. A secretary to the Head of Finance was sacked for her role in bringing the allegations to the notice of the Assistant General Secretary and as a result took the union to an industrial tribunal to establish unfair dismissal. As a consequence, a series of damaging revelations appeared in the press detailing possible fraud, and giving a picture of the General Secretary's alleged expenses-filled lifestyle (for comprehensive coverage, including depositions to the tribunal, see www.rogerlyons.com). The tribunal found in favour of the applicant and the union was forced to pay her £50,000 tax-free, plus costs. A further case, shortly afterwards, saw the union making a settlement of £200,000 plus a car to another official making related allegations. Estimates make the accumulated costs associated with these cases around £750,000.

More important than the money, the spectacle of internal disputes cannot have encouraged members to further effort and sacrifice. If anything, they associated the union with personal privilege and a lifestyle far removed from the experiences of most members. As a direct result over half of the Regional Councils of the union have passed critical resolutions calling for an inquiry and/or the resignation of the General Secretary.

It is hard to imagine senior leaders genuinely committed to the organizing model, and asking for members to take risks with their futures, acting in such a narrow and self-seeking way. The failure of *Organising Works* to inform the perspectives of the union in any other than a formal sense is also indicated in its merger plans. The union came close in 1997 to merging with the 78,000 strong Institution of Professionals, Managers and Specialists (IPMS). The merger proposal was greeted with the usual claims that it would bring more resources, improved services, and stronger organization (MSF, 1997: 1). In a booklet issued jointly by the unions, only one paragraph in fifteen pages dealt with organizing and recruitment and then with little flair or enthusiasm (IPMS/MSF, 1997). Whatever the limitations of the prospectus, however, the proposed merger was at least in line with the project of building a union for skilled and professional workers, with the IPMS membership being largely drawn from scientific and technical grades within the Civil Service. Furthermore, it held out the prospect of attracting further mergers to consolidate the idea of a general white-collar, professional union, of which MSF would be the core.

The merger was eventually rejected by the IPMS membership and subsequently talk has moved in the direction of merger with the AEEU. The AEEU is a primarily craft-and-manual-worker-based union recruiting engineers and electricians. To see a solution in joining a union that has declined at an even greater rate than MSF, down from 1.3 million in 1979 to 880,000 in 1992, to 730,000 in 1999 is possibly perverse when the areas of growth in MSF have all been outside the manufacturing sector, with the NHS sector leading the way, followed by the voluntary sector. This turn towards a larger, manual-worker-based union makes this a merger of a different order, and one that signals the end of the strategy laid down by ASTMS for the organization of white-collar employees. It also signals a loss of confidence in the union's ability to organize and recruit to produce a vigorous and growing union. The union itself has stated that:

> Whilst our own finances are stable, MSF lacks the substantial resources required for the challenges of the new millennium. Massive increases in subscriptions are not practicable. The 'status quo' is not an option as it would require regular belt tightening – rather than an increase in resources for campaigning, organising, officer and specialist support to members. (MSF, 1999c: 3)

A number of concerns have been raised about the merger with the AEEU. There is some attraction to uniting the membership in the manufacturing sector and, in a sense, reviving the idea of an industrial union. Having heard the same arguments for the formation of MSF, few are convinced that larger means stronger. At no time then did the union advance a strategy for capitalizing on the merger by releasing the enthusiasm and skills of its members and few advances were made. *Organising Works* potentially now places a membership-led strategy on the agenda, but rather than perceiving it this way, the present leadership sees merger as an alternative to the struggle to build the union through activity. Moreover, the AEEU gives no indication other than that it is hostile to membership self-activity.

The merger between TASS and the AEUW ended in hostility largely due to the politics of the respective leaders. The present leadership of the AEEU is even further to the right than the leadership of the AEUW, having acquired the leadership of the most right-wing, and arguably undemocratic, of British unions, the Electrical, Electronic, Telecommunication and Plumbing Union (EETPU). It is the latter tradition that seems to have seized hold of the union and many of the structures and policies of the AEUW have disappeared, including the important role played by lay-led district committees. Meanwhile, some of the policies that caused such hostility to the EETPU have continued, the latest being an attempt to sign a single-union recognition agreement with the *Western Mail* newspaper, thereby disenfranchising National Union of Journalist members and Graphical Print and Media Union members, both of which considerably outnumber the AEEU members.

The logic advanced by the MSF is that a larger union is needed, that the manufacturing members have most to gain and that the unions share the same fundamental approach:

> That is a willingness to look at the future and a willingness to change the way we work if that seems appropriate. It is recognition that, while we can learn from the past, the future might require something different. We are both modern trade unions and are committed to being modern trade unions in the future. We both react flexibly to problems that arise. This is a firm basis for a relationship (MSF, 1999d: 2–3).

It is doubtful whether this firm basis of expediency and flexibility will be enough to satisfy the non-manufacturing memberships who constitute the majority of the union. The union is claiming that the new union will preserve and develop the industrial autonomy and structures that allow members in individual sectors to decide their own policies and priorities (1999d: 3). On the other hand, it continues: 'We are creating a new union that will have its own structures and policies. It will not be MSF and it will not be the AEEU. It will develop its own structures through a process that gives equal representation to MSF and the AEEU. The new structures will determine the new unions policies' (*ibid.*: 3). It is just this looseness of formulation that caused widespread disquiet amongst ASTMS activists when the merger with TASS took place. Similar fears were raised again and this time in the context of a weakened MSF leadership facing a much larger union. The consequences of the union's inability to grow through successfully motivating its membership meant that many people in the union saw no alternative but to merge – not to strengthen organizing but to stall further successive rounds of demoralizing rationalization and cuts in expenditure and resources

It is tempting to blame officials or the nature of the membership for the failure to organize. In order for people to fight, however, members need to believe in the aims and to have confidence in the ability of the organization. The leadership of MSF has given members, representatives and officials little reason for either belief or confidence. From a point at which the leadership appeared to define the adoption of organizing salvation of the union, it has presented contradictory information and a confused image about the union's direction. The effect has been compounded by the emergence of deep divisions within the union and a series of serious allegations about the misuse of union funds by senior officials. With the apparent onset of yet another financial crisis driven by the same loss of members and inability to recruit sufficient others, the union sought a merger with the AEEU. With the merger forming Amicus, formally completed in 2002, it is likely that, in the wake of preoccupations with the internal politics of the organization of the new union, the policy of Organizing Works will be even less of a priority. If, as seems likely, this does occur, the policy of *Organising Works*, born of financial crisis, will almost certainly be dispatched by a final one.

References

Bacon, N. and Storey, J. (1986) 'Individualism and Collectivism and the Changing Role of Trade Unions', in Ackers, P., Smith, C. and Smith, P. (eds) *The New Workplace and Trade Unionism*, London: Routledge, pp. 41–76.

Carter, B. (1983) 'Conservative Militants – The Case of ASTMS', in Hyman, R. and Price, R., *The New Working Class? White Collar Workers and Their Organisations*, Basingstoke: Macmillan.

Carter, B. (1991) 'Politics and Process in the Making of MSF', *Capital and Class*, 45: 35–72.

Carter, B. (2000) 'Adoption of the Organising Model in British Trade Unions: Some Evidence from Manufacturing, Science and Finance (MSF)', *Work, Employment and Society*, 14 (1): 117–36.

Carter, R. (1986) 'Trade Unionism and the New Middle Class: the Case of ASTMS', in Armstrong, P., Carter, R., Smith, C. and Nichols, T. (eds) *White Collar Workers, Trade Unions and Class*, London: Croom Helm, pp. 132–59.

Carter, R., Fairbrother, P., Sherman, R. and Voss, K. (2002) *Made in the USA: The TUC, the Organizing Model and the Limits of Transferability*, in press.

Cooley, M. (1980) *Architect or Bee? The Human/Technology Relationship*, London: Hand and Brain.

Danford, A. and Upchurch, M. (1999) *MSF in the South West: Statistical Analysis*, Report 4, ESRU, Bristol: University of the West of England.

Foley, T. (1992) *A Most Formidable Union: The History of DATA and TASS*, London: MSF.

Heery, E. and Kelly, J. (1994) 'Professional, Participative and Managerial Unionism: An Interpretation of Change in Trade Unions', *Work, Employment and Society* 8 (1): 1–22.

IPMS/MSF (1997) *IPMS/MSF: Prospectus for a New Union*, London: IPMS.

Jenkins, C. and Sherman, B. (1977) *Collective Bargaining*, London: Routledge.

Mortimer, J. (1960) *A History of the Association of Engineering and Shipbuilding Draughtsmen*, Richmond: Association of Engineering and Shipbuilding Draughtsmen.

MSF (1993) *MSF into the 21st Century*, London: MSF.

MSF (1995a) *MSF Strategic Plan*, London: MSF.

MSF (1995b) Circular, London: MSF.

MSF (1996) Circular, London: MSF.

MSF (July 1996) *MSF at Work*, London: MSF.

MSF (1997) *MSF Report*, 25, London: MSF.

MSF (1999a) http://www.tuc.org.uk/vbuilding/msf/

MSF (1999b) http://www.tuc.org.uk/vbuilding/msf/browse/object.exe?714

MSF (1999c) *MSF Report*, 40, London: MSF.

MSF (1999d) *MSF and the AEEU, MSF*, London: MSF.

Roberts, B. Loveridge, R. and Gennard, J. (1972) *Reluctant Militants*, London: Allen & Unwin.

Smith, C. (1987) *Technical Workers: Class, Labour and Trade Unionism*, Basingstoke: Macmillan.

Sunday Times (1999) March 14.

Turnbull, P. (1995) 'Organising Works in Australia – Can It Work in Britain?' *Working Paper No. 97*, Department of Management and Industrial Relations, University of Melbourne.

10 Strategic Dilemma: The State of Union Renewal in Canada

Pradeep Kumar and Gregor Murray

Union organizations in Canada have weathered the past two difficult decades for trade unionism better than many other labour movements. Canadian unions have often been cited as examples of successful organizational renewal in an era characterized by declining union influence (ILO, 1997). In particular, the Canadian union movement has succeeded in maintaining its overall aggregate membership in the face of adverse environmental pressures at exactly the same time as unions in the other national contexts examined in this book have suffered a precipitous decline in membership levels. Even though this membership performance has not kept pace with the expansion of the labour force, it is seen as an accomplishment in comparative terms. Yet, there is ample reason to take stock of the state of union renewal in Canada for it provides a good test case of some of the more voluntaristic prognostics for curing the ills of organized labour elsewhere.

On the positive side of any such assessment, there was an early realization in Canadian union ranks of the need to adopt more proactive strategies (Kumar and Ryan, 1988). Canadian unions have demonstrated a degree of wage militancy, notably in the 1980s, with their no concessions policies, but they have also innovated in the realm of bargaining. Moreover, Canadian unions have been involved in a range of coalition and community activities, thus maintaining a fairly high profile in both the political arena and in civil society. In other words, not only have Canadian unions largely retained their membership, but they have moved away from traditional forms of narrow business unionism towards a wider embrace of innovative practices and structures aimed at renewing workers' commitment to unions and recognizing new labour market and social identities (Kumar and Murray, 2002). Judged by international standards, the Canadian 'grass' might well appear much 'greener' to trade unionists elsewhere, despite the snow banks that cover it for so much of the year.

There is also scope for a more pessimistic interpretation of organized labour's fate in Canada. The environment is incontestably a hostile one and a number of the major provincial governments have pursued a neo-liberal reform agenda despite the opposition of organized labour. Nor, despite wage militancy, is it possible to speak of substantive gains in unionized living standards over the past two difficult decades (Jackson and Robinson, 2000). Moreover, despite the relative stability of union membership levels, overall union density and collective bargaining coverage have experienced a considerable decline over the last decade.

So, to borrow a popular metaphor, is the Canadian union bottle 'half empty' or 'half full'? In order to explore this question and to highlight the strategic challenges and dilemma facing organized labour in what many judge as a 'relatively good', if not 'best', case scenario, this chapter seeks to give an overview and an assessment of the experience of the Canadian union movement over the last decade. In particular, it focuses on two key strategic challenges: first, how to secure access to union representation through increased efforts to recruit new members and ensure the effective participation of members in their unions and, second, how to maintain and develop the union in the workplace through a strategic engagement with workplace restructuring.

Each of these challenges, neither of which is unique to Canada (see, for example, Masters and Atkins, 1999), underscores the profound problems for labour movement renewal. On each challenge, it is possible to point to considerable strategic innovation on the part of the Canadian labour movement. Yet, it is also necessary to emphasize the mixed results flowing from this strategic innovation. In many respects, Canadian unions have been 'running to stand still'. For an international audience, certainly the most sobering aspect of this analysis of union renewal is that many of the ingredients of the current international recipe for union renewal, at least in the predominantly English-speaking countries analysed in this book, are being implemented in one way or another in Canada and are found to offer necessary but insufficient conditions for organizational renewal. In short, an analysis of the Canadian experience usefully allows us to highlight the sources of success but also to focus more sharply on the strategic dilemma facing trade unions in the search for organizational renewal.

Context for union renewal in Canada

This exploration of the challenges facing Canadian labour draws on a range of studies of union renewal but it is systematically informed throughout the chapter by the results of our national survey of Canadian union organizations, the Human Resources Development Canada (HRDC) Survey 1997–1998 – see Kumar, Murray and Schetagne (1998a, 1998b). The survey indicates that unions in Canada, like other industrialized countries (see Olney, 1996), have been affected over the past two decades by unprecedented and interrelated changes in their economic, technological, labour market and public policy environment. These environmental changes, linked to globalization and demography, have had a profound impact on workers and their unions, necessitating significant adaptations in unions' organizational, bargaining and political strategies.

Survey respondents emphasized how very different the current environment for bargaining, servicing, and organizing is compared with the environment a decade ago. They highlighted the negative impacts of this changed environment on levels of union employment and membership, work environment, and the labour-management relationship. However, they also indicated a high degree of confidence in their ability to mobilize their members due to their perceptions of continuing worker trust and satisfaction with union services.

Union strategies in Canada might be described as both defensive and proactive, focusing on the protection of wages and benefits in the case of the former and fostering social unionism through expanded programmes of education and research, new organizing, coalition building and rank-and-file activism in the case of the latter. Given the very adversity of the environment facing unions in Canada, defensive strategies, not to be confused with simple reactive strategies (Gindin and Panitch, 2000) appear to be grounded in the need to protect past worker gains from some of the worst excesses of the new environment. There is considerable evidence of more proactive strategies, but analysis of the degree of success achieved suggests that there are also formidable but surmountable obstacles to the pursuit of more proactive strategies. The strategic challenge seems to be how to find the appropriate fit between defensive and proactive strategies.

Access to union representation and to the life of the union

Overall aggregate union membership in Canada grew fairly continuously from the mid-1960s until the mid-1990s. As in many other countries, the watershed came in the early 1980s when the expansion of the labour force began to outstrip the expansion of union membership, thus translating into

Table 10.1 *Collective bargaining coverage (union members and non-members) by sex, age, employment status and sector in Canada, 1990 and 2000*

	1990 Union coverage		2000 Union coverage		1990–2000 Change	
	Coverage (000)	Density (%)	Coverage (000)	Density (%)	Coverage (000) percentage change	Density net change in percentage points
Sex						
Male	2237	42.0	2124	33.5	−5.1	−8.5
Female	1719	36.1	1866	31.5	+8.6	−4.6
Age						
15–24 years (1990 = 16–24)	358	20.8	292	14.2	−18.4	−6.6
25–44 years	2389	41.0	2151	33.0	−10.0	−8.0
45–54 years	826	49.3	1178	44.5	+42.7	−4.8
55 years or more	384	44.4	369	35.9	−4.0	−8.5
Employment status						
Full time	3440	41.1	3467	34.6	+0.9	−6.5
Part time	517	30.1	519	23.3	+0.5	−6.8
Sector						
Public	n.a.	n.a.	2053	73.7	—	—
Private	n.a.	n.a.	1937	20.5	—	—
TOTAL	3957	39.2	3990	32.6	+0.9	−6.6

Sources: For 1990, annual estimates based on the Labour Market Activity Survey provided by Statistics Canada; for 2000, estimates for January to June from the Labour Force Survey, Akyeampong, 2000 and provided by Statistics Canada.

Note: Collective bargaining coverage includes individual respondents who indicate that they are union members or, if not a union member, that they are covered by a union contract or collective agreement. The 1990 and 2000 estimates are broadly comparable, although the 2000 survey covers workers from the age of 15 whereas the 1990 survey reported results for workers from the age of 16.

a very slight decline in union density in the decade of the 1980s and a much more pronounced decline in the 1990s. Table 10.1 illustrates both the overall stability in aggregate union membership and the decline in union density over this latter decade.

Unions in Canada might typically be described as strongly present in areas where employment is stable or even in decline and weak in areas of employment growth. To illustrate, union coverage in the year 2000 in Canada (that is workers who were either a member of a union or whose wages and conditions of employment were determined by a collective agreement) was estimated to extend to just under four million workers in paid employment or 32.6 per cent of paid employment (Akyeampong, 2000). There was, however, a wide dispersion in the relative union coverage by industry. It was less than 10 per cent in industries such as agriculture (2.7 per cent), accommodation and food (8.3 per cent), and professional, scientific and technical industries (5.1 per cent) and less than 15 per cent in finance (10.4 per cent), management and administrative support (13.5 per cent) and trade (14.8 per cent); whereas it was somewhat more than a third of paid employment in manufacturing (35.2 per cent) and exceeded 50 per cent in healthcare (53.5 per cent), public administration (70.3 per cent), utilities (70.4 per cent) and education (71.8 per cent). Just under half of all union members in Canada (48.3 per cent) can be found in just three sectors: education, health and social services or public administration. The specific challenge, of course, is how to unionize the non-unionized. Less than two out of ten employees not covered by collective bargaining (17 per cent) were in manufacturing whereas roughly seven out of ten employees who were not union members were in the service-producing sectors, especially trade, accommodation and food or finance.

The challenge for union organizations is threefold. First, there is clearly a need to recruit more aggressively new members in order to counter the decline of the union movement over the last two decades. Second, in order to respond to this first challenge and connect with the new labour force, the very geography of the labour movement must shift, which further entails challenges to the practices of union organizations on several levels. Third, as an extension of the second point, there is a need to reinforce the link between existing union members and their organizations or what has often come to be known as 'internal' organizing. Let us examine each of these challenges.

Despite many variations between provincial jurisdictions in the gathering of data, the overall picture of union organizing activity in Canada is one of a downward trend since the peak years of public sector organizing in the 1960s and 1970s until the early 1990s (Martinello, 1996:). Studies by Lipsig-Mumme and Lexer (1998) and Yates (2000) tend to confirm the trend of an apparent drop-off in organizing through the mid-1990s, especially with the chilling effect of a more hostile political climate in Ontario (Martinello, 2000; Yates, 2000). Nonetheless, the success rate for organizing in Canada, as judged by successful certification applications, remains fairly high: ranging from 70 to

75 per cent according to Martinello (1996), but somewhat lower in Ontario in recent years, as reported by Yates (2000). Only in the province of Quebec (Ministère du travail, various years) are there indications of a higher level of organizing activity and success from 1998 through to 2000. In other words, although the labour movement as a whole continues to enjoy a fairly high degree of success in its organizing efforts and tends to organize upwards of 100,000 new members a year, there is not yet any compelling evidence of an overall strategic shift in organizing effort. Case study evidence of particular upward blips in organizing activity in particular unions (Murray, 1998; Yates 2000) has not translated into a significant overall shift in the aggregate numbers. Under adverse economic and workplace conditions, unions face increased demand for membership servicing on issues such as workplace change and downsizing so that union resources tend to be more heavily concentrated on these defensive activities as opposed to proactive policies of new organizing.

A brief look at the recent organizing experience in Ontario, Canada's largest province, provides further illustration of the challenges facing the labour movement and tends to corroborate the above interpretation. In 1999, roughly 37.4 per cent of union members and 42.1 per cent of non-union employees in Canada were located in Ontario. In other words, it is a key jurisdiction for the future of the labour movement. Drawing on figures recently reported by Yates (2000: Table 1), over the last five years (from 1994 to 1999), the Ontario Labour Relations Board granted certifications covering 122,524 employees. Breaking down these certifications by sector, Yates's data reveals a mixed union record in terms of organizing in sectors where union membership is already well established versus in those sectors where employment is growing but unionization rates are low.

Successful new union organizing in Ontario is still more likely to reflect the existing distribution of union membership in manufacturing and the public sector. Although there is some shift towards private services organizing, this effort nonetheless appears relatively small in relation to the scale of shift required to effect a substantial increase in collective bargaining coverage in these sectors.

Our own survey results also point in this direction. Unions report that organizing workers in traditional jurisdictions is a more important priority than organizing workers in new areas of growth: 51.1 per cent of unions reported that organizing in traditional jurisdictions was an extremely or very important priority, as opposed to 36.3 per cent of unions for new areas of growth. Organizing in new areas of growth is not to be done to the detriment of traditional areas of growth since more than 90.9 per cent of the unions indicating that organizing in new areas of growth was a high priority also reported that organizing in traditional jurisdictions was an equally high priority. Roughly a third of the unions participating in the survey (33 per cent) indicated that both traditional and new jurisdictions were a high priority whereas for a quarter of unions (25.3 per cent) neither form of organizing appeared to be a priority. Those unions reporting that organizing in new areas of growth was a high priority were significantly more likely to be large in size (53.1 per cent of such unions, $p = 0.067$) and in the private sector (57.5 per cent, $p = 0.00$), where union membership has been seriously eroded by waves of downsizing and rationalization in the past decade. There is little to distinguish between small unions in the public and private sectors. The contrast between medium-sized unions (1000 to 10,000 members) seeking new areas of growth is particularly great between public (10 per cent) and private sectors (66.7 per cent). Amongst large unions, 35.3 per cent of those in the public sector compared to 73.3 per cent of the private sector attach a high priority to growth in new areas of membership. This finding is consistent with that reported by Yates (2000: 662; also see chapter in this volume) in her survey of organizers in Ontario. She found that industrial unions appear more likely to conduct organizing campaigns in private services (43.9 per cent of campaigns) than in manufacturing (31.9 per cent).

A key focus for organizing renewal must therefore be on the practices and success of these large private sector unions in their organizing practices and efforts. For example, a number of unions have shifted more resources into organizing and appear to demonstrate a greater commitment to new organizing, although this commitment often appears subject to the vagaries of internal politics (see Murray, 1998) and to other economic and organizational exigencies, not least the need to respond to the servicing demands and defensive priorities of existing members on issues such as workplace change. Indeed, it is hard to qualify these nonetheless progressive changes in organizing as a strategic shift of the magnitude purportedly pursued by some US unions, notably the Service Employees International Union (SEIU), which have sought to effect a massive shift of organizational resources towards new organizing. Indeed, it is probably safe to say that Canadian unions have been comforted in their new organizing efforts by the relative overall stability of aggregate union membership. For example, drawing on estimates from Table 10.1, paid employment grew by roughly 20 per cent over the decade of the 1990s but union membership only expanded by 1 per cent, translating into a loss of relative union coverage of 6.6 percentage points (from 39.2 per cent to 32.6 per cent). While the expansion of union membership by Canadian unions can be presented as an achievement in absolute terms and the result of considerable organizing effort, it does not come close to matching overall shifts in employment in the labour market.

Apart from the challenge of enhancing the organizing effort and directing it towards the industries in expansion, a key question is whether it is targeted to reach the new groups in the labour force. A common theme running through many union movements is how to reach and espouse the aspirations of the new labour force, be they women, the young, casual or part-time in employment status, high tech or immigrant. Recent surveys indicate that the willingness to join a union is substantially higher among women, youth, workers of visible minority status, and employees who are less satisfied with their pay and job security and have a 'weak' employment relationship with their employers (Lowe and Schellenberg, 2001). While there is some evidence of the success of recent campaigns in the case of at least some of these target groups, the overall figures suggest that caution is required in affirming overall success.

Changes in the gender composition of the Canadian union movement are reflected in the data presented in Table 10.1. The number of men covered by collective bargaining declined by 5.1 per cent over the past decade whereas that of women has actually increased by 8.1 per cent over the same period; the net loss of union coverage was considerably less for women (4.6 percentage points) than for men (8.5 percentage points). This continues a longer-term trend where newly organized union members in Canada are more likely to be women (Galarneau, 1996). Given the growth in women's participation in the labour market, the increasing presence of women in unions represents a real strategic success in terms of labour movement adjustment. Indeed, it can be argued that this internal transformation is of considerable significance for future labour movement strategies, although several observers argue that this change in membership has yet to work its way through many union organizations (Briskin and McDermott, 1993). Another positive trend in union membership figures shows that the number of part-timers covered by collective bargaining increased at about the same rate as full-time employees.

Lowe and Rastin (2000), recently highlighted the interest of the young in Canada, particularly the youngest age categories, in union representation. There have been a variety of high-profile unionization campaigns in British Columbia and Quebec of young private service sector workers, particularly in the food services industry with high-profile employers such as McDonald's and Starbucks. Yet, despite the visibility of such campaigns, Table 10.1 shows an actual decline in the number of unionized employees of 15 to 24 years of age (–18.4 per cent) as opposed to smaller declines and even expansion for older groups of age over the 1990 to 2000 period. Indeed, union coverage in the 45–54 age cohort in Canada actually increased by 42.7 per cent over the same period. Similarly, the same period was characterized by a decline in union members with short-term job tenure as opposed to longer-term job tenure. It is clear that unionization is much more prevalent among baby boomers than it is among what is popularly called the generations X and Y that followed them.

Recruitment amongst these new groups of workers rests in part on the permeability of internal union structures to new interests and opportunities for participation by these groups. A study of members of the Confederation des syndicats nationaux (CSN) – one of the major union organizations in Quebec province – highlighted the importance of internal factors for union renewal. Drawing on a representative survey of members of the CSN, Lévesque, Murray and Le Queux (1998) investigated whether the new identity groups – women, the young, those with less stable employment, those in private services or those with higher educational attainment – were more likely to be alienated from the union. The response offered a fascinating glimpse of the complexities of union renewal. They found that these new identity groups were as likely as all other members to express strong support for the basic need for unionism. However, this general endorsement of their union did not necessarily translate into an embrace of all of its methods or values. In essence, many of the new identity groups were less likely to express the traditional union value set, for example the importance of the strike as a defence mechanism or of not crossing picket lines. One of the most significant countervailing factors that allowed for these new identity groups to buy into their union culture was participation in their union. In other words, a sense of internal democracy was likely to translate into a closer proximity to the union as an organization and as a social movement.

The theme of enhanced inclusiveness is an important one running through much of the literature and thinking on union renewal in Canada. Many Canadian unions have introduced a wide variety of intermediary representative structures based on new identities such as racial or ethnic orientation, identities based on professional, gender or sexual orientation (see Murray, 1991; Briskin, 1999; Hunt, 1997). As was highlighted by the study of Lévesque, Murray and Le Queux (1998), the challenge is to ensure that these structures provide real opportunities for engagement with and participation in the union, from which new collective values, adapted to the realities of the changing workforce, are likely to emerge.

A simple but telling example emerges from the study of the bargaining priorities of unions in Canada. To what extent does their agenda reflect the concerns of new groups to be organized? The HRDC survey indicated that gender, family and working-time issues tended to come relatively far down the list of bargaining priorities for most unions. Thus, 23.6 per cent of unions indicated that a policy on sexual or racial harassment was a high priority, 18.7 per cent employment equity, 11.2 per cent family-related leave, 11.2 per cent restrictions on overtime, 5.6 per cent flexible working time and 2.3 per cent childcare facilities. Such a priorazation rated far behind the importance attributed to the protection of current wages and benefits (90 per cent of respondent unions), job adjustment issues concerning training, flexibility and the union role in the workplace (more than 40 per cent of unions) and job control and participative mechanisms (at least 25 per cent of unions). Why gender and working-time issues rate so low is a matter for conjecture. Are they seen to be publicly mandated and therefore to be achieved in non-bargaining forums? Do these issues have low ratings because of underrepresentation of those who espouse these issues or the absence of appropriate forums in which to advance them? Irrespective of the explanation, it is important to note that the actual degree of success achieved on such items was in fact very high when these items were a high priority (Kumar and Murray, 2002). This finding again highlights the strategic importance of increased opportunities for participation and internal democracy in the renewal of unions.

To summarize, Canadian unions have engaged in substantial innovation over the past couple of decades in order to reach out to new groups of workers, especially women and part-time workers, but there remain substantial barriers to a quantum shift in the density of union coverage. First, the evolving structure of employment, with the fragmentation of traditional employment relationships into temporary jobs and the drift to forms of independent contracting, raises problems for union recruitment. These are further exacerbated by the public policy framework, which is ill adapted to these new forms of employment (Murray and Verge, 1999).

Second, much of the new organizing is taking place on a fragmentary and decentralized basis. Most national and international unions in Canada have made it clear that they see a very limited role for labour centres in the area of recruitment and organizing. There has not been much attempt to develop a coordinated strategy at this level and, with the exception of the British Columbia Federation of Labour, where efforts to develop a common strategy have taken place, they have generally been rebuffed. The absence of coordination and the predominance of a piecemeal fragmentary approach is likely to bedevil union efforts to effect any significant shift in the level of union coverage in the Canadian economy.

Finally, there remain important internal union barriers to new recruitment activity. Despite some evidence of an increase in organizing resources, such resources need to be expanded even more. Further, to appeal to new identity groups unions need to ensure access to union structures and resources for new members and enhanced opportunities for participation. Although Canadian union structures have proved to be relatively permeable to the expression of new interests and an identity agenda, leading to some success by Canadian unions with these new groups of workers, internal union structural reform needs to continue.

Strategic engagement in the workplace

The relentless pressure for workplace change is a second strategic challenge facing unions in Canada. The drive by management to create 'high-performance organizations' has been characterized by successive waves of restructuring and reorganization to achieve corporate norms of efficiency and flexibility. This trend covers a wide variety of changes in the workplace: numerical and functional flexibility in work processes and structures with an emphasis on flexible job designs and work arrangements, performance- and knowledge-based compensation systems, the decentralization of decision-making authority, increasing employee involvement and peer discipline through team/group work, and the promotion of a non-adversarial employer-employee relationship in order to foster a 'participatory' enterprise culture. This new unitary approach to human resource management has significant implications for the independent workplace role of unions. The approach is more centred on employees than on union representation. It favours efficiency and management control, as opposed to equity and pro-cedural fairness in work allocation. It further implies an enterprise role and partnership in workplace administration, fundamentally different from the traditional 'watchdog' or protective role of unions.

Unions thus face a quandary. To resist change is to stand accused of being dinosaurs – special interest groups intent on the defence of members' privileges. To support such changes and participate in the change process on management terms risk the danger of being 'co-opted' to the corporate competitiveness agenda. To engage strategically in the change process on the basis of autonomous power and an independent agenda of economic and social change, can provide new opportunities for expanded union influence on workplace governance, but it can also associate local union leaders with the negative consequences of some of these changes. In other words, a strategy of engagement can be a source of union renewal but also involves considerable risk. Union leaders in Canada have generally concluded that they have no choice but to be both defensive and proactive on workplace change. This mixed strategy is a product of their vision or values, the environmental context that they face, and the nature of workplace change and its impact on workers, work environment and union power.

First, in terms of values, unions in Canada have espoused productive, safe, secure and healthy workplaces for their members, which are free from discrimination and harassment and that provide opportunities for economic advancement, social interaction, and involvement in decision making. The approaches of individual unions may vary, but the common strand is that strategic involvement in workplace change can advance more effectively these worker goals (CLC, 1992).

Second, the adverse economic, public policy, and bargaining environment also explains Canadian unions' mixed-strategy approach to workplace change. The HRDC survey of unions revealed that Canadian unions see themselves operating in a 'lean and mean' environment of intense competitive pressures and cost cutting with increased management emphasis on cost reduction, closures and mergers, downsizing, outsourcing and contracting out, use of temporary, contract and part-time workers, and privatization. Employer demands for wage and work-rule concessions have increased. These pressures, according to the survey results, are systematically more acute in the highly unionized public sector than in the private sector, and have adversely affected both union bargaining power and the work environment and the quality of life of union members. Another survey of labour leaders, conducted by the Canadian Labour and Business Centre (CLBC) in the year 2000, found that, due to a growing emphasis on 'more work with less people', the workplace climate has deteriorated. This deterioration is manifested in such indicators as working relationships, workplace morale, workplace violence and injuries, stress levels, and work/family pressures (CLBC, 2001). It is perhaps not surprising then, as was apparent in the HRDC survey, that the overwhelming priority of unions is a defensive one. Asked to identify their bargaining priorities in the most recent bargaining round, more than 90 per cent of union respondents identified the protection of current levels of wages and benefits as a high priority (90.6 per cent). To emphasize its defensive nature, this priority contrasts markedly with the improvement of wages and benefits, which was identified as a high priority by only 44.3 per cent of respondents. It is probably not surprising that traditional job control and workplace procedural mechanisms, such as lay-off protections (64.4 per cent) and restrictions on contracting out and outsourcing (47.8 per cent) were also identified as a high priority. However, a more proactive orientation to workplace change was also apparent in the identification of bargaining priorities. Almost half of Canadian union respondents identified an increased union role in decision making (49 per cent), advance notice of organizational change (46.6 per cent), consultation mechanisms on change (44.3 per cent) and improved training and retraining opportunities (42.2 per cent) as high priorities during the last bargaining round.

Third, the extent, nature and impact of workplace change provide additional valuable insights into Canadian unions' choice of strategy. The HRDC survey revealed that the workplace change has been pervasive across Canada, covering both public and private sectors. Unilateral implementation of change by management was the most dominant pattern, although consultation with unions was also customary particularly in the public secotor where unionization rates are very high. Unions supported the changes 'some of the time', when it was felt that change could benefit worker well-being or lead to expanded influence for unions. The survey revealed a mixed pattern of outcomes. Among the most common impacts were a decline in worker confidence in management due to unfilled expectations, a reduction in job or employment security, and a deterioration in the quality of work life. A substantial minority of unions (one-third to two-fifths of respondents) also reported increased union influence and worker control, higher levels of worker confidence in unions, and improved union-management relations. The impacts on unions were also diverse. The change initiatives significantly strained union resources, heightened the need for education, research and rank-and-file communications, diverted attention from organizing and day-to-day activities and created an atmosphere of crisis and/or tension between members and leadership or, in some situations, between locals and national offices. An overwhelming majority of unions surveyed suggested that the change initiatives created modest to significant pressures within their unions to formulate an independent agenda on workplace change. These HRDC survey results on the nature and impact of workplace change are confirmed by a number of other studies (Kumar, 1995; Schenk and Anderson, 2000; Statistics Canada, 1998; Lewchuk and Robertson, 1997; Lévesque et al., 1997).

Just as in the case of organizing discussed in the previous section and unlike a number of other countries, Canada's main labour centre – the CLC – does not articulate a particular workplace agenda of its own. Although the CLC has been engaged in promoting education and research on work restructuring through its provincial and local bodies and in developing a national training strategy, individual affiliated unions are left, and no doubt prefer, to develop their own policy agenda according to their particular needs and circumstances. Such policies reflect their values, goals, priorities, organizational culture and the history of their relationship with employers in their major sectors. Labour's agenda on workplace changes, as illustrated by formal statements of Canada's three large private sector unions – the Canadian Autoworkers Union (CAW), the United Steelworkers of America (USWA) and Communications, Energy and Paperworkers Union of Canada (CEP) – nonetheless present a number of common elements. These include a clear statement that labour and management have different goals, priorities and interests in workplace change; a focus on major improvements in work environment through union participation in job designs and technological change; expanded opportunities for training and joint control of training to enhance accessibility, ensure the provision of generic portable skills, and expand union influence on the delivery of training; a meaningful input in the conception, development and implementation of change; access to resources, training and information to negotiate effectively and participate in the change process; inclusion of employment equity and work-time flexibility initiatives; the maintenance of a basic wage as a primary form of negotiation; and an insistence on negotiated change (see Kumar, 1995).

In pursuit of this agenda, unions developed a number of policies and guidelines, as well as support systems, to help locals negotiate change and build their capacities, skills, and competencies in dealing with management. They have also modified their bargaining priorities to give effect to these policies. Our survey showed that over one-third of the unions reported having developed a comprehensive workplace change policy. Large unions are more likely to have such comprehensive policy guidelines than the small or medium-size unions. A majority of unions also have specific policies on training and retraining, outsourcing/contracting out, and employee involvement.

The HRDC survey further revealed that a majority of unions in Canada conduct educational programmes and/or offer courses to train leadership and rank-and-file activists on change issues. Membership surveys to solicit and analyse members' views on problems, possibilities, and the impact of change are also quite common. A majority of unions also report that their national offices provide technical assistance to help locals in negotiating workplace change. A few unions have also designated exclusive staff resources to deal with work reorganization and training-related matters. The survey also showed that unions with a comprehensive policy agenda, primarily large unions with more than 30,000 members, are more likely to have expanded support systems to guide and coordinate the activities of their locals. It would appear that the more extensive resources associated with large unions are an important factor in the development of proactive workplace change strategies.

Canadian unions have not limited their engagement strategies to the workplace level. They are also working with employers and governments to regulate the process of economic restructuring, in particular to expand their influence and opportunities in the area of labour adjustment and training, venture investment funds and research and education. For example, they have participated actively in sectoral training councils (Gunderson and Sharpe, 1998), labour-sponsored investment funds (Quarter *et al.*, 2001) and university research initiatives. Unions also make extensive use of the Internet to strengthen communication with rank-and-file membership. Active involvement in activities of the CLBC, the only national centre jointly administered by business and labour, is another example of unions' proactivity on their strategic engagement in the change process. The CLBC conducts research on workplace change and related issues and acts as a forum for consensus building on labour market and productivity issues.

It is still too early to make any definitive pronouncements on the success of this combined union strategy of defensive and proactive engagement in workplace change. However, it is fair to say that the union experience has so far been mixed. A first indicator of limited success is perhaps the chilling effect on employers of unions taking more consistent and comprehensive positions on these issues. Union resistance and willingness to participate in the change process has probably forced employers to be cautious in unilaterally implementing change and to reassess their proposals in order to accommodate union concerns. Indeed, the union factor is advanced as the reason why workplace change in Canada, relative to the USA and other countries, has been slow and uneven (see OECD, 1999). It can be argued that unions have been successful in slowing down the pace of change on such practices as performance- and/or knowledge-based compensation, job rotation, and team concepts. However, there is also some evidence that the predominant mode for the implementation of workplace change remains unilateral imposition by management. In the HRDC survey, nearly two-fifths (39 per cent) of the unions surveyed indicated that initiatives were implemented by management unilaterally most of the time and almost one-half (47.6 per cent) said they were unilaterally implemented some of the time.

Despite this cautionary note, there is mounting evidence of a growing incidence of information sharing and communication in industries undergoing significant restructuring (Verma and Chaykowski, 1999). Perhaps more significant is the increasing frequency of negotiations over quality, work methods, scheduling, and training as well as the establishment of labour-management committees in a vast majority of recent collective agreements (Payette, 2000). It appears that through their strategic participation in the change process some unions in Canada have been able to demonstrate that union involvement in the change process can ensure more stable change and better outcomes in terms of economic benefits, labour relations and work environment (Holmes and Kumar, 1998; Lapointe *et al.*, 2000); Lévesque and Murray, 1998).

However, it is also apparent that negotiating workplace change and work reorganization is not an easy task when union and employer goals, interests and priorities diverge significantly. Beyond the rhetoric that workers are their most valuable resource, management's primary goals are improved productivity, enhanced product/service quality, and greater cost-efficiency and control. Management interest in improving work environment, meaningful employee empowerment, and better quality of work life – the primary goals of unions in participation in workplace change – is secondary (Kumar, 1995, 2000). This clash of objectives is clearly reflected in the recent CLBC survey of labour and management views on what constitutes a 'healthy workplace'. While high productivity, low absenteeism, high morale, high motivation, the ability to attract and retain employees and good working relationships are the key criteria for a healthy workplace for business; a safe/secure workplace, worker ability to balance work and family pressures, low levels of injuries and manageable stress are the priorities for labour (CLBC, 2001). High morale and good working relations are common indicators, but business and management differ markedly in their evaluation of their recent evolution. Labour reports the deterioration in the two indicators while business believes that there has been a significant improvement in both worker morale and working relationships over time. Similarly, whereas unions stress that in order to have an effective impact over workplace change they must be involved in long-term discussions on production/service delivery methods and technological change, employers appear unwilling to foster exchange on strategic production and investment issues and implementation of technological change and give up their management prerogatives to manage the workplace.

This management resistance to an expanded union role in workplace change is probably the reason why unions have had much less success at the bargaining table on workplace control issues. The HRDC survey indicated that although unions have been able to achieve a high degree of success on traditional bargaining objectives, they have had much less success in negotiating an enhanced role in workplace change. Even those unions that attached a high degree of priority to negotiating an enhanced role in workplace change were unlikely to achieve a high degree of success (Kumar and Murray, 2002).

There is evidence, however, that unions achieve a higher degree of success in their strategic engagement in the workplace when they can mobilize internal and external resources in the pursuit of these objectives Thus, unions able to increase local union capacity through education and research, expanded communication and opportunities for debate and discussion are more likely to achieve their desired results in the negotiation of workplace change. Local unions are more effective in negotiating workplace change when they develop close horizontal and vertical relationships with their own and other unions (Murray *et al.*, 1999) and have internal democracy, measured by the 'degree of responsiveness of local unions' leaders to the interest of the membership and by the broad based activity of its membership' (Frost, 2000) or what Lévesque and Murray (1998, 2002) call internal and external solidarity. The resource power base stemming from internal cohesion, democracy and external alliances with other unions and social groups in the community, Lévesque and Murray (2002) argue, could be the most effective tool for expanding union influence over workplace change and enabling union renewal.

If Canadian unions' strategic engagement in workplace change has only had a mixed success, it is perhaps not because a proactive strategy does not work but because unions must give an even greater priority to building local union power and capacity. Indeed, it is safe to state that many unions have not really put serious efforts into building inter-union and community alliances. The basic strategic challenge for Canadian unions in the realm of engagement in the workplace is thus twofold: finding an appropriate balance between their defensive and proactive strategies, and building their local unions' capacity for a more effective policy agenda on work reorganization and enforcing it through a synergetic use of internal cohesion, external alliances and union democracy.

Conclusion: Avenues for renewal

Union renewal is not a simple technical question of readjusting servicing or organizing strategies. The complexity of finding appropriate voices and structures for new and renewed types of interest intermediation indicates that there is not a single, magical formula for union renewal. On the basis of the two strategic challenges examined, the strategic challenge for Canadian unions seems to lie in finding the appropriate balance between defensive and proactive strategies. Defensive strategies, grounded in workplace contingency, are a necessary but often insufficient response to the changing environment. Proactive strategies are clearly central to the continuing renewal of labour organizations in Canada and their ability to respond to this new environment on behalf of their members. Such proactive strategies promise to break new ground, but they also risk greater resistance both from the external environment and within unions themselves. This points to the need to broaden alliances and to deepen the dialogue within the membership about the need to emphasize certain kinds of goals in the pursuit of union renewal. As for the dialogue amongst the membership, democracy must be conceptualized as a vital source of union power. The success of proactive strategies thus appears to depend on the building of capacity at several levels of the labour movement. It is to the long-term building of such capacity that union 'renewalists' must turn their energies if they are to secure more fundamental changes for the role of workers and their representative organizations in their societies.

Acknowledgements

The authors wish to acknowledge the financial support of Human Resources Development Canada (HRDC), the Social Sciences and Humanities Research Council (SSHRC) and the Fonds pour la formation de chercheurs et d'aide à la recherche (FCAR) in Quebec in the research reported in this chapter. The views expressed in this chapter are those of the authors and do not necessarily reflect those of the organizations supporting this research.

References

Akyeampong, E. (2000) 'Non-unionized But Covered by a Collective Agreement', *Perspectives on Labour and Income*, Statistics Canada 2000 Special Labour Day Release, pp. 3–19.

Briskin, L. (1999) 'Autonomy, Diversity and Integration: Union Women's Separate Organizing in North America and Western Europe in the Context of Restructuring and Globalization', *Women's Studies International Forum*, 22 (5): 543–54.

Briskin, L. and McDermott, P. (eds) (1993) *Women Challenging Unions: Feminism, Democracy and Militancy*, Toronto: University of Toronto Press.

Canadian Labour and Business Centre (CLBC) (2001) *Viewpoints 2000: The Healthy Workplace*, Ottawa.

Canadian Labour Congress (CLC) (1992) *Economic Policy Statement: 19th Constitutional Convention*, Ottawa.

Frost, A. (2000) 'Explaining Variation in Workplace Restructuring: The Role of Local Union Capabilities', *Industrial and Labor Relations Review*, 53 (4): 559–78.

Galarneau, D. (1996) 'Unionized Workers', *Perspectives on Labour and Income*, Ottawa (Spring), Statistics Canada, Catalogue no. 75-001-XPF, pp. 43–52.

Gindin, S. and L. Panitch (2000) 'Rekindling Socialist Imagination: Utopian Vision and Working-class Capacities', *Monthly Review*, March, pp. 36–51.

Gunderson, M. and Sharpe, A. (1998) *Forging Business–Labour Partnerships: The Emergence of Sectoral Councils in Canada*, Toronto: University of Toronto Press.

Holmes, J. and Kumar, P. (1998) 'Recent Patterns of Production and Investment in the Canadian Auto Industry: Reflections on Management Strategy', in Babson, S. and Núñez (eds) *Confronting Change: Auto Labor and Lean Production in North America*, Detroit: Wayne State University Press, pp. 95–115.

Hunt, G. (1997) 'Sexual Orientation and the Canadian Labour Movement', *Relations industrielles/Industrial Relations*, 52 (4): 787–811.

ILO (International Labour Organization) (1997) *World Labour Report: Industrial Relations, Democracy and Stability*, Geneva, Switzerland: International Labour Office.

Jackson, A. and Robinson, D. (with Bob Baldwin and Cindy Wiggins) (2000) *Falling Behind: The State of Working Canada*, Ottawa: Canadian Centre for Policy Alternatives.

Kumar, P. (1995) *Unions and Workplace Change in Canada*, Kingston, Ontario: IRC Press, Queen's University.

Kumar, P. (2000) 'Rethinking High Performance Work Systems', in *Incomes and Productivity in North America: Papers of the 2000 Seminar*, Washington: Commission for Labor Cooperation, North America Agreement on Labour Cooperation.

Kumar, P. and Murray, G. (2002) 'Canadian Union Strategies in the Context of Change', *Labor Studies Journal*, 26 (4): 1–28.

Kumar, P., Murray, G. and Schetagne, S. (1998a) 'Adapting to Change: Union Priorities in the 1990s', *Workplace Gazette* (Fall), pp. 84–98.

Kumar, P., Murray G. and Schetagne, S. (1998b) 'Workplace Change in Canada: Union Perceptions of Impacts, Responses and Support Systems', *Workplace Gazette* (Winter), pp. 75–87.

Kumar, P. and Ryan, D. (1988) *The Canadian Union Movement in the 1980s: Perspectives of the Leaders*, Kingston, Ontario: Industrial Relations Centre, Queen's University.

Lapointe, P.-A., Lévesque, C., Murray, G. and Jacques, F. (2000) *Les Innovations en milieu de travail dans l'industrie des équipements de transport terrestre au Québec: rapport synthèse*, Quebec: Ministère du travail.

Lévesque, C. and Murray, G. (1998) 'La régulation paritaire à l'épreuve de la mondialisation', *Relations industrielles/Industrial Relations*, 53 (1): 90–122.

Lévesque, C. and Murray, G. (2002) 'Local versus Global: Activating Local Union Power in the Global Economy', *Labor Studies Journal* 27(3): 39–65.

Lévesque, C., Murray, G. and Le Queux, S. (1998) 'Transformations sociales et identités syndicales: l'institution syndicale à l'épreuve de la différenciation sociale contemporaine', *Sociologie et sociétés*, XXX (2): 131–54.

Lévesque, C., Murray, G., Le Queux, S. and Roby, N. (1997) 'Workplace Restructuring and Worker Representation: The Impact of Work Reorganization on the Local Union', in Chaykowski, R., Lapointe, P. A., Vallée, G. and Verma, A. (eds) *Worker Representation in the Era of Trade and Depregulation*, Québec: ACRI/CIRA, pp. 115–30.

Lewchuk, W. and Robertson, D. (1997) 'Production without Empowerment: Work Organization from the Perspectives of Motor Vehicle Workers', *Capital and Class* (Fall): 37–64.

Lipsig-Mumme, C. and Lexer, K. (1998) 'Organizing and Union Membership: A Canada Profile 1997', York University CRWS Working Paper No. 18.

Lowe, G. and Rastin, S. (2000) 'Organizing the Next Generation: Influences on Young Workers' Willingness to Join Unions in Canada', *British Journal of Industrial Relations*, 38 (2): 203–22.

Lowe, G. and Schellenberg, C. (2001) *Changing Employment Relationships in Canada: A CPRN Research Report*, Ottawa: Canadian Policy Research Networks Inc.

Martinello, F. (1996) *Certification and Decertification Activity in Canadian Jurisdictions*, Kingston, Ontario: Industrial Relations Centre, Queen's University.

Martinello, F. (2000) 'Mr. Harris, Mr Rae, and Union Activity in Ontario', *Canadian Public Policy*, 26 (1): 17–33.

Masters, M. F. and Atkins, R. S. (1999) 'Union Strategies for Revival: A Conceptual Framework and Literature Review', in Gerald R. Ferris (ed.) *Research in Personnel and Human Resources Management*, vol. 17, Stamford CT, JAI Press Inc., pp. 283–314.

Ministère du travail (various years), *Rapport annuel*, Quebec: Gouvernement du Québec.

Murray, G. (1991) 'Exceptionalisme canadien? L'évolution récente du syndicalisme au Canada', *La Revue de l'I.R.E.S.*, no 7, pp. 81–105.

Murray, G. (1998) 'Steeling for Change: Organization and Organizing in Two USWA Districts in Canada', in Bronfenbrenner, K., Friedman, S., Hard, R. W., Oswald, R. A. and Seeber, R. L. (eds) *Organizing to Win*, Ithaca, NY: Cornell University/ILR Press, pp. 320–38.

Murray, G., Lévesque, C., Roby, N. and Le Queux, S. (1999) 'Isolation or Integration? The Relationship between Local and National Union in the Context of Globalization', in Waddington, J. (ed.) *Globalization and Patterns of Labour Resistance*, London: Mansell, pp. 160–91.

Murray, G. and Verge, P. (1999) *La Représentation syndicale*, Sainte-Foy: Les Presses de l'Université Laval.

OECD (1999) 'New Enterprise Practices and Their Labour Market Implications', OECD Employment Outlook, June, pp. 177–223.

Olney, S. (1996) *Unions in a Changing World*, Geneva: Switzerland: International Labour Office.

Payette, S. (2000) 'What Is New in Workplace Innovations', *Workplace Gazette* (Spring), 3 (1): 110–19.

Quarter, J., Carmichael, I., Sousa, J. and Elgie, S. (2001) 'Social Investment by Union-based Pension Funds and Labour-sponsored Investment Funds in Canada', *Relations industrielles/Industrial Relations*, 56 (1): 92–115.

Schenk, C. and Anderson, J. (2000) *Reshaping Work 2: Labour, the Workplace and Technological Change*, Ottawa: Canadian Centre For Policy Alternatives.

Statistics Canada (1998) *The Evolving Workplace: Findings from the Pilot Workplace and Employee Survey*, Catalogue No. 71–583-XPE.

Verma, A. and Chaykowski, R. (eds) (1999) *Contract and Commitment: Employment Relations in the New Economy*, Kingston ON: Queen's University IRC Press.

Yates C. (2000) 'Staying the Decline in Union Membership: Union Organizing in Ontario, 1985–99', *Relations industrielles/Industrial Relations*, 55 (4): 640–74.

11 THE REVIVAL OF INDUSTRIAL UNIONS IN CANADA: THE EXTENSION AND ADAPTATION OF INDUSTRIAL UNION PRACTICES TO THE NEW ECONOMY

Charlotte A. B. Yates

Introduction

The breakdown of the post-war regime, based on growth in manufacturing and deepening domestic demand, has led many industrial relations scholars to argue that industrial unions face inevitable decline 'in the face of changing technology, workforce diversification and economic restructuring' (Cobble, 1994: 285). Built out of the adversarial industrial climate of mass production industries, industrial unions are said to have outlived their usefulness. Entrenched industrial union practices and structures arguably do not fit the new flexible, cooperative employment relations of contemporary workplaces, or industrial unions lack the experience and capacity to represent the needs of a more diverse and growing service sector workforce (Towers, 1997; Kochan *et al.*, 1986; Freeman, 1993; Cobble, 1994). Cobble concludes that 'just as industrial unionism superseded craft unionism as technological change and economic restructuring transformed the workplace, so too must industrial unionism give way to other alternatives' (Cobble, 1994: 195).

These conclusions are premature and fly in the face of mounting evidence that industrial unions are adapting successfully to new economic conditions and workforce demographics. This chapter develops two arguments about industrial union capacity to change, basing its argument on experience in Canadian unions. First, the chapter offers evidence that industrial unions have been as successful, if not more so, than other unions in Canada, in organizing and representing workers in the service sector and female and racially mixed workplaces. Second, the chapter contradicts conclusions about the outmoded nature of industrial union structures and practices, demonstrating instead that many industrial union practices are highly effective in protecting non-industrial workers' interests, and in particular those employed in the private service sector. This shifts one of the key issues in debate from the inadequacy of industrial union practices and structures to one about the conditions under which these unions can transfer existing structures and practices into new sectors. Overall, the chapter concludes that a new form of unionism is emerging. But this new form of unionism is arising out of the transformation of industrial unions, rather than from their supersession.

Although the following tale is a Canadian one, its importance to debates on union renewal are not limited to Canada. Most of the pressures that have necessitated change by industrial unions in Canada are being experienced elsewhere. Emergent new forms of unionism arising in Canada are likely therefore to resonate with experiences in other countries. Further, although Canada is like other 'liberal' countries where labour has never held the privileged position of political and economic influence in countries such as Sweden, the Canadian labour movement differs from those in Britain, Australia, New Zealand and the USA in having achieved relative stability in union membership over the last ten to twenty years (see Chapter 10). Thus the strategic responses of Canadian industrial unions may offer a road map to the future of unions in these countries.

The fate of industrial unions

Critics of unions more generally, and industrial unions in particular, have predicted that industrial unions would become the dinosaurs of the new economy, incapable of adapting to new economic conditions and eventually becoming extinct. These arguments have been based on an analysis of changes to the labour market that have eroded core memberships of industrial unions in heavy industry, in particular manufacturing, and arguments that existing union practices and structures do not 'fit' features of emerging employment relationships and economic realities. Through an examination of each of these two arguments this chapter challenges the evidence upon which arguments about the disappearance of industrial unions are based. Using evidence from interviews with union staff and leaders, a survey of union organizers in Ontario (the industrial heartland of

Canada), documentary evidence and observation of several unions, this chapter argues that industrial unions are being reborn by extending and adapting existing practices and structures into new growth industries. Rather than the dinosaurs of the new economy, industrial unions are engaged in a process of revitalization to emerge once again as counterbalances to increasingly powerful employers.

Heavy industry, especially manufacturing, on which industrial unions relied for the bulk of their memberships, have been hard hit by economic recessions in the early 1980s and early 1990s, and more systematically by industrial restructuring accompanying investment in new labour-saving technology. The immediate result was lay-offs of thousands of industrial union members and plummeting industrial union membership. The United Steelworkers of America, which lost 55,000 members of a total 180,000 in Canada between 1980 and 1983 was one of the unions hardest hit by this decline (CALURA, selected years; Murray, 1998). Although by the end of the 1990s, employment in manufacturing and other goods-producing industries in Canada was on the increase due to new investments and a boom in the automotive industry, the proportion of unionized workers in the manufacturing sector continued to decline. The biggest pool of non-unionized workers lies in the growing private service sector.

As important to union fortunes as these labour market and economic changes were, shifts in employer strategies and union responses to new conditions were as important in precipitating a crisis for industrial unions. The early 1980s were marked by employer demands for concessions from unions, which opened the door to significant restructuring of collective bargaining relationships between employers and industrial unions. Concession bargaining began as a means of offering firms temporary cost relief through reduced wages and benefits. Yet, as employers began to appreciate the depth of restructuring needed in order to survive competition and the underlying shift in balance of power away from unions, they used industrial unions' initial compliance over concessions to demand replacement of institutionalized bargaining relations with a new non-adversarial 'flexible' model of industrial relations (Drache, 1991; Mahon, 1991). Master and pattern bargaining and job control unionism, especially seniority provisions, came under attack. Accompanying these pressures was the articulation of a new ideology, couched as 'common sense', which portrayed unions as having outlived their usefulness. Only if they abandoned existing structures and practices might they survive.

The effects of these and related political economic changes on industrial unions were profound. Persistent high unemployment in Canada undercut the capacity of industrial unions to resist or bargain back many of the concessions that they had initially seen as temporary measures intended to restore the economic health to their employers. Declining real wages and the dismantling of entrenched institutions of collective bargaining placed into question the *raison d'être* of industrial unions. Many unions were left strategically disoriented. Industrial unions came under further pressure as their own members often blamed union strategies of concessions and cooperation with management for wage and benefit losses and declining working conditions. Changes in employment patterns towards non-standard and service sector work confronted industrial unions with the fact that membership renewal could no longer rely upon expansion in the manufacturing and resource industries. Further, the growth in labour market participation by women and workers from diverse ethnic and racial communities challenged established industrial union practices and identities (Yates, 1998b; Hyman, 1994).

Industrial unions initially responded defensively to the economic, political and social changes of the late 1970s and early 1980s. They sought to protect existing members from economic insecurity and to hang on to the vestiges of industrial unionism even while being forced in many instances to accept concessions and a devolution of union influence. As the crisis enveloping industrial unions deepened, however, these unions scrambled to adapt their strategies and rebuild their organizations. Rebuilding has meant both expanding membership to include workers from a more diverse range of industries, especially workers in the service sector, as well as the extension of industrial union structures and practices into new sectors.

Industrial unionism: the archetypical form of unionism in Canada

To appreciate the ways in which industrial unions have adapted to new political and economic conditions it is first important to sketch out the broad characteristics of this form of unionism, which became the dominant and hence archetypical form of unionism in post-World War II Canada. Industrial unions grew out of workers' struggles against the exclusive membership and conservative political practices of craft unions and out of the desperate economic and political conditions of the 1930s Depression. They were also a product of changing economic practices primarily associated with the rise to dominance of mass production. Workers employed in mass production industries were denied entrance into craft-based workers' organizations and sought protection and workplace rights in a new industrial form of union.

The industrial union model can be characterized along four dimensions – membership composition, union strategy, organizational structure and culture. Although variations on each of these dimensions arise out of the historical legacy and political struggles of individual unions, this typology is useful in identifying the key features of industrial unions.

Membership composition

Membership in industrial unions was organized on the basis of industry. Workers, whether skilled or unskilled, who were employed in an industry, were organized into single unions. Although membership in more than one industry developed as common practice, accepted conventions and sets of rules enforced by central labour bodies established industrially based jurisdictional boundaries within which unions organized and represented workers. The strength of industrial unions was based on the depth and spread of union organization within an industry or sector and associated capacity to regulate internal labour markets through the negotiation of common wage rates, work rules and working conditions. In practice, industrial unions tended to rely for organizational strength upon the unionization of large employers in heavy industry, especially manufacturing. They often ignored the organization of small employers on the assumption that near full employment in the post-war period forced these small non-union employers to pay union rates in order to secure a labour supply. This limited the effect of the non-union workplaces on wages and working conditions in the primary labour market. Few industrial unions organized the white-collar office workers employed in industries. These strategic choices by industrial unions meant that few women, and proportionally fewer workers from ethnic and racial minorities than were active in the labour force became members of these unions. These strategic choices also shaped in part the remaining characteristics of industrial unions, including their strategic orientation, organizational structure and collective identity. Until the 1980s, membership in industrial unions was remarkably stable in terms of numbers and the industries and employers that were organized. This stability rested on the continued dominance and periodic expansion of employment in the already unionized sectors, rather than union organizing efforts.

CHARLOTTE A. B. YATES

Industrial union strategy

Industrial union strategy became characterized beginning in the 1950s by its economism. Industrial unions focused their strategic energies primarily on collective bargaining and servicing of individual union members. Collective bargaining until the 1980s centred on the negotiation of wages and benefits and was 'generally predicated on what has been labelled "job-control" unionism' (Murray, 1998: 323). Job-control unionism entails bargaining detailed sets of work rules for each job in a workplace and controlling movement of workers from one job to another, whether due to promotion, changing production requirements or lay-off, through application of the seniority principle (Katz, 1985; Kochan *et al.*, 1986). As strikes in mid-contract were made illegal in Canada in the 1940s, legally mandated grievance procedures became the primary means through which unions upheld collective agreements in between sets of negotiations and individual members channelled their complaints. The result of this process was threefold. First, lengthy, technically detailed collective agreements were put into place that required specialized staff to interpret and uphold. Second, a passive servicing model of unionism tended to develop as individual union members relied on full-time union service representatives to resolve their complaints and problems. Third, this collective bargaining regime reinforced tendencies towards responsible unionism and depoliticized union goals, framing them instead around an economistic discourse and practice.

Industrial union goals of controlling the internal labour markets of particular industries or sectors have been achieved through a combination of seniority provisions and master and pattern bargaining of wages and working conditions. Master and pattern bargaining involve targeting a company or worksite for winning breakthroughs in collective bargaining. Gains made in a collective agreement at a targeted company/worksite are then used as a pattern for unions to negotiate similar agreements on other sites of the same employer or throughout a sector. Pattern bargaining encourages centralization of bargaining activities and reinforces reliance upon union leaders and specialists.

The political strategy of industrial unions became dominated by reformist, usually social democratic party politics. Industrial unions tended to develop formal ties with social democratic parties. Yet, other than periodic bursts of political activism at election time in support of their partisan allies, industrial unions left politics largely to the political party (Brodie and Jenson, 1988), focusing their energies on collective bargaining and membership servicing.

Organizational structure

Industrial union structures grew out of the ascendency of responsible unionism and came to reflect a union strategy dominated by collective bargaining. Industrial unions, which started as international unions with headquarters in the USA but with memberships that spanned national boundaries, developed as large, hierarchical organizations in which union locals were subordinate to national or international head offices. Union locals, with some exceptions, tended to comprise one certified bargaining unit which covered employees in one workplace, a model of unionism that has elsewhere been described as enterprise unionism.

International, national and regional union offices housed large staffs of service or 'business' representatives who undertook the day-to-day servicing of collective agreements and specialists in such areas as education, health and safety and pensions. These staff, who were more often appointed than elected, were responsible to union leaders. Union organizational structures tended to reflect corporate industry structure and the prevailing economism of industrial unions. Union departments corresponded either to specific companies or to specific technical divisions of the internal labour market and productive activities. Politics, organizing and education became 'ancillary services' (Murray, 1998: 324) to the main business of collective bargaining and controlling internal labour markets.

The second pillar of industrial union structure is its representative democratic structure. Instituted in part in reaction to the exclusive and leadership-dominated structures of older craft unions, industrial unions based the development of their internal structures on a model of representative democracy borrowed from the broader tenets of liberal democratic states. Representative democracy gives primacy to individual franchise, secret ballots, constitutionally protected regular elections and the role of the elected representative in speaking on behalf of his/her constituency. These rights and responsibilities are enshrined in union constitutions. For Peter Fairbrother such representative democracy encourages a

> view of democracy where the elected person is most frequently seen as a representative for a constituency rather than as a delegate of a constituency. As a representative the spokesperson has the authority to speak on behalf of their constituency without direct reference to that constituency ... Thus, the emphasis is on procedure and representation. (Fairbrother, 2000, p. 325)

Activities and forms of mass action outside these formal political structures were delegitimized, therefore having the effect of containing membership activism and militancy (Yates, 1993). Although industrial union strategy and structure arose in part out of internal union struggles, they were also heavily influenced by employer expectations of responsible union behaviour and economic efficiency and government regulation of union activities.

Collective identity

The final characteristic of industrial unions is their domination by a collective identity articulated around whiteness, male paternalism and physical brawn (Cockburn, 1991). This identity grew out of three sets of relationships, namely the 'brute' physical nature of work done by industrial union members, segmented labour market relations between white men, men of colour and women and the antagonistic relationship with management. In contrast to skilled workers, whose identity was constructed through a celebration of their skill, and hence superiority to other manual workers, industrial workers defined themselves in relationship to the physical nature of their work. Manliness defined through strength in physical work became a defining feature of industrial union identities. This process of identity construction through strength was reinforced by and rationalized racial and sexual segmentation of labour markets. Physical strength differentiated male industrial workers from women who were defined by their speed, dexterity and femininity (Jenson, 1989; Cockburn, 1988). At the same time, strength was graduated such that raw 'brute' strength required for certain types of work, such as foundry work, was identified with certain racial and ethnic groups whose 'inherent' characteristics made them more able to perform this type of work. The experience of labour market segmentation as physically separate spheres of work reinforced these identities.

But the identity of industrial unions also grew out of the antagonistic industrial relations in heavy industry. Maleness and physical strength became the basis upon which workers proved themselves capable of doing the work assigned to them by management (Lewchuk, 1993) while also providing a discourse through which to build collective support and legitimacy for combative union strategies such as strikes and picket lines. Through struggles and the telling of historic union battles, brawn, maleness and whiteness became conflated with the virtue of the production worker and industrial unionism. Maleness in industrial unionism was further reinforced by broader cultural and labour market practices that identified the family wage and the male bread-winner as the key to post-war prosperity and social stability.

The industrial union model, albeit in more complex and varied forms than is suggested above, persisted as the dominant form of unionism until the 1980s. Initially under pressure from women and people of colour mobilizing for change in the 1970s, industrial unions only underwent significant change in the aftermath of the 1981–2 recession. This recession shifted the balance of power between labour and capital and precipitated the unravelling of many features of the post-war regime, including dramatic changes in economic organization and management practices, shifts in government policy towards neo-liberal market-driven solutions and struggles to dismantle the existing collective bargaining regime. As conditions that secured the privileged post-war position of industrial unions were eroded, the viability and relevance of industrial unions and the working class to the new economy and society came into question, both in Canada and abroad (Laxer, 1984, 1996; Gorz, 1982). The remainder of this chapter examines how industrial unions responded to these challenges and the possibility for their renewal.

Industrial unions in the throes of change

After an initial period of retrenchment and disarray in the 1980s, industrial unions have tried to adapt to economic and political-cultural changes. Patterns of membership expansion discussed below suggest a tendency for industrial unions to become general unions, a tendency that supports the 'end of industrial unions' thesis. Yet, bargaining practices, emergent organizational structures and ways that industrial unions have of seeing their new members suggests instead that industrial unions are attempting to extend the industrial union model into new industries and adapt within rather than against the industrial union form. The industrial union form is proving resilient due to the relative success of industrial union structures and practices in defending and representing workers in the previously unorganized private service sector. Four areas of adaptation are discussed below: 1) organizing the unorganized, 2) bargaining, 3) restructuring of internal union organizations, and 4) changes to union identity. Not all unions have embraced change on all fronts. Moreover, some industrial unions are changing in ways that erode the industrial union model while others are more systematically trying to adapt and extend this model to new groups of workers.

CHARLOTTE A. B. YATES

Organizing

By the end of the 1980s, most industrial unions in Canada renewed their commitment to organizing the unorganized in efforts to reverse the precipitous declines in their memberships. The initial thrust of organizing lay in extending the industrial union principle by organizing smaller and newly established shops in existing industrial jurisdictions. This organizing strategy was intended to restore union density to core industries which had been declining due to employment growth in non-union companies such as Japanese transplant auto plants and new non-union competitors (Yates, 1998a; USWA, 1998). Although this approach paid off, it did not tackle a number of challenges identified by industrial unions. Employment in the private service sector was growing at a rate greater than employment in traditional areas of union strength. With exceedingly low unionization rates, the private service industry was seen as a prime source of new members for industrial unions. Further, a growing literature based on polls of workers showed that women were consistently more predisposed to joining unions than men (USWA, 1998: 17). Yet, industrial unions had hitherto ignored women and their workplaces as potential sources of membership. Several industrial unions therefore saw organizing amongst women as crucial to their future, necessitating not only different types of organizing strategies and targets but also wider reformation of industrial union structures and practices. These realizations drove industrial unions to expand the scope of their organizing drives beyond core industries and traditional groups of workers.

In the last five years, this has meant a growing concentration of industrial union resources into organizing in the service sector, including the fast-food industry, healthcare, casinos, universities, cleaning and security (Yates and Ewer, 1997; Yates, 1998a; Yates, 2000b). Based on industrial union responses to a survey of union organizers in Ontario, only 32 per cent of organizing drives by industrial unions that resulted in applications for certification to the Labour Board between 1 May 1996 and 30 April 1998 were in the manufacturing sector and 8.2 per cent in the transportation and storage industries. This compared to 46 per cent in private services, of which 14.2 per cent of total organizing drives were in retail trade, 10.2 per cent in accommodation, food and beverage services and 13.7 per cent in 'other services'. Of the total organizing drives launched in the private service sector in the province of Ontario, industrial unions were responsible for almost 60 per cent. Proportionally more of the total organizing drives undertaken by industrial unions were launched in female-dominated workplaces (defined as workplaces where 60 per cent or more of the workers were women) than by non-industrial unions. Industrial unions are also more likely to organize work-places where the majority of workers are people of colour. In light of this focus on organizing amongst women, people of colour and in the service sector, it is not surprising that during organizing drives, industrial unions emphasize issues of job security, the need for a voice in decision making, dignity and justice and scheduling and hours. These data demonstrate clearly that industrial unions are both adapting their organizing strategies to target new workforces but are also proving capable of shifting their priorities so to represent service sector workers, women and people of colour.

This shift in the type of workplace and workforce organized has necessit-ated a revision in organizing strategies used by industrial unions. Fuelling this shift in organizing strategy is the need for industrial unions to adapt to increasingly effective anti-union employer strategies and more restrictive labour laws. Innovations in organizing strategies are devised to overcome barriers in gaining access to workers in small workplaces and appealing to diverse groups of workers. Strategies tend to be more rank-and-file intensive, pay greater attention to the diversity of the workforce and in some cases build new alliances between unions and social movements.

Rank-and-file intensive tactics encompass many of those strategies asso-ciated with the organizing model. Although not necessarily new to unions, these strategies are being employed in a more systematic and tactical man-ner. Based on survey results, the two rank-and-file strategies with the greatest positive effect on the outcome of an organizing drive were making initial contact with a group of unorganized workers through another rank-and-file worker and building an inside organizing committee made up of workers from the workplace being organized. Based on the idea that workers have greater credibility than union staff with other workers and a better under-standing of workplace problems, these strategies assign a primary role in the organizing drive to workers themselves. In addition to this tactic, unions continue to use other rank-and-file intensive tactics such as holding small group meetings, phoning and making house calls to workers. These strate-gies increase in effectiveness according to the proportion of workers con-tacted (Yates, 2000a) and in some cases have quite different effects in female- and male-dominated (more than 60 per cent women or men) workplaces.

Two common ways in which industrial unions have adapted their strategies in recognition of growing labour force diversity are the adoption of a dis-course of equality in their appeals to workers and the employment of organizers that 'mirror' the demographics of the workplace being organized. The latter has been achieved in Australia and the USA by hiring university students, often associated with various social movements, as union organizers. This strategy has been rejected by most unions in Canada. Canadian unions, supported increasingly by unions in Australia and the USA, argue that university students lack the work and life experience to empathize with and build trust amongst workers (Lerner, 1999; LeBeau and Lynch, 1999; Early, 1999). Moreover, university student organizers tend to be parachuted into communities, reinforcing arguments made by employers that unions are outsiders, with no real knowledge or commitment to the long-term economic health of communities. Most Canadian industrial unions have achieved representativeness in their organizing drives by training hundreds of rank-and-file workers as organizers, involving them either as volunteers or temporary paid organizers in organizing drives (Yates, 2000b: 657–8). This strategy has the advantage of providing unions with trained organizers with diverse workplace experiences and demographic characteristics who also have experience in particular communities. Unions can then match the composition of their organizing committee with that of the workplace being organized. In British Columbia, the involvement of the Organizing Institute, modelled on the US experience, in training organizers on behalf of unions allows unions to create a common pool of union organizers. This overcomes a problem faced by many industrial unions that lack internal membership diversity at the outset and therefore have few workers from diverse communities who they can train as organizers.

A handful of industrial unions, such as the Canadian Autoworkers Union (CAW) and Union of Needletrades, Industrial and Textile Employees (UNITE) have also adopted a strategy of community unionism that is aimed at building long-term links between unions and communities in anticipation that this will build union credibility and further break down barriers of access to workers in 'new' communities. Community must not be misconstrued as being limited to spatial communities. The community in community unionism has a much broader application, including spatial as well as gender, ethnic and racial communities. Community unionism is a long-term strategy wherein unions first focus on building alliances between unions and community organizations, sometimes offering services such as legal aid or education to non-union workers. Only much later do unions expect to reap increased membership benefits. Links with diverse communities have been established in a variety of ways. The CAW established a store-front union office in downtown Toronto where non-union workers could drop in for advice on such matters as employment rights. For its part, UNITE built alliances with ethnic and immigrant community groups, especially the Chinese community from which large numbers of homeworkers are employed by the textile and clothing industries, by offering services such as legal aid, English as a second language classes and access to community kitchens to non-union workers (Borowy and Johnson, 1995). Unfortunately, these strategies have proven expensive and difficult to sustain, especially in an environment where unions want immediate membership gains from organizing expenditures. For this reason UNITE has abandoned many of its initiatives. For its part, the CAW has modified its approach, separating community union recruitment strategies from the broader political project of building social movement unionism whereby it establishes long-term working relationships with social movements around particular issues, such as daycare and free trade (Gindin, 1998).

The combined effect on industrial unions of changing membership targets and adaptive organizing strategies is highly diverse union memberships and proportional declines in core union memberships. For example, CAW membership amongst auto workers declined from 85 per cent to 40 per cent of total union membership within a ten-year time span while membership increased amongst workers in the service and other industrial sectors (Yates, 1998a). During the 1980s, one Canadian district of the USWA increased female membership by 341 per cent (Murray, 1998: 329).

Growing membership diversity within industrial unions puts pressure on the coherence of the industrial union model by eroding the membership principle of one industry, one union. Yet, whether these membership changes signal the end of industrial unions depends upon the direction of change pursued by these unions in attendant modifications of union struc-ture, strategy and union identity. Some industrial unions have seen the dis-cussed changes to their membership as merely expanding the principle of industrial unionism, to embrace a number of additional industries, in par-ticular the service industry. In this way, they seek to sustain the form of industrial unionism. The challenge for them lies in successfully extending existing structures and practices to these new industries, while modifying their collective identity to become more inclusive and representative of diverse memberships including women and ethnic and racial minorities. It is to a discussion of these other dimensions of change that we now turn.

Changing bargaining capacity: industrial unions and diverse memberships

The data on organizing by industrial unions, presented earlier in this chapter, underscores the shifts taking place in the type of workforce being organized by industrial unions. Yet, key to the long-term adaptability and survival of industrial unions is their capacity to bargain effectively for new groups of workers, thus retaining them as members. Survey results show that industrial unions are as likely to get a first contract for private service sector workplaces as unions in the total population. Although the numbers are small, industrial unions have an even greater likelihood of gaining a first contract in the government/public sector (82 per cent) than all unions surveyed (70 per cent). While industrial unions have expanded their bargaining agenda and wins to include such issues as protection against sexual and racial harassment, paid maternity leave and childcare, they have also extended many traditional industrial union benefits to service sector workers, most notably seniority provisions and job ladders. The extension of these 'traditional' benefits to workers in the service sector offers the potential for recognition of currently hidden and undervalued skills of workers while also building career ladders for service workers (Probert, 1992). In so doing, industrial unions put pressure on secondary labour markets to adopt many of the internal labour market advantages currently offered only in the male-dominated primary labour markets.

Organizing in the private service sector has confronted industrial unions with the problem of developing methods of bargaining that are effective for multiple small and dispersed bargaining units. Problems include the high cost of bargaining for and servicing these workplaces and the difficulty in mobilizing adequate pressure on employers when workforces are small. Industrial unions have proved particularly effective in meeting these challenges by extending the industrial principle of master bargaining to the service sector. Examples of this include the USWA's master contract for Pinkerton's security guards who work in workplaces ranging from one to 100 workers, CAW master contracts for more than 50 Kentucky Fried Chicken outlets in British Columbia and several Starbucks coffee bars, and United Food and Commercial Workers (UFCW) master contracts for several store chains such as Zellers. Once these unions establish master contracts, newly organized bargaining units are conjoined into the existing contract, thus providing much better terms and conditions for the newly organized workers. Master bargaining has several advantages, including its cost-effectiveness, improved capacity to regulate internal labour markets and enhancement of union bargaining leverage with employers. Master bargaining reduces the likelihood that employers refuse to bargain or can destroy the union workplace by workplace. To use this bargaining strategy, however, industrial unions have to organize and represent a critical mass of workers in the service sector, whether by employer or particular sub-sector such as coffee houses, which requires overcoming significant employer opposition and many legal obstacles. This in turn means maintaining a commitment to the principle of industry-based membership expansion, whereby the service sector is treated as one more industry in which unions seek to regulate internal labour markets.

Some unions have attempted to deal with the bargaining weakness of stand-alone service sector workplaces by mobilizing the power resources of large industrial workforces to back up the demands of newly unionized workplaces. For example, when the CAW organized a casino in 1998 in Windsor, a city dominated by automobile production and CAW union membership, the president of the Chrysler automobile local was centrally involved in bargaining. This not only increased the bargaining expertise of the Casino local but signalled to the employer that the CAW was willing to extend its full resources to back up these workers' demands. When bargaining broke down, the CAW used successfully the power of its large auto membership numbers to threaten widespread workplace action in support of Casino workers and a consumer boycott of the Casino, which relied heavily upon business from autoworkers. This strategy has a number of advantages. It opens up bargaining strategies that use the consumer power of large industrial union memberships to pressure service sector employers into bargaining fairly. This strategy also increases the bargaining strength and cost-effectiveness of servicing small units by relying upon the resources and expertise of large local units, rather than the central union office. The limitation of this strategy is that it only works under conditions where a union is dominant in a community and has a commitment to and capacity for solidaristic action. The latter means that established union members must be willing to take action, and hence risks, in supporting the demands of other workers in their community. This requirement reinforces the imperative that industrial unions need to rebuild internally at the same time as extending their organizations to new workplaces.

A final problem in bargaining arises from the costly methods adopted by industrial unions for delivering benefits to their members. The delivery of benefits has been based on a model of buying individual-based benefits from private sector providers. Such arrangements are expensive, posing an insurmountable barrier to low-paid workers employed by small employers. In the absence of adequate state-provided benefits, industrial unions must find ways of 'socializing' the costs of benefits across multiple independent employers. The USWA has experimented with providing basic dental benefits to security guards by establishing clinics at which the union hires dentists to work a certain number of hours, performing a limited range of dental procedures, the cost of which are socialized across several employers.

Industrial unions are proving themselves capable of shifting their bargaining priorities and representing successfully the interests of a more diverse set of workers. Moreover, the extension of several industrial union practices to the service industry offers solutions to employment and bargaining leverage problems that are particularly acute in service sector and small workplaces. The determining issue of union success in breaking into new territory may have less to do with abandoning industrial unionism and more to do with extending this model of unionism outside traditional heavy industry.

Changing union structure

Industrial unions continue to be characterized by hierarchical, bureaucratic structures in which locals are subordinate to national or international unions. Some industrial unions are rationalizing local union structures, pressuring locals to amalgamate with one another into larger units, with the objective of making them more self-sufficient and therefore less dependent on central resources. Many industrial unions seek to encourage industry-wide communication and coordination through the establishment of multiple sectorally based deliberative bodies, which bring together workers throughout the union on an industry basis, providing a forum through which specific demands of workers in different industries can be articulated for the purposes of bargaining with employers and within the union. Very few industrial unions have shifted their organizational structure away from the servicing model, arguing that servicing continues to be pivotal in maintaining membership support for their union.

The biggest changes to industrial union structure have been driven by the need to meet the demands for representation by women and people of colour. In the last ten years, industrial unions have appointed more women and people of colour to staff positions, have offered special leadership training courses and have developed facilitative practices such as provision of child care at union meetings in their efforts to increase the representative nature of their organizations. None of them has been willing to challenge liberal-democratic-based structures and practices, largely eschewing affirmative action-type policies, which have been popular in union federations (White, 1993).

Action on leadership representation is a first step towards making industrial unions more responsive to diverse groups, but it is not a panacea. The focus on leadership tends to shift responsibility for change from the union as a whole to the shoulders of the new leaders. These leaders have neither the resources, the time nor the power within the union effectively to take on all these responsibilities alone. In the absence of extensive formal and informal networks, progress is slow and burnout amongst these leaders is high. Further, changing the composition of leadership does not necessarily challenge existing bureaucratic structures and practices, which are often at the root of a union's lack of responsiveness in the first place. Finally, women and people of colour are disproportionately found in appointed or specialist-staff positions such as education and health and safety, which lack a rank-and-file base (White, 1993; Yates, 1996). Without this membership base of support, advancement of these activists is limited as is their capacity to mount serious challenges to incumbent leaders and established practices.

Industrial union economic strength has been derived from centralized union structures which have enhanced their capacity to mobilize power resources tactically in support of collective efforts. This centralization continues to be a source of strength – one that industrial unions are attempting to extend to new sectors. The problem for industrial unions lies in their ability to combine the structures that facilitate centralized strategic capacity with ones that enhance representativeness and active inclusion of new members in agenda setting and decision making. This rests in part on more rapid and complete structural change inside industrial unions, but it also rests on more subtle changes to union discourse and identity.

Identity reconstruction

Collective identity refers to an interpretive framework built upon shared values, experiences, social networks and objective characteristics of groups of individuals. Collective identities weave into their framework notions of a union's history, which includes reference to heroic actions and past strategies as ways of offering symbolic and strategic limits to what actions and alliances are possible. By providing members of the collectivity with a lens through which to interpret and act in the world, collective identities shape goal formation and strategic direction. Thus different union collective identities offer different frameworks within which workers structure and define their relation to other workers, to their union and to their community and employer.

Collective identities are built over time, never static although often stable, and occasionally subject to dramatic change. Pressures from more diverse memberships have combined with structural economic and cultural-ideational changes to fragment workers' interests and erode existing industrial union solidarities (Hyman, 1991, 1994; Yates, 1998b). At the same time, unions have become increasingly aware that their cultural 'image' is outdated and fails to appeal to young, women, racially and ethnically diverse workers.

Industrial unions in Canada vary in the degree and type of shifts in their identity, some having embarked on a conscious strategy of identity reconstruction whereas others hold on to existing world views. In most cases where conscious identity reconstruction has taken place, these are leadership-driven initiatives, involve limited and controlled membership participation and rely upon re-education of union members in an effort to shift their orientations. We can identify three types of identity reconstruction in industrial unions out of which flow different models of unionism: 1) rights-based, 2) nationalist, working-class identity, and 3) simple rank-and-file unionism.

A 'rights-based' identity draws on contemporary social movements articulation of equality strategies based on human rights (Leary, 1996). Employment rights, regardless of gender, race or creed, become human rights, which it is the job of unions to uphold. The Steelworkers in Canada have begun reconstruction around a rights-based identity, captured in the phrase 'everybody's union'. This union's rights-based discourse and identity combines recognition of diversity with individual rights. It overlays existing union subcultures with a web of workers' rights in the workplace and union, and union responsibilities that limit the expressions and practices of exclusion that characterized industrial unions in the post-war period. The USWA-Canada has promoted this rights-based discourse and practice throughout its education offerings and bargaining practices. This rights-based identity has simultaneous advantages and disadvantages. In championing the rights of all individual workers, the union has constructed an inclusive identity that can accommodate both the special interests of new groups of workers joining the union as well as redefining means of protecting incumbent members' rights. Further, a human rights discourse has the potential to bridge individualistic and collectivist elements in the union. The limitation of this rights-based identity is its tendency towards procedural strategies and its openness to individualistic tendencies, both of which may limit union capacity to build broad-based solidarities.

The second path of identity reconstruction is based on a reaffirmation and expansion of class-based identities, where class becomes inclusive of all workers regardless of gender, race or ethnicity. Although not limited to expression by industrial unions (White, 1990), this class-based discourse and identity is the path chosen by the Canadian Autoworkers. Through its education programmes, communications and leadership strategy and mergers with left-wing unions the CAW has built an identity around notions of class and radical nationalism. The primacy of social class manifests itself in CAW support for and celebration of militant workplace strategies, including mass strikes and plant occupations. Nationalism interplays with class, seen in the CAW's articulation of its strategies as an alternative to multinational capital's neo-liberal agenda. To increase its mobilizational capacity and cross-cutting appeal to all workers, the CAW has built alliances with community and action groups over such issues as daycare articulating them as class-based needs. Yet the CAW is bedeviled with the age-old problem that class-based identities and action sit uneasily with recognition of other bases of inequality, especially race and gender. A class-based identity which is built on paid work and employer-worker relations elides other power struggles and differences that centre on the home, woman-man relations and race and ethnicity.

The third basis for union identity reconstruction relies upon the celebration and primacy of rank-and-file workers in building their union and realizing their own goals and objectives. This form of new identity initially grew as a defensive action in small, financially vulnerable unions, such as the Hotel and Restaurant Employees Union (HERE) and UNITE, that have struggled to retain their place in a rapidly changing labour market and within a labour movement increasingly dominated by a handful of large and powerful unions. These are also unions more explicitly influenced at the leadership level by the organizing model. By relying upon membership activism and control, which is reinforced by involving new members immediately in a range of union activities, including organizing, these unions are constructing strong solidaristic bonds between members and their union and among workers themselves which in turn reinforce the growth of democratic practices. The question for these unions is whether they can survive in the long term, given their small size and weak financial base.

Notwithstanding these examples of industrial unions which have embarked on a conscious strategy of identity reconstruction, many industrial unions in Canada have reaffirmed a business union identity. These unions articulate service-based relationships between the individual worker and the union and define their scope narrowly in economistic frames of reference. Whereas both the rights-based and nationalist class-based identities offer possibilities of change to more activist roles for individual union members, an identity based on business unionism reinforces a passive role for members and expects new members to 'fit' in to existing structures and practices which are deemed as generic rather than industrial or patriarchal and paternalistic.

Embedded within each of these identities are frames and clues for emergent models of unionism that differ in terms of structure, relationship between union members, leaders and bureaucracies and broader political strategy. None of them seeks to dismantle the form of industrial unionism but rather to modify it. The question remains whether existing collective identities based on paternalistic relations, male bravado and aggressive combative tactics are an essential part of the industrial union form and therefore their undoing in terms of the capacity of this model to transform. Moreover, with the exception of the simple rank-and-file unionism model, it is unclear how deeply changes to the union identity have penetrated union memberships, raising the possibility of internal union conflict and resistance to change.

Conclusion

Industrial unions are not destined to be the dinosaurs of the new economy. Rather than sitting on the sidelines of economic change and workforce diversification, watching their own demise, industrial unions are adapting rapidly to new economic and political conditions, thus paving the way to their possible revival. Industrial unions are doing as good if not a better job of organizing and responding to the needs of service sector workers and women and people of colour. Part of this success lies in changes made by industrial unions to established ways of representing workers. But part of this success also lies in defending and extending industrial union structures and practices beyond their traditional boundaries. For example, by struggling to erect centralized bargaining practices in the service sector, industrial unions may undercut many of the ways in which capital employs these workers to achieve workplace and labour market flexibility and may transform these bad jobs into good jobs, in which workers can find job security, decent wages and career opportunities.

Yet, there remain hurdles to industrial union adaptation. One of the biggest hurdles lies in their capacity to undergo internal structural and identity change, which will break down the barriers between old and new union members and therefore expand unions' capacity for solidaristic action. Although these unions have experienced leadership-driven change to internal structures and identities, it remains to be seen how deeply these changes penetrate into the local level and undo the sexism, racism and paternalism that has characterized industrial unions for so many years.

A second but no less significant hurdle is the growing conflict between industrial unions in Canada. Jurisdictional disputes and political-ideological differences between the CAW and other industrial unions have in the first year of the new millennium resulted in an all-out war between unions in Canada. This not only drains resources away from organizing the unorganized but has nobbled central labour bodies and strengthened the hands of governments and employers determined to destroy the influence of unions in the labour market. As unions can rely less and less on supportive legislation and government action to bolster their position, they must build upon their own resources, which in part rely upon the capacity for concerted collective action by their members. Such collective action becomes more difficult as unions wage war on one another.

Industrial unions have one advantage over many other unions – access to considerable financial and organizational resources amassed during the 'golden' years of post-war economic growth. Even though union financial and organizational resources have been shrinking under pressure of political and economic change and membership declines, industrial unions continue to have considerable resources at their disposal, which make organizing in new sectors and amongst diverse groups of workers more viable in the medium to long-term. Rather than industrial unions being unsuited to contemporary political-economic conditions, they may be the only organizations capable of extending the benefits of unionization into new sectors and amongst new groups of workers in the face of increasingly hostile governments and employers.

Acknowledgement

The author wishes to acknowledge the financial support by the Social Sciences and Humanities Research Council (SSHRC) for the research reported in this chapter.

References

Borowy, J. and Johnson, T. (1995) 'Unions Confront Work Reorganization and the Rise of Precarious Employment', in Schenk, Chris and Anderson, John (eds), *Re-Shaping Work: Union Responses to Technological Change*, Toronto: Ontario Federation of Labour, pp. 29–47.

Brodie, J. and Jenson, J. (1988) *Crisis, Challenge and Change: Party and Class in Canada Revisited*, Ottawa: Carleton University Press.

CALURA (Corporations and Labour Unions Returns Act) (selected years), *Part II-Labour Unions*, Catalogue 71–202, Ottawa: Statistics Canada.

Cobble, Dorothy (1994) 'Making Postindustrial Unionism Possible', in Sheldon Friedman *et al.*, *Restoring the Promise of American Labor Law*, Ithaca, NY: ILR Press, pp. 285–302.

Cockburn, Cynthia (1988) *Machinery of Dominance: Women, Men and Technical Know-how*, Boston: Northeastern University Press.

Cockburn, Cynthia (1991) *In the Way of Women: Men's Resistance to Sex Equality in Organizations*, Ithaca, NY: ILR Press.

Drache, D. (1991) 'The Systemic Search for Flexibility: National Competitiveness and New Work Relations', in Drache, D. and Gertler, M. (eds) *The New Era of Global Competition: State Policy and Market Power*, Montreal and Kingston: McGill-Queen's Press, pp. 249–69.

Early, Steve (1999) 'Membership-based Organizing', in Mantsios, G. (ed.) *A New Labor Movement for the New Century*, New York: Monthly Review Press, pp. 82–103.

Fairbrother, Peter (2000) *Trade Unions at the Crossroads*, London: Mansell.

Freeman, Richard (1993) 'What Does the Future Hold for US Unionism?' in Jenson, Jane and Mahon, Rianne, *The Challenge of Restructuring: North American Labor Movements Respond*, Philadelphia: Temple University Press, pp. 361–80.

Gindin, Sam (1998) 'Notes on Labour at the End of the Century: Starting Over?' in Meiksons, E. Wood *et al.*, *Rising from the Ashes? Labor in the Age of 'Global' Capitalism*, New York: Monthly Review Press, pp. 190–202.

Gorz, Andre (1982) *Farewell to the Working Class*, London: Pluto Press.

Hyman, Richard (1991) 'European Unions: Towards 2000', *Work, Employment and Society*, 5 (December): 621–39.

Hyman, Richard (1994) 'Changing Trade Union Identities and Strategies', in Hyman, R. and Ferner, A. (eds) *New Frontiers in European Industrial Relations*, Oxford: Basil Blackwell, pp. 108–39.

Jenson, Jane (1989) 'The Talents of Women, the Skills of Men: Flexible Specialization and Women', in Woods, S., *The Transformation of Work?* London: Unwin Hyman.

Katz, Harry (1985) *Shifting Gears: Changing Labor Relations in the US Automobile Industry*, Cambridge MA: MIT Press.

Kochan, T., Katz, H. and McKersie, R. (1986) *The Transformation of American Industrial Relations*, New York: Basic Books.

Laxer, James (1984) *Rethinking the Economy: Canadian Politics after the Neo-Conservative Assault*, Toronto: New Canada Publications.

Laxer, James (1996) *In Search of a New Left: Canadian Politics after the Neo-Conservative Assault*, Toronto: Viking Press.

Leary, V. (1996) 'The Paradox of Workers' Rights as Human Rights', in Compa, L. and Diamond, S. (eds) *Human Rights, Labor Rights and International Trade*, Philadelphia: University of Pennsylvania Press, pp. 22–47.

LeBeau, Josephine and Lynch, Kevin (1999) 'Successful Organizing at the Local Level', in Mantsios, G., *A New Labor Movement for the New Century*, New York: Monthly Review Press, pp. 104–18.

Lerner, Stephen (1999) 'Taking the Offensive, Turning the Tide', in Mantsios, G. (ed.) *A New Labor Movement for the New Century*, New York: Monthly Review Press, pp. 69–81.

Lewchuk, Wayne (1993) 'Men and Monotony: Fraternalism as a Managerial Strategy at the Ford Motor Company', *Journal of Economic History*, 53 (4): 824–56.

Mahon, Rianne (1991) 'Post-Fordism: Some Issues for Labour', in Drache, D. and Gertler, M. (eds) *The New Era of Global Competition: State Policy and Market Power*, Montreal and Kingston: McGill-Queen's Press, pp. 316–32.

Murray, Gregor (1998) 'Steeling for Change: Organization and Organizing in Two USWA Districts in Canada', in Bronfenbrenner, K., Friedman, S., Hurd, R., Seeber, R. and Oswald, R. (eds) *Organizing to Win: New Research on Union Strategies*, Ithaca, NY: ILR Press, pp. 320–38.

Probert, B. (1992) 'Award Restructuring and Clerical Work: Skills, Training and Careers in a Feminized Occupation', *Journal of Industrial Relations*, 34: 436–54.

Towers, Brian (1997) *The Representation Gap: Change and Reform in the British and American Workplace*, Oxford, New York: Oxford University Press.

USWA (United Steelworkers of America) (1998) 'Report of the Organizing Task Force', report presented to the 29th Constitutional (International) Convention. Las Vegas, Nevada, August 10–13.

White, Julie (1990) *Mail and Female: Women and the Canadian Union of Postal Workers* Toronto: Thompson Educational Publishing.

White, Julie (1993) *Sisters and Solidarity*, Toronto: Thompson Educational Publishing.

Yates, Charlotte (1993) *From Plant to Politics: The Autoworkers Union in Postwar Canada*, Philadelphia: Temple University Press.

Yates, C. (1996) 'Neo-Liberalism and the Working Girl: The Dilemmas of Women and the Australian Union Movement', *Economic and Industrial Democracy* (November): 627–65.

Yates, C. (1998a) 'Unity and Diversity: Challenges to an Expanding Canadian Auto-workers' Union', *Canadian Review of Sociology and Anthropology*, 35 (February): 93–118.

Yates, C. (1998b), 'Defining the Fault Lines: New Divisions in the Working Class', *Capital and Class*, 66: 119–47.

Yates, C. (2000a) 'Union Organizing in Ontario: What Works? What Doesn't?', report prepared for the Ontario Federation of Labour, Toronto: OFL, February 24.

Yates, C. (2000b) 'Staying the Decline in Union Membership: Union Organizing in Ontario, 1985–1999', *Relations industrielles/Industrial Relations*, 55 (4): 640–74.

Yates, Charlotte and Ewer, Peter (1997) 'Changing Strategic Capacities: Union Amalgamations in Canada and Australia', in Sverke, M. (ed.) *The Future of Trade Unionism*, Aldershot: Ashgate, pp. 131–48.

12 Social Movement Unionism: Beyond the Organizing Model

Christopher Schenk

Introduction

As we enter the twenty-first century a key debate in the labour movement concerns the changes in outlook and practice necessary for union renewal. This debate, initiated in the USA, has spread to Australia, Britain, Canada and beyond, is structured around the counterpositioning of a business-union 'service model' to an 'organizing' model of unionism. This chapter moves beyond both models of unionism by focusing on the need for building unions through more in-depth democratic practice and the development of alternative perspectives. It argues for unions to take up the challenge of social movement unionism.

There is a vital need for changes in union direction and structure to ensure effective solutions in the face of multiple challenges: workplace restructuring and downsizing, the rise of a contingent workforce, persistent unemployment, decreased government intervention in the economy and anti-worker legislation.

A discussion of social movement unionism is part of the larger debate on union renewal. There are a number of reasons why the issue of union renewal is important. The first arises from unions' current declining membership and influence. As the introduction to this book shows, union membership across the five countries under investigation is in decline. Dramatic declines are evident in Australia, New Zealand and the USA. Decline in Britain has been more gradual whereas Canada, long remarkable for its stable albeit middle-range unionization level, now shows definite signs of slippage.

Second, although unionization rates have declined, the evidence suggests as strongly as ever that unionization is a key way to improve living standards. The advantage of working in a unionized workplace, as opposed to a non-union workplace, is referred to as the union premium or union advantage and is seen in better wages and benefits in unionized establishments and greater protections from arbitrary management decisions – see Mishel, Berstein and Schmitt (1999: 185) and Jackson and Robinson (2000: 100). Further, unionized workers have a voice in the workplace and some control over wages and working conditions.

A third reason why the subject of union strength is important concerns a little-known but important range of studies demonstrating that a strong labour movement, defined in terms of high union density is associated with more income equality both before and after taxes, lower levels of unemployment, a lower level of inflation, more extensive social welfare legislation, a higher percentage of government employment primarily to deliver needed social programmes, and lower levels of poverty (Robinson, 1994: 661). Much of this labour movement effect is due to labour market factors such as lower unemployment and a more generous spread of higher-wage jobs. Some is due to a higher social wage, such as more progressive taxation, universal healthcare and other social policies (Cameron, 1998: 219–59). The evidence also suggests, surprisingly to some, that this pattern holds for the USA as well as other OECD countries. As Lerner (1996: 3) puts it: 'A just, democratic society depends on a powerful workers' movement.'

The service model versus the organizing model

The 1980s and 1990s saw a dramatic growth in inequality and economic restructuring – most often involving corporate downsizing, policies favouring flexibility, new human resources management, increased unemployment, minimal compensation particularly in non-standard work, deregulation, privatization, an ongoing technological revolution and cuts to social services (Kumar *et al.*, 1998). It is under these circumstances that the search for union renewal and systemic alternatives was reborn. As Bill Fletcher and Richard Hurd (1998: 37) note in reference to the American labour movement:

> The post-World War II labour movement, founded on a social truce with capital and the apparent inevitability of a rising living standard, has hit a bulkhead-piercing iceberg of dramatic proportions.

It took many years of union decline in the USA before the 'bulkhead' would begin to be confronted. Across Canada, with a relatively stable unionization rate, it is only in the 1990s with the election of explicitly right-wing anti-worker governments and the belated unravelling of the post-war settlement, that a serious re-evaluation is being undertaken. Given the earlier decades of decline of American unions and the attempts to reverse it, it is only natural that Canadian, Australian, New Zealand and British unionists, looked to the USA for ideas on union renewal (Pocock and Wishart, 1999).

In 1988 the AFL-CIO published an organizing manual entitled *Numbers that Count* in which the debate on union decline was reconceptualized by counterposing the servicing model of local union leadership – 'trying to help people by solving problems for them' – to the organizing model – 'involving members in solutions' (Diamond, 1988: 6). The following year Andy Banks and Jack Metzger in *Labor Research Review* (1989) equated the servicing model to stale unionism, an overreliance on union staff and the grievance and arbitration process and a passive membership. The organizing model on the other hand, visualized focusing on collective action and militancy. Banks and Metzgar (1989: 50) held that through the involvement of 'many more people in [its] daily life ... [the union] would be able to take on and solve more problems.' Later issues of *Labor Research Review* explored the two models; particularly noteworthy was Teresa Conrow's (1991) article 'Contract Servicing from an Organizing Model'.

Whatever its limitations, contrasting the debate in this manner caught the imagination in US labour circles and formed the basis of an ongoing vigorous debate. Russo and Banks (1996) clearly describe the distinction between the servicing and organizing models:

The service model

1. Union leaders solve problems for members.
2. The union relies on the grievance and arbitration procedures.
3. Membership is passive or limited to responses to leader requests for cooperation.
4. Members rely on specialists, experts and union staff.
5. The union develops secretive and closed communication channels.
6. Union structures are centralized and top heavy.
7. The union grows dependent on and is reactive to management.
8. Distinctions are made between internal and external organizing activities.

The organizing model

1. Stimulates and involves members in problem solving in group process or collective actions.
2. Is not limited to the bargaining process.
3. Is committed to education, communications, and member participation in the union.
4. Develops and depends on members' skills and abilities.
5. Shares information and develops open communication channels.
6. Has a decentralized organizational structure.
7. Operates independently of management, and is proactive.
8. Makes no distinction between internal and external organizing activities.

Implementing the organizing model has proved more difficult than theorizing about it. Concerns have been and continue to be raised on a number of levels as unions and locals attempt to operationalize the change to an organizing model. Some of these problems have already been documented (Fletcher and Hurd, 1998, 2001).

Indeed as Fletcher and Hurd (1998: 43) note: 'In practice ... there is a constant tension between the organizing model and the servicing magnet.' Many union members proved more interested in servicing for purposes of their grievance/arbitrations and their collective bargaining for a new agreement than using their union dues to assist in organizing the unorganized. Further concerns arose internally as staff skilled in service work now found their skills and value diminished. Staff was confronted with new expectations of membership involvement and organizing. Moving to the new organizing model was found to create more work, longer hours inclusive of evenings and weekends – particularly for the increased number of members and staff assigned to organizing. This, in turn, led to a higher level of staff burnout. Operationalizing the organizing model involved a sea change in union functioning and structure and constant re-evaluations. At the same time there was, and remains, a lack of clarity as to specifically which changes were necessary and why. As Fletcher and Hurd (1998) further document, the best of unions only moved gropingly down the path of the organizing model, not quite knowing concretely how to get there or even what was 'there'. Additionally, unions and locals differed in approaches given traditions, size, sector, level of commitment, leadership and particular circumstances.

These concerns regarding the organizing model have made the task of pursuing this model more difficult. Yet, underlying these problems lie even greater challenges concerning union democracy and the importance of articulating an alternative ideology that can guide unions in their efforts to further social and economic change. There is a concern amongst many that the organizing model itself will become utilitarian rather that a genuine step toward a culture of solidarity. It is to these key concerns that we now turn our attention.

Democracy and alternative visions

As indicated earlier, unions today are under increasing attack from governments and employers. To keep from becoming marginal institutions of narrow appeal they will have to undergo significant change in structure and perspective. At the same time such external factors limit union choices. The focus of this chapter is largely within these limits, where 'the internal dynamics of unions determine the course of action chosen' (Yates, 1990: 75). Below, some choices concerning union democracy are outlined, followed by those concerning the development of a critical alternative vision.

If our goal is to build strong, powerful unions, in order better to protect and change the lives of union members and working people as a whole, democracy will need to be strengthened. Why? The short answer is that there is an important link between union growth and power and union democracy. As Moody (1997: 4) notes: Social movement unionism:

> goes beyond the 'organizing model' of unionism used in the U.S. in opposition to the older 'service model' of American business unionism by asserting the centrality of union democracy as a source of power and broader social visions and outreach as a means of enhancing that power.

Social movement unionism seeks to redraw the 'frontier of control' by its own restructuring and practice aimed at empowering membership participation and democratic control, by allying with key community coalitions active in struggles for change, and through the development of an alternative ideological vision enabling a critical assessment of wider social issues and unifying strategies to effect them. In collective bargaining, social movement unionism is inclusive of both workplace specific issues and society-wide issues. As Gindin (1995: 268) says:

> Movement unionism includes the shape of bargaining demands, the scope of union activities, the approach to issues of change, and above all, that

sense of commitment to a larger movement that might suffer defeats, but can't be destroyed.

While the focus of social movement unionism has traditionally been on extra-parliamentary action, alliances with political parties are not excluded and under certain circumstances can be mutually beneficial. Finally, this essential understanding of social movement unionism leaves open the specific terms of alliance between labour and other social movements and a recognition of other forms of oppression (race, gender) that exist within the conflictual dynamic of capital and labour.

Experience in the labour movement strongly suggests that the more members have a real say in their union, the greater their involvement in decision making, the higher the potential for a membership educated and interested in the issues of the day, and consequently the more vital the union. In confronting dominant corporate and social forces, democracy can be a strong instrument for building solidarity, a renewed solidarity built on a foundation of an empowered membership. Truly empowered members make a stronger union. Unions need this increased power to fulfil their members' needs for better pay and working conditions as well as to pursue the goals of social change. Advancing workers basic needs and aspirations, in turn, further activates members and attracts non-unionized workers. Thus we see an integral link between becoming a social movement union and organizing the unorganized. As Eisenscher (1999: 218) notes:

> The battle for union democracy is an integral part of the effort to rebuild labour's ranks and influence. *Activism and empowerment must be wed if unions are to be transformed and labor rejuvenated.* (emphasis added)

For unions to move from a 'service model' to an 'organizing model' is both a giant step and a substantive improvement. Yet to counterpose the two models in this manner limits debate in several ways. In attempting to initiate the process of membership participation and empowerment, the 'organizing model' *per se* contains little assistance for members and leaders in further democratizing their union. Yet, the very engine of labour revitalization is to be found in the democratization of unions. Only a more educated, involved membership develops the capacity and confidence to run their union and in so doing overcome the sectionalism of a stratified workforce divided into numerous bargaining units with separate collective agreements, particular cultures and consequent distinct solidarities. Only as union members themselves begin more directly to control their own union (democracy after all means rule by the people) will we see the scope and weight of unelected administrative apparatuses mediating between those that are 'elected to govern' and those that have to live with their decisions, diminish. This notion of rank-and-file particpatory democracy must necessarily be distinguished from the parliamentarist models with their exclusive reliance on indirect, individual franchise proposed in earlier literature (Lipset *et al.*, 1956).

To achieve these goals change must move beyond greater activism and militancy and even the formalities of democracy (elections, etc.) as important as they are. Activism and rank-and-file control must be combined as Eisenscher (1999: 218) notes. He further explains:

> In confronting more powerful economic and social forces, democracy is an instrument for building solidarity, for establishing accountability, and for determining appropriate strategies – all of which are critical to sustaining and advancing worker and union interests. *Union democracy is not, however, synonymous with either union activism or militancy*. Members can be mobilized for activities over which they have little or no control, for objectives determined for them rather than by them. The quality of democratic participation and the consequences of that participation for the operation and strategic direction of unions are vital to union success and labour's continuing relevance. (emphasis added)

In the long run what one might term a top-down 'faucet' approach to union building and mobilization does not work. People cannot be turned 'on' for a particular campaign or organizing drive and then turned 'off' and returned to passivity only to be asked to turn 'on' again for some new endeavour. Strong unions cannot be built by turning members on and off like a tap or by the flick of a switch. Experience suggests it takes patient discussion, meaningful participation and renewed solidarity forged in action.

Second, while the organizing model rejects a passive service model with the intention of stimulating rank-and-file activity, education and participation, it does so, as we have noted, without any clear alternative perspective or even an awareness that such is important. This is a significant omission. A common alternative vision facilitates the development of unifying strategies at both the bargaining table and on broader social issues. The labour movement needs a worker-centred way of seeing the world and comprehending the events and social forces unfolding within it. It helps link our daily experience and the failings of the present to our imagined ideal – to conceive of what Daniel Singer (1999: 6) calls 'realistic utopias'.

Viewed from another perspective, the strength of the organizing model is not so much in providing a map for change, but in its initiation of the change process – its focus on rank-and-file involvement and organizing the unorganized. Yet, as Moody (1997: 276) notes casting the debate as simply either/or models 'focuses exclusively on the union as an institution'. As such, success or failure is assessed primarily on the basis of collective bargaining and organizing outcomes. While these goals are important, social movement unionism encompasses a vision that extends beyond a particular workplace to the labour movement and society as a whole. It is necessary to make such links in our increasingly globalized world so as to assess more accurately one's situation and thereby be in a better position to improve it. Social movement unionism, says Gindin (1995: 268):

> means making the union into a vehicle through which its members can not only address their bargaining demands but actively lead the fight for everything that affects working people in their communities and the country.

A prime example of this type of development in North America would be the Ontario Days of Action, which consisted of twelve city-wide shutdowns of workplaces and demonstrations across the province by labour and community groups in 1996 and 1997. The central issues concerned the defence and improvement of a universal healthcare system, protecting quality public education and restoring and maintaining vital social services in the face of government fiscal restraints. Also forming a part of the alternative platform was the need for government full-employment policies, a more equitable distribution of wealth and basic necessities of life such as affordable housing. Each of these issues affected union members and non-union members alike setting a new agenda in the face of a conservative government. They encouraged thinking about the state of society as a whole: what's right about it and what's wrong about it? Could what's wrong about the society be changed? If so, how? With what? How do we overcome the chasm between what is and what could be? As in struggles elsewhere, new alternative perspectives began to develop out of these mobilizations. New structural venues also surfaced during the Ontario Days of Action, enabling greater rank-and-file participation in decision making.

The importance of raising and discussing new ideas in the face of particular issues should not be underestimated. The struggle for trade union renewal is in large measure a battle for the hearts and minds of working people. Put another way, social change necessitates a contest of ideas and over time the ideological hegemony of right-wing ideas will have to be confronted.

Beginning the change process

So where to start? With the core notion of democracy how does one initiate union renewal? As we have argued, democracy is about membership power over the things that matter. Union constitutions, elections, votes, motions, rules governing meetings and the like should be designed to facilitate democratic membership control.

Fortunately, we have something to build on. In key unions, mainly located in industry, resources and the public and broader public sector (hospitals, education) and organized in the Canadian Labour Congress (CLC), the AFL-CIO, the Australian Council of Trade Unions (ACTU) or the British Trades Union Congress (TUC), a culture of union democracy already exists, albeit an incomplete one. A number of unions also have significant elements of movement unionism. The question therefore becomes how to build on the already existing elements of democracy and social movement unionism?

One might first ask how union democratic processes can be expanded with the intent of enhancing rank-and-file control. Several changes come to mind including: the direct election of more positions inclusive of key staff positions; the right to recall elected officials under specific circumstances that need to be clearly defined; horizontal structures enabling direct democracy, and the introduction of some form of job rotation. The latter could occur between local activists, elected officers and staff positions. Activist members should have the opportunity to carry out full-time union work for specified periods and then return to their workplace and union local. Full-time staff should have collective agreements maintaining their links to the workplace, enabling and periodically requiring them to return there and reintegrate themselves with workplace life and with rank-and-file union politics. The intent is to develop new and renewed layers of activists with more grounded experience – worker activists who both participate in making decisions and in carrying them out.

Experience with various union activities from handling local grievances to leading union-wide campaigns further develop individual and collective capacities. They enable new critical perspectives particularly when combined with in-depth union education. Questions arise such as 'what are the constraints imposed on union members by corporate power?' and 'what are the constraints of labour relations legislation and state structures?' The logical next questions are: 'how do we challenge such constraints?' and 'what are the alternatives to them?'

Real union democracy means that unionism is integral to what one does and how one operates in the workplace and with fellow workers each and every day. Democratic practice has to be learnt. It is only people with the experience of running their own union affairs who can readily develop the confidence and capacity to participate in the wider community, to take their burgeoning culture of solidarity and resistence with them into other arenas.

These two issues – democracy and alternative vision – speak to the larger picture of change, to the *directions* necessary if we are to set a new course, to develop members' own capacities and assist each other in taking charge of our social and economic destinies. The specifics vary from place to place but there are two further general points we need to make space for: one concerns the role of elected leaders; the other affects union staff.

One might begin by stating what should be obvious, namely, leadership is vitally important. At this stage of human development, given people's busy lives, each of us do not have the time, the desire or yet the skill to do everything. Yet there will be a changed role for union leaders with grassroots membership empowerment. The process of democratization will pose uncomfortable challenges for some. But these challenges are surmountable. In the long run leaders will enjoy a more exciting, visionary and powerful union. Leadership will involve setting directions, articulating the democratically agreed vision and goals and then leading their strategic implementation. These will of necessity be decided upon within the framework of continued debate and pluralism – a pluralism that is inclusive of both different perspectives and multiple identities. The need to respect people's various identities as feminists, environmentalists, or members of a particular ethnic community and concomitantly to create the necessary unity to defend their needs and aspirations as workers, is still before us. This will involve some new leadership skills. Leadership will need to be more accountable and inclusive than before, more accessible than before, and concur with the new reality of a membership with increased input and authority. Such change is as difficult as it is possible.

Key to easing this process is having leaders who come to accept and embrace change. As Eaton (1995: 6) suggests, leadership involves a relationship, one that is 'transformational to both leaders and followers, and that leadership is empowering rather than dominating.' As members become more interested in new ideas and directions and as they carry them out, the interest in the petty politics of the personal will diminish. New networks and membership caucuses can be expected to develop, disappear and reoccur. Again, this can be problematic from one perspective, but from another it is part of the renewal process and if properly focused and directed can help replenish the democratic life of unions with new ideas, directions, activists and, yes, sometimes new leaders.

Union staff will also find themselves caught up in this process of bottom-up change. As union members engage in the exchange of ideas, set new directions and take more control over carrying out the agreed activities, staff can either resist thus further complicating the change process or enter the change process with an open mind. The process of collectively engaging in constructing an alternative vision, setting new directions, bringing new members into the union and creating new democratic structures to further membership control can be liberating.

Social movement unionism in action

To elaborate further the functioning and practice of social movement unionism one might best start at the local union level. This is particularly true in Canada, the USA and the other countries with decentralized bargaining systems (Adams, 1995; Fudge, 1993; O'Grady, 1992). For most members the workplace – their local – is 'the union.' It is here that members experience workplace relations on a day-to-day basis, can best articulate their views, and will more likely come to a consensus or at least a conclusion as to a course of action. It is here that the average member can most easily exercise democratic control over their work affairs and defend themselves against employer attacks. It is also on this level that many membership goals will be realized or lost.

In many countries collective bargaining occurs with some exceptions on a workplace-by-workplace level. Yet many local issues can and need to be articulated as broader-based struggles, capable of forging alliances between unions and their communities. Contracting out (or outsourcing) is often seen as an issue particular to workers in a specific workplace only. In the private sector work is contracted out for a number of reasons central to which is cost and often involves work being sent either to non-union workplaces or 'offshore' to countries where labour costs are even lower. Unionized workers bargain against outsourcing in an effort to save their jobs, but like many other issues, outsourcing needs to be made into a public issue as it has significant public implications. Within a social movement union perspective a union local could take this issue into the community. Protecting and expanding good jobs in a workplace unit needs to be seen as defending and maintaining quality jobs for everyone in the community.

For workers in the public or broader public sector the issue of contracting out is highly related to the issue of privatization as most outsourcing is to the private sector. Again, the question of cost – not service – is paramount to employers and government. The issue can be made public as it speaks to the maintenance, and in some cases expansion, of services and jobs in the community. For workers, contracting out and privatization far too often involve job losses and wage cuts and working harder for longer hours under worse conditions. For the public it often involves reduced services and user fees. In short, profitability, not need, dictates the provision of such services. Public awareness campaigns, in revealing the true effects of service cutbacks, can potentially enable the union both better to defend public services and improve their bargaining leverage.

A second example of how to broaden the appeal of unions can be found in debates on work time. There is growing evidence that the labour markets in many countries are increasingly unequal in terms of hours of work and income. The standard work week and typical union member have seen their work world stretched at both ends: at one end, is the rise of contingent work that is part-time, contract, seasonal and now work done by the 'self-employed'; at the other end, one finds increased hours of work. This is particularly evident in the English-speaking countries. *The Growing Gap* report on inequality in Canada found that in 1973, the richest 10 per cent of families had an income nine times more than the poorest 10 per cent of families. By 1996, the richest 10 per cent of families made 312 times more than the poorest 10 per cent of families. The report notes: 'A remarkable symmetry is emerging. One in five jobs are now part-time. Similarly, almost one in five employees work overtime in any given week in 1997' (Yalnizian, 1998). Given that employment and hours of work are the main determinants of income it should come as no surprise that the inequality gap is growing.

There are steps to be taken to mitigate and even reverse this drift (O'Hara, 1993; Hayden, 1999). Some avenues involve the role of government and legislation whereas others of direct concern here involve union initiatives. There are a number of examples of unions negotiating reduced work time. In the pulp- and paper-mills of towns across northern Quebec and Ontario, Canada, employees with relatively high pay cheques have agreed to a reduction of work hours and income levels, provided the employer uses the savings to hire more employees. The intent of these unionized employees is to create employment for young people in their resource-based communities (CEP, 1997; White, 1999).

A further example is seen in the Daimler-Chrysler minivan plant in Windsor, Ontario, where the Canadian Autoworkers (CAW) negotiated the establishment of a permanent third shift. This eliminated the massive over-time of the first two shifts, reduced the hours of work for the daytime shift to seven-and-a-half hours for eight hours' pay, and created hundreds of new full-time jobs. The latest round of bargaining gained an increase of Scheduled Paid Absence or SPA days, which are in addition to vacations. The additional employment from this reduced work time is estimated at 2500 jobs.

The more working people in full-time well-paying jobs can win reductions in work time, the more they can spend time in other activities, such as with their families and in various leisure pursuits. By gaining some respite from work, people also gain some democratic space in which they can engage in community volunteer work and in various forms of democratic administration such as decision making within their union, within the workplace and within society at large (Albo *et al.*, 1993).

The examples noted above are indicative only. The point is that goals of social movement unionism can be furthered in significant part by the bargaining demands selected and the manner in which they are formulated and projected. By articulating union issues within a framework of community needs and interests, unions can begin to overcome their own sectionalism and consequent sectional solidarities (nurses identifying with other nurses only, electricians with other electricians only, and so on) and become more central in members' lives and more attractive to non-union members of the community. The approaches outlined begin the process of *harmonizing* the interests of workers covered by collective agreements and those in the community who are not. In so doing they begin to move unions toward a broader social agenda with the public at large. Such new approaches to common concerns create new activists, develop new capacities, help bring new members to the union and propel new dynamics for change.

There are additional union structures on a city-wide, regional and national level that are potentially significant for union renewal. Beyond national unions themselves they include provincial (or state), and federal central labour bodies and local labour and trades councils. In the face of major government and employer attacks, labour councils have shown themselves to be centres of strike solidarity, conducting limited cross-union debates and mobilizations. However infrequently on the part of some and unevenly on the part of most, such councils have also proved central to reaching out beyond labour's ranks and linking up with community coalitions – anti-poverty groups, affordable housing and tenants rights coalitions, immigrant support groups and feminist and environmental coalitions to name but a few. This activity, in turn, not only creates, broadens and strengthens the voice and effectiveness of working people, it helps change who and what we are. Who we are in terms of the diversity of backgrounds and interests now allied in a common purpose and what we are in the sense of the changing notions of self and collective that occur as, together, people go through the experience of developing new ideas and joint activities and setting new directions. As Heckscher (1988: 177) points out from a slightly different perspective, to be effective unions need to 'build unity around a general vision rather than a fixed contract'. What is necessary, he says, is 'a kind of unionism that replaces organizational conformity with coordinated diversity'.

Lastly, there is a further important dimension to the development of social movement unionism that deserves exploration, namely international solidarity. Developments on this level increasingly influence even the most routine collective bargaining. Substantive union activity in various parts of the world can, in turn, influence broader political-economic developments. A coherent analysis of how each influences the other and the resulting balance of economic and political (class) forces can inform unionists of what goals can most likely be accomplished and what may have to wait. This chapter will only highlight certain trends and the importance of operationalizing strategic international links.

International solidarity

As corporate power and capital mobility have expanded with the aid of enabling technologies, as global competition has intensified and assaulted workers' living standards, unions need to develop innovative ways to fight for social justice (Schenk and Anderson, 1995, 1999). This holds for unions in the broader public sector, fighting cuts to social programmes, as much as for private sector unions fighting concession bargaining in transnational corporations. The hard choice facing trade unions is whether to accommodate government policies and corporate priorities or to challenge them.

The fear of capital mobility and the threat of corporate relocation to countries with low labour costs, such as Mexico, has led some to respond by 'partnering' with management in an ill-fated attempt to defeat 'worker competitors' (Bronfenbrenner, 1996). While many are suspicious of such productivity alliances, the fear of management's ruthless concern for the 'bottom line', corporate relocation and the resulting unemployment often proves stronger. The changed circumstances of more integrated world economies, however, demand a different response: not one of competition between workers as management would favour, but one of international solidarity and resistance. Borderless capital demands borderless unionism. This solidarity, built on strong local and community group links can maximize peoples leverage, win victories, however small, and change agendas and outlooks. As Wells (1998: 22) notes:

> The same global integration of production that makes it possible for employers like Ford to get workers in different countries to compete against each other, also makes it possible for workers to ally with each other.

The question for unions today is how to transform themselves into rank-and-file controlled, democratic, social movements on the international level as well as the local, provincial (state) and national levels. Unionism has historically held that its basic principle is collective solidarity. This principle holds notwithstanding the uniqueness and deserved respect of culture, race, religion, colour, gender, age and language. It holds within a workplace, a country or nation and it holds across borders. What is crucial is that struggle for human betterment needs to be *internationalized*, not isolated and fractured.

The complexities of the most appropriate institutional forms and structures, such as national trade union federations and international bodies such as the International Confederation of Free Trade Unions (ICFTU), deserve fuller consideration than can be given here. Nonetheless, in keeping with our theme of expanding local union and community links and focusing on issues in a manner that both speaks to their specific workplace needs and their societal impacts, new membership structures such as international solidarity committees or networks, are a necessity.

It is important for union leaders and staff to develop formal and informal links with their counterparts internationally. It is also necessary for them to exchange visits and see for themselves the actual working conditions and struggles that working people in low-wage countries confront. However, it is increasingly evident that international solidarity has to move beyond such visits to worker-to-worker exchanges and coordinated bargaining strategies – particularly when confronting the same transnational corporation. Workers confronting the same global corporation need to coordinate their bargaining strategies just as management already sets its bargaining framework and guidelines from its head office as well as on site. Workers in the broader public sector need to learn the lessons from each other's victories and defeats when facing cutbacks and other policies of neo-liberal governments. These new needs necessitate new forms of worker collaboration and new enabling structures. According to Wells (1998: 490): 'Labour's best hope is a *coordinative unionism* which combines the mobilization capacity of the workplace and community with the scope of national and transnational strategies' (emphasis added).

Conclusion

The emphasis of this chapter has been on transforming unions themselves, rather than on transforming union organizing *per se*. The two are far from being mutually exclusive. Rather, they are highly interdependent with each impacting on the other in a manner that can be mutually reinforcing. Nonetheless, many unions across several countries, taking their cue from debates and practices in the USA, have focused on transforming organizing only – more resources, new tactics and strategies. Such change is necessary and important. Unions need to organize more than ever, but when undertaken in isolation from the more daunting challenge of transforming unions themselves, is insufficient.

Strengthening rank-and-file membership control over decision making – that is, deepening union democracy (both representative and direct democracy) and developing an alternative vision for the union and society at large – will involve both organizing the organized – activating members – and attracting unorganized workers to the union movement. The approaches to bargaining outlined above, emphasizing both particular bargaining unit needs and broader societal concerns, are examples of the manner in which union and community activists can begin to link together, overcome sectional cleavages and harmonize their issues in common actions for mutual benefit. The division that Flanders (1970: 5) spoke to when he stated that 'Trade unions have always had two faces, sword of justice and vested interest' must and can be overcome. Social movement unionism aims to make unions centres of working-class life. It means to accomplish this by actively leading the fight for everything that affects workers both in the workplace and in the community at large. Negotiating better wages, working conditions and benefits is central to this, but as has been argued, there is more – much more.

Finally, any commitment to change has obviously to be concretized in specific actions before change can be realized. It cannot remain at the level of abstract conception. Further democratization of unions and the development of alternative visions is necessary to assist such change, but it is people actively engaged in alternative politics that bring it about. In so doing, they not only modify and develop their alternative visions, rethink their union strategies and structures in the light of experience, but change themselves. 'The very process of struggle is one of producing new people', says Lebowitz (1992: 143) 'of transforming them into people with a new conception of themselves – as subjects capable of altering their world.' In other words, *in the process of changing one's circumstances and setting aside worn and outdated ideas for new ideas one is also engaging in changing one's individual and collective self* through new experiences. By gaining confidence in the viability of debate and common action, in winning new adherents to the union and to the movement for change, a new solidarity is forged with new possibilities for the future.

References

Adams, R. (1995) 'Canadian Industrial Relations in Comparative Perspective', in Gunderson, M. and Ponak, A. (eds) *Union-Management Relations in Canada*, third edition, Don Mills, Ontario: Addison-Wesley, pp. 495–526.

Albo, G., Langille, D. and Panitch, L. (eds) (1993) *A Different Kind of State? Popular Power and Democratic Administration*, Toronto: Oxford University Press.

Banks, A. and Metzgar, J. (1989) 'Participating in Management: Union Organizing on a New Terrain', *Labor Research Review*, 14 (Fall): 1–55.

Bronfenbrenner, K. (1996) *The Effect of Plant Closing or Threat of Plant Closing on the Right of Workers to Organize*, report submitted to the Labor Secretariat of the North American Commission for Labor Cooperation, 11 September.

Cameron, D. (1998) 'Politics, Public Policy and Distributional Inequality: A Comparative Analysis', in Shapiro, I. and Reeher, G. (eds) *Power, Inequality and Democratic Politics*, Boulder CO: Westview Press, pp. 219–59.

Communications Energy and Paperworkers Union of Canada (CEP) (1997) *More Jobs, More Fun: Shorter Hours of Work in the CEP*, Ottawa: CEP.

Conrow, T. (1991) 'Contract Servicing from an Organizing Model: Don't Bureaucratize, Organize!' *Labor Research Review*, 17: 45–59.

Diamond, V. (1988) *Numbers That Count: A Manual on Internal Organizing*, Washington DC: AFL CIO.

Eaton, S. (1995) 'Union Leadership Development in the 1990s and Beyond', *Workplace Topics*, 4 (2): 5–16.

Eiseinscher, M. (1999) 'Critical Juncture: Unionism at the Crossroads', in Nissen, B. (ed.) *Which Direction for Organized Labor?* Detroit: Wayne State University Press, pp. 217–245.

Flanders, A. (1970) *Management and Unions*, London: Faber & Faber.

Fletcher, B. and Hurd, R. (1998) 'Beyond the Organizing Model: The Transformation Process in Local Unions', in Bronfenbrenner, K., Friedman, S., Hurd, R., Oswald, R. and Seeber, R. (eds) *Organizing to Win: New Research on Union Strategies*, Ithaca NY: Cornell University Press, pp. 37–53.

Fletcher, B. and Hurd, R. (2001) 'Overcoming Obstacles to Transformation. Challenges on the Way to a New Unionism', in Turner, Katz, B. and Hurd, R. (eds) *Rekindling the Movement: Labor's Quest for Reference in the 21st Century*, Ithaca, NY: Cornell University Press.

Fudge, J. (1993) 'The Gendered Dimension of Labour Law: Why Women Need

Broader-based Bargaining', in Brisken, L. and McDermott, P. (eds) *Women Challenging Unions: Feminism, Democracy and Militancy*, Toronto: University of Toronto Press, pp. 231–48.

Gindin, S. (1995) *The Canadian Auto Workers: The Birth and Transformation of a Union*, Toronto: James Lorimer & Company.

Hayden, A. (1999) *Sharing the Work, Sparing the Planet: Work Time, Consumption and Ecology*, Toronto: Between the Lines.

Heckscher, C. (1988) *The New Unionism: Employee Involvement in the Changing Corporation*, New York: Basic Books.

Jackson, A. and Robinson, D. (2000) *Falling Behind: The State of Working Canada, 2000*, Ottawa: Canadian Centre for Policy Alternatives.

Kumar, P., Murray, G. and Schetagne, S. (1998) 'Workplace Change in Canada: Union Perceptions of Impacts, Responses and Support Systems', *Workplace Gazette*, Ottawa: Human Resources Development Canada, Winter, pp. 75–87.

Lebowitz, M. (1992) *Beyond Capital: Marx's Political Economy of the Working Class*, New York: St Martin's Press.

Lerner, S. (1996) 'Reviving Unions', *Boston Review*, Democracy Project, pp. 3–8.

Lipset, S. M., Trow, M. and Coleman, J. (1956) *Union Democracy: The Inside Politics of the International Typographical Union*, New York: Anchor Books, Doubleday.

Mishel, L., Bernstein, J. and Schmitt, J. (1999) *The State of Working America, 1998–1999*, Ithaca NY: Cornell University Press.

Moody, K. (1997) *Workers in a Lean World: Unions in the International Economy*, London and New York: Verso.

O'Grady, J. (1992) 'Beyond the Wagner Act, What Then?', in Drache, D. (ed.) *Getting on Track: Social Democratic Strategies for Ontario*, Montreal and Kingston: McGill-Queen's University Press, pp. 153–69.

O'Hara, B. (1993) *Working Harder Isn't Working*, Vancouver: New Star Books.

Pocock, B. and Wishart, J. (1999) 'Organizing Our Future: What Australian Unionists Can Learn from US Labour's Fight Back', Centre for Labour Research, Research Paper Series No. 9. Department of Social Inquiry, University of Adelaide, Australia, January.

Robinson, I. (1994) 'NAFTA, Social Unionism and Labour Movement Power in Canada and the United States', *Relations industrielles/Industrial Relations*, 49 (4): 657–93.

Russo, J. and Banks, A. (1996) 'Teaching the Organizing Model of Unionism and Campaign-based Education: National and International Trends', paper presented at AFL-CIO/Cornell University Research Conference on Unions Organizing, Washington DC, April.

Schenk, C. and Anderson, J. (eds) (1995) *Re-shaping Work: Union Responses to Technological Change*, Toronto: Ontario Federation of Labour, Technological Adjustment Research Programme.

Schenk, C. and Anderson, J. (eds) (1999) *Reshaping Work 2: Labour, the Workplace and Technological Change*, Ottawa: Canadian Centre for Policy Alternatives/Garamond Press.

Singer, D. (1999) *Whose Millennium? Theirs or Ours?* New York: Monthly Review Press.

Wells, D. (1998) 'Building Transnational Coordinative Unionism', in Juarez Nunez, H. and Babson, S. (eds) *Confronting Change: Lean Production in the North American Auto Industry*, Detroit: Wayne State University Press, pp. 487–505.

White, J. (1999) 'Workers' Attitudes to Shorter Hours of Work', in Schenk, Christopher and Anderson, John (eds) *Reshaping Work 2: Labour, the Workplace and Technological Change*, Ottawa: Canadian Centre for Policy Alternatives/Garamond Press, pp. 157–71.

Yalnizian, A. (1998) *The Growing Gap: A Report on Growing Inequality between Rich and Poor in Canada*, Toronto: Centre for Social Justice.

Yates, C. (1990) 'The Internal Dynamics of Union Power: Explaining Canadian Autoworkers' Militancy in the 1980s', *Studies in Political Economy*, 31 (Spring): 73–105.

13

GLOBALIZATION, TRADE UNION ORGANIZATION AND WORKERS' RIGHTS

Huw Beynon

Introduction

It is well known that Karl Marx and Frederick Engels concluded *The Communist Manifesto* with the words: 'The proletariat have nothing to lose but their chains. They have a world to win. *Working men of all countries unite!*' In his excellent biography of Marx, Francis Wheen reflected:

> The only fetters binding the working class today are mock-Rolex watches, but these latter day proletarians have much else that they would hate to lose – microwave ovens, holiday time-shares and satellite dishes. They have bought their council houses and their shares in private utilities; they made a nice little windfall when their building society converted into a bank. In short we are all bourgeois now. Even the British Labour Party has gone Thatcherite. (Wheen, 1999: 4)

This has become an accepted view amongst Western intellectuals and politicians. However in their stress upon the affluence of workers in the West and the decline of employment in the manufacturing industries, many points are missed or understated. One of the many subtleties of Marx related to his understanding of capitalist exploitation and of the role of wages and the labour process in this process. In his view, surplus extraction and with it a variety of attendant political processes operated upon the worker 'be his wages high or low'.

It was also argued (following Lenin) that imperialism had enabled the capitalist states to distribute part of the surplus exploitation in the colonies to their northern workers in the form of higher wages. This formed the hallmark of the 'social imperialist' explanation of reformist politics in the northern states and the establishment of citizenship rights to workers through state reform.

In this context therefore, and in contrast to Wheen, it is important to note the number of writers who have begun to comment on the diminution of these rights and also of the wages of manual workers in the advanced capitalist states.

The attack on workers' rights

The issue of 'rights', especially the rights of workers, in the context of ongoing global economic changes, has emerged as a major issue for social scientists and political and social activists. In New York, Ethan Kapstein, Director of Studies at the Council on Foreign Relations, wrote of the break in the 'post-war bargain' built around the Bretton Woods agreement:

> The global economy is leaving millions of disaffected workers in its train. Inequality, unemployment and endemic poverty have become its handmaidens. Rapid technological change and heightening international competition are fraying the job markets of the major industrialised countries. At the same time systemic pressures are curtailing every government's ability to respond with new spending. Just when working people need the nation state as a buffer from the world economy, it is abandoning them. (Kapstein, 1996: 16)

In London, Joe Rogaly, the columnist for the *Financial Times* noted that:

> In the old days, many employees could look to a union for help. Only an eighth of the world's workers are organised now ... The lions have had their teeth drawn ... We are left alone with our new masters, the large corporations, the ones who will do you down if they can get away with it. (Rogaly, 1998: III)

The previous year, on hearing of the plan by Bill Gates (Microsoft Corporation) to launch 300 communication satellites, the same author had depicted the future in this way:

> Corporations that operate in many countries are able to pay taxes where they are lowest. Always cognizant of the costs of being found out, these giants can choose where to do what. They drift naturally to where the laws

are most amenable. This journey away from the rule of law will be accelerated by the network. The chances are that during the coming decade the boards of the planet's 100 largest companies will become more powerful, more relevant to individual lives, than the governments of the 100 largest countries. . . . . We are witnessing the start of a greater triumph for the free market than the proponents of capitalism can have dreamed of. (Rogaly, 1997: III)

Others, while agreeing with Rogaly as to the crisis in workers' rights, have a more complicated understanding of the situation. Charles Tilly, writing in a special issue of the *Journal of International Labor and Working Class History* identifies the expansion of employee rights with the expansion of the state and of democracy. In the context of globalization, he argues, both the state and democracy is weakened. Historically, in the West, he argues:

Rights to strike, to associate, to call down sanctions against poor working conditions, to seek legal enforcement of contracts, to collect unemployment benefits, to earn pensions all depended not on the general ethos of Europeans or Westerners, but on some particular state's readiness to validate the rights in question. (Tilly, 1995: 12–13)

He adds:

The actual exercise of rights depended heavily on the state's capacity and propensity to discipline capital. Much of labour politics in Western countries indeed pivots precisely on the demands that the state enforces such rights in the face of capitalist resistance. (Tilly, 1995:13)

In Tilly's view the globalization of capital and the creation of 'powerful supranational organisations' have undermined the capacity of states to 'discipline capital'. In summarizing his argument he says:

My analysis indicates that the substantial acquisitions of rights made by workers in capitalist countries after 1850, now face devastating reversals. Nothing in the analysis suggests that a new cycle of acquisition is about to begin. As states decline, so do workers' rights. (Tilly, 1995: 21)

Unless new ways of organizing can be found argues Tilly, democracy itself runs the risk of being trampled 'by capital's new oligarchies' (p. 13). Or, in the language of Rogaly:

> You can rely upon management to be beastly to employees, customers, officials and everybody else whenever circumstances so dictate. That is a fundamental proposition whose truthfulness cannot be denied. (Rogaly, 1998: III)

Wallerstein agrees with this view, and uses the language of warfare in his own approach to the ascendance of this oligarchy. In his view it has been a case of attack and counter-attack:

> What is important to realise is that this 'counter-attack' is a major reversal of strategy by the privileged classes, or rather a return to the pre-1848 strategy of handling workers' discontent by indifference plus repression. After 1848 and up to 1968 roughly, the privileged classes tried the road of appeasing the working classes by the institution of the liberal state combined with doses of economic concessions. The strategy was politically successful. They only reversed this strategy when the bill became too high, which was only recently. (Wallerstein, 1995: 26)

These texts make grim reading. They suggest that we are entering a period in which the rights of workers in the OECD states and around the world are in peril.

The elements of repression

Accounts of the forces that have produced this downward pressure upon workers' rights identify three main agencies associated with the repression and control of workers:

Multinational corporations

The increasing significance of transnational corporations in national economies is not a new phenomenon. Capitalism has always had an international agenda. In the current period however, an awareness of the impact of these corporations upon arrangements within manufacturing industry became clear in the 1960s and this accelerated as the century developed. The ending of the Soviet Union and the liberalization of the economies of China, South Africa and Brazil have stimulated the development of their activities on a global scale.

In the 1960s, for example, workers in Ford's factories in the UK became aware of the ways in which Ford's international operations affected their working lives. In the factory at Halewood in Liverpool, work rates began to be compared with those at Ford's equivalent plant in Cologne, which employed migrant Turkish workers. This pattern increased with work measurement and output levels of different plants being used in 'league tables' as workers were encouraged to compete with other workers (Beynon, 1984). The currency crisis of 1976 combined with excess manufacturing capacity in Europe to create a severe downturn in employment and with it the development of bargaining strategies by companies that severely weakened trade union organization.

On one occasion Hyster – a fork-lift truck producer – made clear that one of its three European plants would have to close and the choice depended upon the level of wage concessions each was prepared to make. Soon after, Ford announced that it wished to locate a component factory in Dundee in Scotland but that it would only do so if the trade unions agreed that the wage rates and conditions in this plant would not be part of the national agreement that applied to all Ford factories. This factory was finally located in the Philippines. The depressing impact of developments such as these in manufacturing upon trade union organization and workers' sense of their power and rights is obvious.

The process of plant closure and the relocation of employment has affected many branches of manufacturing industry. In sectors as diverse as clothing, vehicle and chemical manufacture, job losses have been linked with geographical relocation of production sites. It was seen dramatically in the operations of such giant manufacturing corporations as ICI, which in the early 1980s changed the balance of its production from one that was dominated by its British plants to a truly diverse international operation. Its employment base altered in similar ways creating severe job losses in its main British locations on Teesside and Merseyside (see Beynon *et al.*, 1994). As a *quid pro quo*, the UK has offered suitable production sites for the branch plants of US and German corporations as well as those from Japan, South Korea and Taiwan. These companies have formed the basis of the UK electronics and computing industries. Similar processes have affected the position of workers in other countries, including all of those studied in this book. Often, the mere threat of plant closure has been enough to get workers to agree to wage cuts in order to retain jobs.

Generally, the manufacturing plants which have arrived and those others that have remained open have been managed in ways, which have seen their labour forces dramatically reduced. This process is often referred to as *downsizing* (occasionally *rightsizing*). Machines (robots and computers) have been replacing jobs at a pace which has led to some observers predicting *The End of Work* (see Rifkin, 1995). The World Bank commented on this instability in its 1995 Report:

> Transformations involve profound structural reforms. They create new opportunities as well as risks which will of necessity generate winners and losers ... Labor does tend to suffer during the initial period of adjustment and possibly more than capital ... labor is less internationally mobile than capital. So when an economy crashes, labor is likely to bear the brunt of the shock, while capital flees ... Major transformations are associated with massive employment restructuring – many jobs can be destroyed and new ones created. (World Bank, 1995).

Commentators in the USA have come to refer to the emergence of a new form of economy they term *Turbo-Capitalism* (Luttwak, 1999). The key feature of this new system rests on the fluid way in which money and fixed capital moves around the globe altering the landscape of local places and the lives of people who work for a living. One such account was documented in *Business Week*:

> Ask David K. Hayes about the impact of globalisation on his life and you'll hear the story of a painful roller-coaster ride. The Goodyear Tire and Rubber Co. factory in Gadsden Alabama where he had worked for 24 years, decided to shift much of its tire-making to low wage Mexico and Brazil early last year. The plant slashed its workforce from 1,850 to 628. The 44 year old father of two was lucky and landed a job paying the same $36,000 salary at another Goodyear plant 300 miles away. Hayes' wife did not want to quit her $30,000 nursing job, so Hayes rented a small apartment in Union City Tennessee seeing his family on weekends. Then in October, Goodyear reversed course and rehired nearly 700 people in Gadsden, including Hayes. It's good to be home he says but he is constantly fearful that the company will switch again. 'It has been nerveracking' he says. 'We try to be cautious on spending because I don't know if I'll have a job in six months'. (Bernstein, 2000: 42)

Events such as these have led researchers to argue that 'turbo-capitalism' is linked closely with the emergence of new kinds of regimes based upon *insecure employment* (Heery and Salmon, 2000). The increasing insecurity of employment for workers – especially those employed in manual trades – has weakened the capacities for trade unions to organize effectively

International agencies – the IMF

Internationally organized capitalist firms are one critical part of the changing situation. Another is the collapse of the understandings that underpinned the Bretton Woods agreement. This has been associated with the increasing dominance of the International Monetary Fund (IMF) as an agency of financial orthodoxy. In the past twenty years the fund has intervened in the operation of states in a variety of ways. In moments of crisis it has mobilized supporting funds and credits, but increasingly such help has been part of a package that commits the particular state to the introduction of orthodox monetary policies. Such policies have resulted in declining real wages, increased interest rates and drastic cuts to public spending, thus exacerbating crises in many countries including Russia, Mexico and Brazil, to name a few.

Less commented upon is the critical role that the IMF played in the UK devaluation crisis in 1976. The intervention of the IMF in 1976 seriously restricted the options open to the (then) Labour government in the midst of a severe recession (Burke and Cairncross, 1992) and committed it to public expenditure cuts of £8 billion between 1977 and 1979. The experience convinced the government that Keynesianism was at an end. The then Prime Minister, Jim Callaghan, in a provocative speech to the 1977 Labour Party Conference, made this extremely clear:

> We used to think that you could spend your way out of a recession, and increase unemployment by cutting taxes and boosting Government spending. I tell you in all honesty that that option no longer exists, and that in so far as it ever did exist, it worked on each occasion since the war by injecting bigger doses of inflation into the economy, followed by a higher level of unemployment as the next step ... Now we must get back to fundamentals. (quoted in Panitch and Leys, 1998: 117)

The IMF's intervention in 1976 was strongly influenced by opinions in Wall Street that the UK economy had 'run out of rope'. Paul Krugman has commented upon the influence of opinions such as these. In his view international fiscal policy develops in the context of an elaborated dominant discourse. He put it like this:

the endless round of meetings, speeches, and exchanges of *communiqués* that occupy much of the time of the economic opinion leaders. Such interlocking social groupings tend at any given time to converge on a conventional wisdom, about economics amongst other things. People believe certain stories because everybody important tells them, and people tell these stories because everyone important believes them. Indeed when a conventional wisdom is at its fullest strength, one's agreement with that conventional wisdom becomes almost a litmus test of one's suitability to be taken seriously. (Krugman, 1995: 36)

The dominance of a discourse and practice rooted in monetarist orthodoxy, which has been especially evident in the Anglo-Saxon countries studied in this volume, restricts policy options available to governments, in particular those that would maintain or strengthen workers' rights and wages and give primacy to employment over tight monetary policies and fiscal restraint.

Deregulating national politics

This combination of an unregulated global capital and the coordinating activities of international agencies dominated by the USA and a neo-liberal economic agenda form two important parts of the pressure on workers' rights. They were enforced by dramatic changes in the operation of political parties and the changing political strategies of nation states themselves. Here, attention has normally been directed towards Thatcher and Reagan and conservative parties. However the transformation of social democratic parties have been of fundamental importance. We have seen how this operated in the British Labour government of the 1970s. However the phenomenon of social democracy uniting with neo-liberalism seems to have affected all of the (so-called) Anglo-Saxon capitalist states, including New Zealand, Australia and Canada. In many ways, these parties either picked up or laid the ground work for the policies that have become know as Thatcherite and Reaganomics.

In considering the character of these policies in the UK, Alan Budd, Professor of Economics at the London Business School, and close adviser to Mrs Thatcher outlined the philosophical underpinnings of the strategy followed by her governments as they went 'back to basics'. In June 1992 Budd participated in a television programme where he commented:

Raising unemployment was a very desirable way of reducing the strength of the working classes ... what was engineered – in Marxist terms – was a crisis in capitalism which recreated the reserve army of labour and has allowed the capitalists to make profits ever since. (Beynon, 1996: 10)

Another of Mrs Thatcher's advisers – Maurice Stone, confirmed Budd's account. As professor of modern history at the University of Oxford, Stone was asked by *The Sunday Times* to offer an assessment of the twentieth century and with it the political and social significance of each of its ten decades. For him, the 1980s was the time when 'capital struck back'. Both these accounts point to the importance of politics and of political mobilization in this process of economic change. Thatcher and Reagan, with their advisers and Think Tanks, embarked on a political project, which comprehensively excluded other options. Mrs Thatcher's catch-phrase was TINA – there is no alternative – and it was pushed with powerful rhetorical effect.

Such a 'conventional wisdom' took hold of policy decision making in the USA, UK and elsewhere in the 1980s. It contained powerful rhetorical devices that laid great emphasis upon notions of the past, identifying trade unions and their leaders with a bygone age. Trade union leaders in Britain and Australia were commonly referred to as 'barons'. Other allusions were toward the Mafia, and attendant notions of power and corruption. Together these ideas combined to identify trade unionism, (and by extension, notions of the working class) as essentially out of date and living in the past. Newspaper headlines commonly associated trade union leaders with dinosaurs. In the aftermath of Spielberg's movie Jurassic Park, trade unionists and leftists came to be referred to as 'the Jurassics'.

The notion of trade unions as outdated and impediments to change built on a growing frustration with public sector strikes and the overburdening of daily life with rules and regulations. Deregulation, privatization and the championing of consumer sovereignty and individual over collective rights offered new avenues through which individuals could be unburdened and the tyranny of unions ended.

An alternative future

This account is one that emphasizes the ascendance of capitalism and of the capitalist system. It contrasts the expansion of a global economy with the insecurities and vulnerabilities of workers and their families living in local places.

It is a worrying and depressing account from which there seems to be little room for manoeuvre. The interlinkage between the three elements has taken on a form that encourages Thatcher's view that 'there is no alternative'; human beings and social institutions need to adapt themselves to these changed and powerful economic forces. In this context the pressures upon the human psyche increase. In 1998 *Harper's Magazine* held a symposium on the winners and losers in the global economy. Bill Greider expressed the view that:

> In America at least, the process of disfranchisement – the decline in real wages, the decay of representative government and organized labor – has been under way with ups and downs for twenty five years. But that process has had the opposite effect, it has created depoliticization. It's convinced a lot of people that politics is run by somebody else and the hell with politics. (Greider, in Fishman *et al.*, 1998: 50)

He went on to predict a right-wing backlash. In a similar vein, Bernard Crick, the author of the definitive biography of George Orwell, has commented on the re-emergence of 'the mob' in contemporary British life. Drawing upon Hannah Arendt's writings in *Origins of Totalitarianism*, he distinguishes between 'the people' and 'the mob'; indicating that whilst the people seek true representation and to be included in the polity, the mob 'hates the society from which it is excluded' (Crick, 1980). There have been examples of the mob at work on deprived housing estates in the UK in 2000. Inflamed by the tabloid press mobs have turned on suspected paedophiles and 'bogus asylum seekers'. In their accounts Greider and Crick echo some of the worries of Kapstein mentioned earlier. In his long view of history, Kapstein sees in the depression and transformation that took place in Europe in the 1870s the origins of World War I and the subsequent rise of Hitler and the Nazi Party.

Is there an alternative way of seeing these developments? Are there alternative developments and strategies that could provide a different and alternative view of the future?

Trade unionism and global capitalism

In the dominant discourse, trade unions are seen either as villains or as outdated. They are generally seen to have been superseded by developments in the organization of capitalist production and in the changing nature of capitalist societies. Here it is common to refer to the declining influence of trade unions in national politics; their declining membership; the difficulty they have as national organizations in dealing with global systems of production and distribution; and the ways in which workers are increasingly understanding themselves as consumers rather than producers.

This account has been assisted through exaggeration. While trade union membership has declined in the main capitalist states it has still maintained significant membership. Between 1998 and 1999, it increased in the UK and the USA (see Chapter 1, Table 1.1). Furthermore there is strong evidence to support the view that workers in their working lives still see management's power as of fundamental concern and in need of curtailment. Undoubtedly the rhetoric of 'globalization' points to real problems of establishing collective action of 'workers of the world'. At the same time, it masks the fact that trade unions have grappled with the problems involved in linking up and creating strategies that go beyond national boundaries (illustrated in all the chapters in this book).

These initiatives are varied. A formal international organization has been developed in the chemical industry with the aim to coordinate trade union activities in ways that parallel the growing concentration and international operations of the chemical companies. In a different way rank-and-file trade union groupings in the automobile sector began to build international links in the 1970s, often with important and interesting effects. The Ford workers in the UK produced a 'Fraud' tee shirt as part of their 1978 strike campaign; this was picked up in the Philippines three years later and again by workers in Brazil.

Although many rank-and-file linkages broke down in the late 1980s there are signs that they are re-emerging in different ways. The UK interactive website 'Cyber Picket' (http://www.cf.ac.uk/socsi/union/) receives thousands of 'hits' each year. In Europe, productive formal links are being built up as a consequence of membership of the EU, and the need for common agreements and understanding in relation to the implementation of EU directives. In the south an important meeting of the *Southern Initiative on Globalization and Trade Union Rights* took place in Johannesburg in October 1999. As Fairbrother has noted:

> A distinguishing feature of the conference was the integration of labour movement activists and academic researchers, informing each other in a productive and mutually supportive way. (Fairbrother, 1999)

The main achievement of the conference was the signing of a 'statement of intent' between the Maritime Union of Australia and the Transport and General Workers Union (TGWU) of South Africa for a programme of exchange and policy development involving shop stewards and members from the ports of Durban (South Africa) and Fremantle (Australia). More formal international linkages are also being established through international organizations such as the International Metalworkers Federation (IMF), the International Transport Federation (ITF) and the International Committee of Free Trade Unions (ICFTU). While these types of international labour solidarity action and networks have been in place, albeit sporadically, for decades, there is also a 'new' form of international linkage emerging between labour groups and social movements. In what has now become a classic text, André Gorz wrote in 1967 of *A Strategy for Labour*. He pointed out that the trade union movement formed the best organized force within progressive politics. The support it gave to other broader social movements was seen to be decisive: for the broader 'movement' and also for the trade unions themselves. As he put it:

> According to whether the trade union movement opposes them or whether it seeks a common alliance and common course of action with them, these other elements will be part of the left or will break with it, will engage with it in collective action or will remain minorities tempted to resort to violence. (Gorz, 1967: quoted in Panitch, 2000: 368)

Furthermore 'the attitude toward the other social movements ... will determine (their) own evolution' (Gorz, 1967: quoted in Panitch, 2000: 368).

Over the last 30 years, trade union organizations have most often seemed to be at odds with these social movements. One activist's recollections of the mass demonstrations in Seattle that halted WTO meetings highlights the gulf separating labour and new social movements.

> Walked out on to the street one last time. The sweet stench of CS gas still flavored the morning air. As I get into my car for the journey back to Portland, a black teenager grabbed my arm. Smiling he said 'hey man does this WTO thing come to town every year?' I knew immediately how the kid felt. Along with the poison, the flash bombs and the rubber bullets there was an optimism, energy and camaraderie on the streets of Seattle that I hadn't felt in a long time.

In reflecting on this optimism, he writes: 'In the annals of popular protest in America these have been shining hours, achieved entirely outside the conventional arena of orderly protest.' He contrasts their actions on the streets of Seattle with 'white paper activism and the timid bleats of the professional leadership of big labour and environmentalism' (St Clair, 1999: 96).

Yet there are also signs that clear changes are taking place in the relationship between unions and social movements, which are having significant effects on labour strategy. In the UK, remnants of the coal-miners' union, building upon their experiences in the year-long coalfield strike, have joined with environmental activists in protests over the development of opencast coal-mining (Beynon *et al.*, 2000). Others have cooperated with poverty action groups in relation to work in the informal sector. More generally, Shelia Rowbotham and others have documented the ways in which trade union organizations in India, South Africa, Madeira, and Australia have taken a positive attitude toward the organization and support of home workers. These activities and the role of HomeNet in securing the role of home workers within the International Labour Organization (ILO) Convention in 1996 are documented through its newsletter (Rowbotham, 1999; see also Rowbotham, 1993). In the USA, Ruth Milkman has confirmed the effectiveness of unionizing campaigns that develop some of the thinking of the social movement activists and involve them in organizing roles. This has been particularly effective in the organizing of immigrant workers (Milkman, 2000; see also, Chapters 2, 3, 7 and 9 in this volume). In Brazil, the Central Unica dos Trabalhores (CUT) has been concerned for many years to organize around the ILO core labour standards and to build strong links with social movements and workers in the informal sector.

This increased receptiveness by some trade unions to new ways of organizing has in part been influenced by the severe collapse in the membership brought about by plant closures and the development of new kinds of work processes, work contracts and working conditions. But it is also the result of recognition of the influence of globalization on workers' lives and jobs and the need for cross-border solidarity.

The signing of the North American Free Trade Area (NAFTA) has given rise to the 'anti-sweat shop' movement which involves both labour and student groups. The United Electrical Workers – now a small and much reduced union – has established a *Strategic Organizing Alliance* with the Frente Autentico del Trabajo (FAT) in Mexico that has developed educational work through student exchanges (on FAT, see Hathaway, 2000). This Alliance aims at building a degree of solidarity between the workers of North America and those who work in the new branch plants in the South. The Milwaukee Labor Council organized a benefit dinner to assist cross-border work. Developments from this include:

- a cultural exchange of artists each of whom worked with local people in producing a mural that represented labour in its various forms;
- detailed contacts between trade unionists in the North and South relating to the role of multinational corporations, the nature of the agreements on wages and conditions;
- information and support (via boycotts and lobbying) in relation to strikes over social clauses, working conditions, trade union victimization and so forth.

Counter-hegemonic globalization

Recently writers in the USA and the UK have begun to question the ways in which globalization has been understood to operate as a hegemonic force within politics and social theory. Peter Evans and Doreen Massey have each written of ways in which globalization when viewed from the perspective of workers and the people 'at the bottom' can be interpreted in new and important ways. Hence Evans writes:

> Why shouldn't the burgeoning growth of communication and, movement across national boundaries create new global strategies aimed at well being and equity at the same time as it stimulates transnational finance and trade? (Evans, 2000: 230)

And Massey:

> We are faced here with a problem of language. The word 'globalization' has been hi-jacked to mean only the particular form of globalization (neo-liberal and overwhelmingly concerned with the economic) that we suffer at the moment. But 'globalization' really just means global interconnected-ness, and it could take other forms, on different terms and embodying different kinds of power relations. Perhaps, indeed, there are the begin-nings of ideas about how this might work in the decidedly international networks already being invested with the radical protest movements themselves. Either way we need to wrest the term back for ourselves and argue for and imagine not the local rather than the global but a different form of globalization. (Massey, 2000: 19)

Massey points to the significant role played by nation states in the creation of the specific form of 'globalization' that currently exists. Panitch emphasizes this point in a recent essay that deals with the 'Strategy for Labour'. He writes:

> Globalization is not an objective economic process which labour needs to catch up to, as so many seem to think. It is a political process advanced by identifiable interests for clear purposes. The failure to see the strategic political nature of globalization reflects an economism which needs to be overcome. National states are not the victims of globalization, they are the authors of globalization. States are not *displaced* by globalized capital, they *represent* globalized capital, above all financial capital. (Panitch, 2000: 374)

Panitch concludes that the foundations of a new strategy need to begin within nation states. But here the kinds of progressive alliances that labour has sought to make with its 'national bourgeoisie' are no longer a credible option. For: 'The state more and more represents a set of (domestic and foreign) internationally orientated capitalist classes' (Panitch, 2000: 375).

How can these ideas help? To begin with, in pointing to globalization as a particular kind of ideological construct, they assert new ways of thinking and understanding and the importance that this can have in considering the kinds of options that are available. For example a considerable literature now exists upon the ways in which 'transnational communities' are being built by people who travel around the world in various ways in search of, or as part of, employment, or retaining contacts with friends and kin (see Evans, 2000). Working migrants through their remittances make a significant contribution to the balance of payments of their 'home' states. Evans sees in these Diasporas a kind of 'globalization from below' worthy of consideration:

> Globalization from below allows ordinary citizens, especially those from poor countries, to build lives that would not be possible in the more traditional world of bounded states. (Evans, 2000: 230)

But, as he points out:

> the surprising resilience and adaptive ability of ordinary people whose lives have become transnational does not necessarily challenge the dominant global rules, the ways these rules are made, or the economic ideology that legitimates them. (Evans, 2000: 230)

However it is clear that this 'transnational awareness', has become a feature of many institutional forms and practices that might well affect these rules.

Evans singles out three forms that he considers worthy of careful consideration:

- *Transnational advocacy networks.* These are particularly effective in relation to the environment and to women's rights. They involve attempts to transmit information transnationally and to regulate the behaviour of the powerful through the invocation of norms. Evans sees this to have been particularly effective in north-east Brazil (women's rights) and in relation to the lives of the rubber tappers. These networks facilitate the spread of information which can then be used as a weapon; they also enable a process of 'venue shifting' to take place – where injustices in one place are raised and pressurized in another.
- *Purchasing power and consumer boycotts.* Information on the working conditions of Nike's labour force in Indonesia and Vietnam produced a major crisis for the corporation. By the end of 1997–8 fiscal year its earnings had dropped to half of the previous year's and its stock value had fallen by 40 per cent. Researchers indicated that direct labour costs accounted for no more that 2 per cent of the price of a $100 shoe. Nike's vulnerability derived from the fact that its sales related to the image and the brand.
- *United world workers.* One of the side agreements of NAFTA allowed trade unions in each of the three participating countries to file complaints based on labour rights violations. This has led to interesting and important collaboration between the official trade unions (one involving 50 separate unions) of Canada, the USA and Mexico, in ways that might not have been predicted. It also provided the basis for a shift in the thinking of some Northern Unions – seeing the Mexicans as collaborators in struggle rather than 'job thieves'. Similar possibilities exist with the WTO's insistence on rejecting 'core labour standards' (Evans, 2000: 231–7).

Each one of these areas commends an inversion of the rule: think globally act locally. They suggest that there is much to be gained by *acting globally*. The underlying principle rests on the possibility of establishing worldwide norms that can apply to relationships in the formal and informal economy. This might not be easy; especially in a world made up of very different religious beliefs and cultural practices. As Massey puts it: 'In a situation of social and cultural variation and economic inequality, can any abstract set of rules be adequate?' (Massey, 2000: 19). She asks poignantly in relation to the new rules of free trade:

If we vote for total free movement of both trade and people, is it 'fair' that it will be the relatively poor of the First World who will lose their jobs and find their council house stock coming under pressure? Judging between the relative poor of the First World and the ferociously poor of the Third World shows the lack of adequate relation between these rules and the social actors and their highly differentiated powers, who are the agents of globalization. (Massey, 2000: 19)

Massey favours 'acting globally' but prefers to think in terms of goals and principles such as those relating to equality and the environment. And, as Evans is quick to point out, 'acting globally' will produce few positive results unless it is linked with local organization. Consumer boycotts and pressure of human rights and labour standards are vulnerable to the counter-claim that they are simply protectionism by another name. For this charge to be countered, local trade union and community groups also need to be organizing around the new 'world norms'. This, of course, is where Panitch comes in. In his trenchant view:

If internationalism is conceived in a way that is an alternative to, or a substitute for, changes that are necessary at the national level the results can only be negative, if not disastrous. There can be little tolerance for the kind of invocations of global working class unity that, as was first made so tragically clear in 1914, has always produced more rhetorical heat than effective transnational solidarity and understanding. (Panitch, 2000: 388)

At the beginning of the twenty-first century it does not seem overly optimistic to suggest that some institutionalized practices are in place that might build important new levels of international understanding. Workers' organizations in the south – especially in Brazil and South Africa – have been important in providing examples of new forms of organizing in most difficult circumstances. There is a possibility that organizations in the north will now make their own contribution to the extension and development of a more humane and equitable form of global society.

References

Bernstein, A. (2000) 'Backlash: Behind the Anxiety over Globalisation', *Business Week*, April, pp. 38–44.
Beynon, H. (1984) *Working for Ford*, new edition, Harmondsworth: Penguin.

Beynon, H. (1996) 'A destruicao do classe operaria inglesa', *Revista Brasileira de Cientas Socias*, 10(27: 5–18.

Beynon, H., Cox, A. and Hudson, R. (2000) *Digging up Trouble: Opencast Mining and Environmental Protest in the UK*, London: Rivers Oram.

Beynon, H., Hudson, R. and Sadler, D. (1994) *A Place Called Teesside*, Edinburgh: Edinburgh University Press.

Burke, K. and Cairncross, A. (1992) *Goodbye Great Britain: The 1976 IMF Crisis*, London: Kogan Page.

Crick, Bernard (1980) *George Orwell: A Life*, London: Secker & Warburg.

Evans, P. (2000) 'Fighting Marginalisation with Transnational Networks: Counter-hegemonic Globalisation', *Contemporary Sociology*, 29 (1): 230–41.

Fairbrother, P. (1999) *Report on the SIGTUR Conference*, mimeo, Cardiff School of Social Sciences, Cardiff University, Cardiff, Wales.

Fishman, T., Garten, J. and Greider, W. (1998) 'Global Roulette: In a Volatile World Economy Can Everyone Lose?', *Harper's Magazine*, June, pp. 39–50.

Gorz, A. (1967) *Strategy for Labour: A Radical Proposal*, Beacon Books, Boston, quoted in Panitch, L., 'A Strategy for Labour', in *Socialist Register 2001*, London: Merlin Press, 2000.

Hathaway, D. (2000) *Allies across the Border: Mexico's 'Authentic Labor Front' and Global Solidarity*, Cambridge MA: South End Press.

Heery, E. and Salmon, J. (eds) (2000) *The Insecure Workforce*, London: Routledge.

Kapstein, E. (1996) 'Workers and the World Economy', *Foreign Affairs*, May/June, 1996, pp. 16–35.

Krugman, P. (1995) 'Dutch Tulips and Emerging Markets', *Foreign Affairs*, July/August, 74, (4): 28–44.

Luttwak, E. (1999) *Turbo-Capitalism: Winners and Losers in the Global Economy*, London: Texere Publishing.

Marx, K. and Engels, F. (1968) 'Manifesto of the Communist Party', in K. Marx and F. Engels, *Selected Works*, London: Lawrence and Wishart, pp. 31–63.

Massey, D. (2000) 'The Geography of Power', *Red Pepper*, July, pp 18–21.

Milkman, R. (ed) (2000) *Organising Immigrants*, Ithaca, NY: Cornell University Press.

Panitch, L. (2000) 'Reflections on Strategy for Labour?' *Socialist Register 2001*, London: Merlin Books, pp. 367–92.

Panitch, L. and Leys, C. (1998) *The End of Parliamentary Socialism: From New Left to New Labour*, London: Verso.

Rifkin, J. (1995) *The End of Work: The Decline of the Global Labor Force and the Dawn of the Post-market Era*, New York: A Tarcher/Putnam Book.

Rogaly, J. (1997) 'No Spot on Earth Will Be Microsoft-free', *Financial Times Weekend*, 3–4 May, p. III.

Rogaly, J. (1998) 'Time for a New David to Tackle Goliath', *Financial Times Weekend*, 18–19 April, p. III.

Rowbotham, S. (1993) *Homeworkers Worldwide*, London: Merlin Press.

Rowbotham, S. (1999) 'New Ways of Organising in the Informal Sector: Five Case Studies of Trade Union Activities', London: HomeNet.

St Clair, J. (1999) 'Seattle Diary: It's a Gas, Gas, Gas', *New Left Review*, 238 (November–December): 81–96.

Tilly, C. (1995) 'Globalisation Threatens Workers' Rights', *Journal of International Labor and Working Class History*, 47 (Spring): pp. 1–23.

Wallerstein, I. (1995) 'Response: Declining States, Declining Rights', *Journal of International Labor and Working Class History*, No. 47, Spring, pp. 24–7.

Wheen, F. (1999) *Karl Marx*, London: Fourth Estate.

World Bank (1995) *World Bank Development Report 1995: Workers in an Integrating World*, New York: Oxford University Press.

INDEX